The First American Frontier

AYER COMPANY, PUBLISHERS, INC.
SALEM, NEW HAMPSHIRE 03079

HOUSTON PUBLIC LIBRARY

R0160124288
SSC

Reprint Edition, 1986
AYER Company, Publishers, Inc.
382 Main Street
Salem, New Hampshire 03079

Reprinted from a copy in
The State Historical Society of Wisconsin Library

LC # 70-146414
ISBN 0-405-02878-4

The First American Frontier
ISBN for complete set: 0-405-02820-2

See last pages of this volume for titles.

Manufactured in the United States of America

BOONESBOROUGH

ITS FOUNDING,
PIONEER STRUGGLES, INDIAN EXPERIENCES, TRANSYLVANIA
DAYS, AND REVOLUTIONARY ANNALS

GEORGE W. RANCK

LEXINGTON, KENTUCKY

Member of The Filson Club

FILSON CLUB PUBLICATIONS No. 16

BOONESBOROUGH

ITS FOUNDING,
PIONEER STRUGGLES, INDIAN EXPERIENCES, TRANSYLVANIA
DAYS, AND REVOLUTIONARY ANNALS

With Full Historical Notes and Appendix

BY

GEORGE W. RANCK

Member of The Filson Club
Author of

"The Bivouac of the Dead and Its Author," "The Travelling Church,"
"History of Lexington, Kentucky," "The Story of Bryan's
Station," "Girty, the White Indian," etc.

Illustrated

LOUISVILLE, KENTUCKY
JOHN P. MORTON & COMPANY
Printers to The Filson Club
1901

COPYRIGHTED BY
THE FILSON CLUB
1901

PREFACE.

BOONESBOROUGH, like a mist of the morning, has vanished, and the place which knew it once will know it no more forever. Not a cabin of the thirty that formed the parallelogram of the fort; not a picket of the bullet-battered lines that encompassed the station, and not a pale of the stockades between the cabins is left. Not even a chimney, the last of a human habitation to perish, is left standing or shows the little mound of debris at its base as survivor of its fall. Its former site is an unromantic cornfield, where is seen the cultivated soil and the gathered crop, instead of preparations for aggressive war or stolid defense. So thoroughly has the station disappeared that it affords no perch for the owl and no hiding-place for the fox. Neither fire nor flood, nor earthquake nor ruthless time has ever more completely swept a town from the face of the earth. Other towns in Kentucky, like Lystra and Franklinville and Ohiopiomingo, have vanished, but they never had any except a paper existence, while Boonesborough was a reality.

Preface

The sites of some of the greatest cities of the world were occupied by accident and yet succeeded, while intelligent design selected others that utterly failed. It is easy enough to choose a site and lay off a town, but it requires inhabitants and manufactures and trade and perseverance to make it a success. When General George Rogers Clark, in 1776, led the opposition against the Transylvania Colony, and Virginia asserted her old law forbidding private citizens to purchase lands from the Indians, Transylvania was doomed, and with it Boonesborough. It was then only a question of time when the town and the fort would transfer their prestige to Harrodsburg and become things of the past. Boone could roam through the untrodden forests in search of game, and could fight the Indian behind the trees of his native woods or on the open plain, but he lacked the municipal tact and persistence which builds up towns and turns them into cities, and most of his companions were like unto him.

But gone forever, as it is, Boonesborough yet holds a place in the memory and the heart of the living. Imperishable recollections hover over its desolate site and bind it with chains of steel to our memories. It was here that civilization took its firm stand in the transmontane wilderness. Men had earlier roamed over the country as hunters and explorers and traders, but in Boonesborough

Preface

they had their wives and children with them, and formed there the family circle, without which any attempts at civilization are mockeries. The blood that flowed through the veins of these fearless and hardy pioneers and warmed their hearts and nerved their strong arms yet courses through the veins of their descendants and makes the site of the old vanished station hallowed ground. As the zealous Mohammedan, when journeying to the Beit Allah of Mecca, sees in the mirage of the desert the minarets and domes and spires of the sacred Mosque, so the loyal descendant of the Boonesborough pioneers sees in the mists of tradition the fort and stockade and cabins of the vanished town as they were when occupied by his ancestors. The classical scholar reveres not more the sites of departed Troy and Pæstum and Thebes than does the descendant of the first settlers the site of Boonesborough. Here the Boones, the Hendersons, the Calloways, the Harts, and Floyd and Kenton and Ballard and Stoner and Holder and Rawlings and Pogue stood like an impregnable wall and rolled back the fierce tide of savage warfare until civilization and Christianity were established in the primeval forest. It is the recollection of the hardships endured and the courage displayed by our ancestors there that makes Boonesborough dear to us and gives it a sure place in our memory and heart.

Preface

Every Kentuckian has some conception of vanished Boonesborough, and imagines that he carries an image of it in his memory like unto it as it once existed. It is well, however, while we are cherishing conceptions of this town of the past, that we hold to a conception rightly formed. It has now been one hundred and twenty-six years since Boonesborough was founded, and during this long period no full or adequate history of it has been written. It has been reserved for a member of The Filson Club, an hundred years after the town had perished, to gather the conflicting traditions from their scattered sources, and, after separating the true from the false, to weave the facts into an exhaustive narrative. This Mr. George W. Ranck, the author of the work which follows this preface, has done, and here presents Boonesborough as it began and progressed and declined and finally disappeared from the face of the earth. He who reads Mr. Ranck's narrative will learn more about this vanished town than any one has known since its day in the land. And the reader will not only learn much that is new about Boonesborough, but he will learn something too important not to be known about pioneer life in Kentucky, about the attempt of Henderson and Company to establish a proprietary government by the name of Transylvania in Kentucky, and about the brave men and women who left

Preface

comfortable homes on the Atlantic slope of the Alleghanies and settled in the wilderness of Kentucky, amid wild animals and wilder savages, with no protection but their own strong arms. Their own courage and skill and daring, practically unaided, won the great West from the British and the Indians and added it to the rich fruits of the Revolutionary War.

Boonesborough was really the creature of the Transylvania Colony, and Mr. Ranck very properly began the narrative with the treaty of Watauga in the spring of 1775, by which the southern half of Kentucky was purchased from the Indians. The building of a protecting fort on the acquired lands on the Kentucky River near the mouth of Otter Creek and the gathering of pioneer families there and the rise of a town around the fort followed in the natural order of sequence. And so did Indian war and sieges naturally follow, with all their heart-rending atrocities and sufferings. The confined life of the fort, however, in spite of the dangers outside of the pickets, soon began to drive the inhabitants to extramural cabins upon lands selected for farms. It was not many years after this process began before Boonesborough was deserted and log cabins with women and children in them on bits of cleared land peeped out here and there from the dark shadows of the surrounding forest. The steady decline and final extinction of the fort and town naturally followed the exodus of their inhabitants to the near and distant farms. The whole historic field has been covered, embracing every fact and tradition that need be known, and including biographic sketches of some of the leading characters in those stirring and perilous times. Old and rare manuscripts and scarce books and forgotten newspapers have been searched, and the whole story told in the book before us as it has never been told before.

Not the least important and instructive part of Mr. Ranck's work is its excellent halftone illustrations. These are not scattered indiscriminately through the book, as illustrations too often are, but appear at the pages where they are described and belong. Fine pictures represent the old fort, the place of meeting of the delegates, the sulphur well, the salt lick, the fresh water spring, the river, the ferry, and other views of the landscape, including the town of Boonesborough itself with its laid-off streets and numbered lots. There is a striking likeness of Boone, and a spirited picture of the treaty men making their way back to the fort after they discovered the treachery of the Indians. The author has thus covered every practicable scene by a suggestive picture.

Still another merit of the work is the Appendix. Extracts from scarce books now inaccessible to the gen-

Preface

eral reader, transcriptions of manuscripts which exist only in single originals at distant places, and articles from old newspapers and pamphlets make up the appendix. Among the selections is the deed by which the Cherokee Indians conveyed to Richard Henderson and his associates for the Transylvania Colony all the southern part of Kentucky, embracing about 20,000,000 acres; the Journal kept by Judge Henderson while on his proprietary land of Transylvania and while going to and returning therefrom; the proclamations of the Governors of Virginia and North Carolina denouncing the Transylvania enterprise; the Journal of the proceedings of the assembly of Transylvania delegates; Felix Walker's diary of his trip to Boonesborough in 1775, and numerous other papers that are valuable to the student of history.

A book without an index is open to many objections in this rapid age. No one has time to turn over the leaves and find what he may want to read. The book under consideration is open to no such fault. Besides separate lists of the illustrations in the text and of articles in the appendix, giving the page of each, it has an ample general index, giving each subject and name, and the page on which it is found. It is an index, too, which gives the initial word with such certainty that we are not disappointed when we turn to the given page.

Preface

It will be seen at a glance that the author has gone to the original sources for his material, that he has given us no rehash of other books and of other writers' opinions, and that British records play in this field their very important part. Another element of strength and value in this volume that no lover of genuine history will fail to appreciate is its full and free citation of authorities. A quibbler would have to contend with these authorities alone — not with the writer of the text.

It seems, therefore, that the book of which this is a preface is a work of merit in all its parts. The history of Boonesborough from its beginning in 1775 to its final extinction in less than half a century afterward is given by it in fullness and in detail. Indeed, the author has told all that had need of being told, and it will be long before any thing new or important can be added to the story as he has told it. The whole historic field has been gone over, and from it gleaned every thing that related to the vanished town or to its connections, or to the men and women who imparted to it their own immortality.

This is the sixteenth publication of The Filson Club. The fifteen volumes which preceded it were issued from year to year, and have gone forth into the world as promoters of history and biography. The club began its

Preface

work in 1884, when it was formed, and it is the intention of its members to continue in the same line of publications until all the important matters in Kentucky are the subjects of monographs and all of the representative men and women have biographies. Those of us now living can form no just estimate of the value of such publications, but those who come after us in the distant future will know their worth and bless us for them.

R. T. DURRETT,
President of the Filson Club.

LIST OF ILLUSTRATIONS.

	PAGE
The Author,	*Frontispiece*
Daniel Boone,	10
The Sulphur Well,	17
The Lick Spring,	19
Site of Fort Boonesborough,	25
Meeting of Transylvania House of Delegates,	30
Plan of Fort Boonesborough,	35
Site of Fort Boonesborough from opposite side of river,	40
The Hills of Clark County,	50
Relics of Daniel Boone,	66
Fort Boonesborough before Siege of 1778,	79
Climax of the Treaty,	89
Sycamore Hollow,	104
The Town of Boonesborough,	110
Residence of Judge Henderson,	115
Boonesborough Ferry,	125
The Old Sycamore,	134

BOONESBOROUGH.

THE spring of 1775 had come. The time had arrived not only for the assertion of American freedom but for its spread, and "Westward the star of empire takes its way." The hour had struck for the permanent settlement of Kentucky,[1] and in widely separated regions the hearts of unconscious instruments of fate had been fired for the work. But in no American Colony was the interest in that distant forest-land keener than in North Carolina,[2] and in no place in North Carolina was it so conspicuous as in the scattered little frontier settlement of Watauga,[3] in what is now East Tennessee.

[1] See Appendix A for "The Name Kentucky."

[2] Which may be accounted for by the fact that Gist, Findlay, Boone, many of the Long Hunters, and other Kentucky explorers were residents of North Carolina.

[3] The scattered settlement, usually mentioned in a general way as "Watauga," straggled, in 1775, with its stockades, cabins, and clearings, for quite a distance along the Watauga River, in the region now known as Carter County, Tennessee, and then included "The Fort," Sycamore Shoals, Colonel Charles Robertson's, "The Old Fields," since occupied by Elizabethton, and other interesting sites. As the name Watauga is connected with sundry things and places in Carter County, it may be well to say that this, the original pioneer Watauga we have described, must not be confused with the new town of Watauga, on the Southern Railroad, six or seven miles from the historic Watauga of which we write.

Boonesborough

Ever since the preceding fall a train of circumstances had kept the minds of its inhabitants on that enticing country. First, their old friend and pilot, Daniel Boone,[1] who had hunted there longer than any one, and who was stopping temporarily at "Snoddy's on the Clinch,"[2] had passed through their settlement more than once on his way down the Valley of the Holston to the principal seats of the Cherokees.[3] Everybody knew of the comradeship between Boone and these Overhill Indians; that he had killed deer with them and had slept in their cabins, but they also knew that the Cherokees claimed the very game lands on which he had hunted so much and where he had recently tried to settle with his family, and somehow the impression was made that something was "going on" about Kentucky. Later there was quite a buzz in the clearings over the news that Boone and two strangers "from across the Ridge"[4] had held powwows with the head men of the Cherokees, and, in December, curiosity became still more lively when a wagon train of "Indian goods" all the way from Fayetteville was stored in Watauga and carefully inspected by six silent, watchful

---

[1] See Appendix B for note on "Boone Before 1775."
[2] See footnote on page 38, and Appendix C, for "Boone's First Attempt to Colonize Kentucky."
[3] Chota, Tellico, and Tellassee.
[4] The Blue Ridge Mountains, which shut off the infant settlement from the old communities of North Carolina.

chiefs of the Overhill tribes. On Christmas Day the whole thing came out, as the shrewd frontiersmen had guessed, when "Richard Henderson, for himself and Company," publicly advertised for "settlers for Kentucky lands about to be purchased,"[1] and Indian runners carried the order of Ocanostota, the head chief of the Cherokees, for a spring meeting of his people at the Watauga settlement to consider, among other things, a grant, already substantially agreed upon, of those same far-spreading lands. Settlers said it was plain now why Boone had kept his big family conveniently near to the Warrior's Path ever since he had been driven back from Walden's Ridge; that he had never once given up his interrupted plan to plant a colony in Kentucky, but to decrease the risks he wanted to make his next start with the full consent of the Cherokees, and so had suggested and urged the formation of this new Company, and would accomplish his purpose as its agent.

Judge Henderson,[2] the ostensible head of the Company, was one of the leading lawyers of the Colony of North

[1] Colonial Records of North Carolina.
[2] Richard Henderson was a native of Hanover County, Virginia, where he was born April 20, 1735, but had been a citizen of North Carolina since 1756, when his father, Samuel Henderson, settled there. He was a self-made man. His education had been deferred and his opportunities came late, but he was gifted with pluck and ability, and when he did start he made rapid progress, and especially in his chosen profession, the law,

Carolina, and had until recently been one of the Associate Justices of its Supreme Court. Though rather showy, he was a man of genuine ability and culture, was self-reliant and a worker, and, though noticeable always for enterprise and ambition, had surprised the Colony by the magnitude and boldness of his present venture. All of the nine members of the Company were citizens of North Carolina and "from over the Ridge." Three of them were residents of the then very extensive County of Granville, viz: Henderson, John Williams, his cousin and a bright lawyer, and Leonard Henley[1] Bullock, ex-sheriff of the county and a connection also. The others, who lived in or near the adjoining County of Orange, and who were mainly in commercial life, were James Hogg, a Scotchman and talented man of affairs; Nathaniel Hart,[1] one of the first of the Company to "sound" the Indians; Thomas and David Hart, his brothers, and John Luttrell and William Johnstone.

The announcement of so novel an enterprise and at

---

and in 1768 was appointed one of the Associate Justices of North Carolina. This position he held until his court was closed in 1770 by the Regulators, who rose against the corrupt and arbitrary exactions of the royal government of the province. After this he is said to have sustained pecuniary losses, and in 1774 he seized upon Boone's suggestion as a means of repairing and augmenting his fortune. (Wheeler, Ramsey, and Draper.)

[1] Nathaniel Hart was born in Hanover County, Virginia, in 1734, but moved to North Carolina in his youth. Like Henderson, he had taken sides against the Regulators in 1771.

such a disturbed and threatening juncture of public affairs created a sensation, and at least one officer[1] of the Colony anxiously inquired "If Dick Henderson had lost his head?" But "Dick" not only still possessed that convenience, but had used it. With the aid of Boone he had carefully investigated Kentucky, and had decided that now was the very time to strike. The Shawanese and other Northern Indians had but recently been defeated at Point Pleasant, and had obligated themselves by treaty to hunt no more on the Kentucky side of the Ohio. This and prior treaties seemed to leave no other Indian claimants to the Louisa[2] country but the Cherokees, and, as to Great Britain, her claim seemed destined to utter extinguishment in the conflict she was so rapidly forcing upon the Colonies. The importance of the movement was plain enough to Josiah Martin, the royal Governor of North Carolina, and on the 10th of February, 1775, he issued a

---

[1] Archibald Nelson, in Col. Rec. N. C.

[2] Kentucky seems never to have been known by any but Indian names until a short time before 1775, when "Louisa" came into limited use among the whites. The generally accurate Bradford helped to perpetuate the error that the Kentucky River was given the English name "Louisa" by Doctor Walker twenty-six years before this treaty, but not only does Marshall declare that Walker did not reach the interior of the country, but later writers assert that it was a tributary of the Big Sandy — as given on Jefferson's map — that the explorer of 1750 so named. It was some time after Walker's tour before the name of this tributary was applied to the country itself, and then, fortunately, it quickly subsided before the original and ancient Indian name — Kentucky.

proclamation[1] denouncing it as "a lawless undertaking," "an infraction of the Royal prerogative," and threatened the Company, if it persisted in its course, "with the pain of His Majesty's displeasure and the most rigorous penalties of the law." The greatness of the political change that had already occurred is evidenced by the fact that this proclamation was completely ignored.

Boone, who had been commissioned by the Company to open a road to the Kentucky River, never ceased collecting woodmen in Powell's Valley for the work, and concentrated them at Long Island,[2] in the Holston. While arrangements for the expedition were being made, provisions for the entertainment of the Cherokees went on to the appointed conference ground, and so did the Indians and the white men, and early in March, 1775, the biggest crowd that had ever gathered in the Watauga Settlement of North Carolina was encamped about the stockaded cabins of Sycamore Shoals.[3] This spot, which took its name

[1] For text of proclamation see Appendix D.

[2] This noted island, which was about twenty-six miles from the appointed rendezvous, is nearly three miles long, is in main Holston River near the junction of its north and south forks, and is included in the present Sullivan County, Tennessee.

[3] Boone, in his Filson memoir, merely states that the treaty took place "at Watauga," without specifying the particular spot in the settlement that was used. Felix Walker, in his narrative, says it occurred "at Colonel Charles Robertson's," whose home tract in 1775 was about a mile west of Sycamore Shoals, but which, with Fort Watauga near by, often at that

from the great sycamore trees which adorned it, which was then the seat of the now famous Watauga Association, and which is distinguished by its historic memories,[1] was on the southern bank of the Watauga River about three miles below "The Old Fields," the site of the present Elizabethton, in what is now Carter County, Tennessee. It was a rendezvous, familiar to the Indians, in a valley that has long been known for its fertility and beauty, and here, on the spacious stretch of rich bottom lands that were bordered on one side by the winding river and on the other by the swelling foothills of Yellow Mountain, tents and wigwams were pitched and the solemn, ceremonious, and deliberate conference was held. The negotiators in behalf of the Company were Henderson and Boone, Nathaniel Hart and Luttrell. The most prom-

---

time designated the general Sycamore Shoals neighborhood. In his Annals of Tennessee, Ramsey, who was personally familiar with the historic spots included in the Watauga Settlement, and who gave these points especial attention, definitely locates the treaty ground at Sycamore Shoals, which seems to be the verdict of both tradition and later investigation, which further specify that it included the land opposite the late residence of Alfred M. C. Taylor and present home of E. D. Jobe. The writer is indebted to the courtesy of Messrs. N. E. Hyder and D. N. Reese, of Carter County, Tennessee, for facts about the topography of the Watauga region.

[1] It was the seat of that famous little republic, the Watauga Association, which was the beginning of the political history of Tennessee; the place where the permanent settlement of Kentucky was assured, and the rendezvous five years after of the patriot riflemen who rode from thence to King's Mountain and victory.

inent representatives of the Indians were Ocanostota, the aged, crippled, and distinguished head of the Cherokees; the remarkable Attacullaculla, withered and even more aged, but still reputed the ablest of the Indian diplomatists; Savanooko, and Dragging Canoe.[1]

Days were consumed in the consideration of the boundaries and extent of the territory the Company desired, the price offered, and the wisdom of making such a sale, and interpreters were kept busy translating "talks" and documents and speeches. Earnest protests against the treaty were made by orators of the Cherokees, and especially by the eloquent and prophetic Dragging Canoe, but without effect, and on the 17th of March "The Great Grant"[2] was signed, and for the merchandise then stored on the ground and valued at £10,000 Henderson and his associates were declared the owners of territory south of the Kentucky River, comprising more than half of the present State of Kentucky.[3] The twelve hundred Indians present assented to the treaty, and, though a few of them grumbled that they had received only one shirt apiece for

[1] Virginia Archives.

[2] So named to distinguish it from the "Path Deed," signed at the same conference, by which the Cherokees granted Henderson and Company another great tract which was on the Holston, Clinch, and Powell rivers. (See United States Register for 1840.)

[3] For full description of the boundary of the Kentucky grant, see copy of the deed in Appendix E.

their share of the territory, the transaction seems to have been open and fair,[1] and certainly they all joined at the close of the meeting in the big feast the Company had provided.

The plans of the Company for taking possession of the magnificent Kentucky domain had already been arranged. A spot had been selected for headquarters directly on the Kentucky River, near the mouth of one of its tributary streams, which was known even then as Otter Creek,[2] and, as a road to it was a matter of immediate necessity, the Company, assured of success, determined to rush the making of it in advance, and Boone left Sycamore Shoals for Long Island before the treaty was concluded, and just as soon as he could be spared, in order to direct the work. His quota of woodmen with their hatchets and axes were all in waiting at the island, and among others there who had cast in their fortunes with the expedition were his brother, the tried explorer, Squire Boone, and his old Yadkin neighbor, Richard Calloway, who was considerably older than Boone,[3] was a native of Caroline County,

---

[1] See deposition of Charles Robertson in Appendix F.

[2] Probably so named by an early hunter from the Peaks of Otter, though the otter itself was found there.

[3] Calloway was born about 1724. Daniel Boone, according to the records of the monthly meeting of Exeter Township (now Berks County), Pennsylvania, was born November 2 (new style), 1734, and Doctor Draper says that date was entered by Boone himself on his family record.

Virginia, had been a captain in the French and Indian War, and was a colonel of the Bedford County militia when he removed to North Carolina.[1] The Company also included Captain William Twetty and seven other adventurous land hunters from Rutherford County, North Carolina.

On the tenth of March, all being ready, this memorable party of thirty mounted men, armed, but mainly for hunting, as no trouble was expected from Indians, and followed by negro servants, loaded pack-horses, and hunting dogs, started out under the command of Captain Daniel Boone to connect buffalo roads, Indian traces, trails of hunters and Indian traders, and the great Warrior Path, to cut through forests and canebrakes that were trackless, blaze the distances on mile-trees, and thus to make the first regular and continuous road through the wilderness to the Kentucky River. Climbing the dreary ridges that loomed up between them and Cumberland Gap, they threaded that sublime defile,[2] forded rivers that for ages had been nameless and swallowed up in a region vast and solitary, were heard of no more until they had toiled over that depression of the since historic Big Hill of the present county of

---

[1] Draper.

[2] Cumberland Gap is one of the grandest of natural passages. Its narrow roadway extends for six miles between mountain sides that rise twelve hundred feet above it.

DANIEL BOONE.

(In his old age.)

From an Oil Painting by Chester Harding, owned by Colonel R. T. Durrett, of Louisville, Kentucky.

Madison, Kentucky, known to this day as "Boone's Gap," and had camped by a forest stream five miles south of the site of the then undreamed-of town of Richmond,[1] Kentucky. Here, on the 25th of March, before daylight, after an undisturbed journey of two weeks, and while confident of continued peace, they were suddenly fired on by Indians, who quickly retired. A negro manservant of Captain Twetty was instantly killed, Captain Twetty himself was mortally wounded and soon died, and a young companion, Felix Walker, was dangerously wounded.[2] Only two nights after this another attack was made, and presumably by the same Indians, and this time on a little detachment which had camped near a stream some distance from the main party. With characteristic imprudence the men had lighted a fire and were drying their badly-soaked moccasins when the savages surprised them, killing and scalping Thomas McDowell and Joseph McPheeters, and stampeding the balance, who ran barefooted through the snow and escaped. One of the men, Samuel Tate, of Powell's Valley, took to the stream to hide his tracks, for it was a moonlight night, and from that day to this the stream has been known as Tate's Creek.[3] Boone, who evidently

---

[1] Walker's Narrative, Appendix G, and depositions of pioneers.
[2] Walker's Narrative, Appendix H, and Boone's letter to Henderson.
[3] Boone. Nat. Hart, junior, in Frankfort Commonwealth of July 25, 1838. Hart errs in date of this attack, which is correctly given in Boone's letter, which was written only four days after the affair.

thought this was the beginning of a serious effort to drive all the white people from the country, and who seems to have been invested by the Company with military powers, posted off a courier at once, ordering "all of the lower companies" of hunters and settlers then in the vicinity of the present Harrodsburg[1] to concentrate at the mouth of Otter Creek, and on the first of April, after the burial of the dead and careful attention to the wounded man, he started a messenger to Judge Henderson, urging him to bring or send aid as soon as possible, and said in his quiet, self-contained way of the excited people who were sure that another Indian war had commenced, that they were "very uneasy," and that he and his men would start that day for the mouth of Otter Creek, and would erect a fort there.

Boone did not even know for certain that Henderson was yet on the road, but he was. Prompt and energetic, he had completed his preparations two days after the treaty was signed, and on the third day, the 20th of March,[2] in spite of a threatened denunciation from another

---

[1] Henderson says in his journal: "These men had got possession some time before we got here."

It is plain from both Boone and Henderson that the site of Harrodsburg had been occupied just before they came, but Boonesborough, organized, garrisoned, and provisioned, was the only substantial settlement in Kentucky in the spring of 1775, and the only one that insured the permanent occupancy of the country.

[2] Henderson's Journal, Appendix I.

governor, Lord Dunmore, he started from sturdy little Watauga toward the distant land of his golden dream. The expedition was a prophecy of permanent occupation, for it included not only forty mounted riflemen[1] and quite a number of negro slaves, but a drove of beeves, forty pack-horses, and a train of wagons loaded with provisions, ammunition, material for making gunpowder, seed corn, garden seed, and a varied store of articles of prime necessity at an isolated settlement. Henderson was accompanied by four other members of the Company, viz: the Harts and John Luttrell, by his brother, Samuel Henderson, and by the patriotic William Cocke,[2] who had recently declined militia service under the royal Governor of Virginia, whose proclamation[3] was issued the very day after they started, threatening the Company with fine and imprisonment if it persisted in the occupancy of crown lands in Virginia "under a pretended purchase from the Indians." Cocke was from Amelia County, Virginia, and had left his young wife at Watauga when he started to "prospect." He was a stranger to Henderson, who little suspected what material was in this black-eyed, black-haired rifleman of twenty-seven. Another member of the party was William Bailey Smith, one of the witnesses of

[1] Walker and Calk.
[2] Appendix, Henderson's Journal.
[3] For text of Dunmore's proclamation see Appendix J.

the recent treaty, who was going out as surveyor.[1] He, too, was a native of Virginia, where he had served as major of militia, but had lately migrated to North Carolina. He was a tall, rollicking, unstable bachelor, energetic and brave, but with quite a turn for embellishing facts.

The expedition, following directly in Boone's tracks, managed in ten days, after clearing the road still more, to get through with the wagons to the last cabin on the blazed route leading up to Cumberland Gap. This log shelter was occupied by Captain Joseph Martin, the Company's agent for the Powell's Valley division of its purchase, who with several men seems to have gone on in advance of Henderson's party. Martin knew that region and the savages who frequented it, for he had explored it as a peltry buyer, and the cabin[2] is said to have been the same one he had used five years before this time when he had established a little trading-post at this distant and lonely spot, from which he had subsequently been driven away by the Indians. Here at Martin's,

[1] Draper.

[2] This cabin or station was in what is now Lee County, Virginia, and is known as Boone's Path Post-office. Captain Martin, who at the above-mentioned time was about thirty-five, was a native of Albemarle County, Virginia. He was a soldier in the French and Indian War, later on was a fur trader, and in 1769 settled in Powell's Valley. He served as captain of a company of scouts in Dunmore's War of 1774, and at its close became interested in the Henderson and Company scheme. (N. Cyclopedia of American Biography, Volume VII.)

Henderson's party was joined by William Calk and four other immigrants from Virginia, and here they had to give up their wagons, hide sulphur, salt, and overplus of other heavy material, and start out with pack-horses only to carry their baggage over the freshly marked but very narrow trace. It was on the 7th of April,[1] when they had just reached the Gap, that Boone's letter about the Indian attack arrived, striking the camp like a small bombshell and causing a few of the men to start on the back track that very night. The next day they met the first of several companies of panic-stricken adventurers who had started from Kentucky at the earliest news of savage troubles, and it became at once vitally important to notify Boone in advance of the slow-moving pack-train that aid was approaching in order to encourage his men to hold their ground. It was the tenth of the month and they had reached the banks of the Cumberland River before any thing was done. There, when most of the force had been further demoralized by the sight of more fleeing refugees, when Henderson despaired of finding a messenger to Boone, and when everybody was expecting to hear that even Boone's party had turned back, the gallant Captain Cocke volunteered[2] to be the

[1] Henderson's letter, Appendix K.
[2] Henderson's letter, Appendix L.

courier to the unterrified pioneer. No one offered to go with him. So, provided with "a good Queen Anne musket, plenty of ammunition, a tomahawk, a large 'cuttoe'-[1] knife, a Dutch blanket, and no small quantity of jerked beef," he started out alone on a ride of a hundred and thirty miles over a wild and solitary path which, according to the stampeded throng, was beset by murderous ambuscades.[2] It was one of the most romantic deeds in the annals of the wilderness, and the hero of it was destined to be heard of again.

But the sturdy and determined Boone had not turned back. He had started, as he said he would, from "the battle-ground," had cut a way through the cane down the meandering course of Otter Creek to the southern bank of the Kentucky River, and had there connected his path with a great buffalo trace which led broad and clear to the site, on the same side of the river, which he had chosen for the official seat of the Company. As the horsemen moved on there was a sudden sound like the trampling of many feet, and when with eager interest they hastened nearer to the selected ground they saw a

[1] Corruption of the French word "couteau" and redundancy besides.

[2] According to Mr. William Chenault, the historical writer of Richmond, Kentucky, Cocke was fortunate enough before he reached Boone's camp to catch up with another horseman named Page Portwood, and the two then journeyed together.

THE SULPHUR WELL.

Outgrowth of the Sulphur Spring that Centred the Ancient Lick in Sycamore Hollow, Boonesborough.

THE LICK SPRING.

(Of fresh water.) As it appeared in the Fall of 1900.

Boonesborough

The spring that was nearest the river was a sulphur[1] one, which soon accounted to the experienced woodsmen for the existence of the lick around it, for they found that the soil had been impregnated for ages with salt[2] which the sulphur water contained. The other spring, which was still further from the river, furnished an abundant supply of fresh water, but, curiously enough, it eventually became known as "The Lick Spring," a name that the sulphur one was naturally entitled to. Not far from them both were grouped some of the grandest trees that ever delighted the human eye. Four of them were especially noticeable. Of these, three were immense sycamores,[3] whose white trunks had been polished by the incessant touch of the salt-hunting elk and buffalo and deer, and one was an elm so magnificent in size and so exceptional in its proportions and in the spread of its far-reaching branches that one who saw it in all its glory, and had a

[1] The terms "salt spring" and "salt lick" are not synonymous, as some authorities on Kentucky seem to have supposed. Filson mentions a salt "spring" at Boonesborough, meaning, probably, a lick, for none of the actual settlers of the place record the existence of a spring of that kind in the locality, and so far as now known the lick was the result of the salt precipitated from the water of the sulphur spring, and not from a common salt one. Felix Walker, writing in his old age, speaks of both springs as sulphur ones, an error which the waters themselves make plain.

[2] Chloride of sodium, or common salt.

[3] The occidental plane tree, called in some American localities the buttonwood tree.

soul to appreciate it, called it "divine."[1] Near by the ancient river ran solemn and beautiful, deep down between the rugged steepness of its southern side and the wooded heights and everlasting hills that shut in the other shore. The natural charms of the distant treaty ground of Sycamore Shoals were strangely duplicated in the camping-ground of "Sycamore Hollow." And here, on the 1st of April,[2] 1775, about a mile and a quarter below the mouth of Otter Creek, Boone and his harassed and tired woodsmen unloaded their horses, cooked a simple meal, and, after a good long rest, began the erection of several log huts for temporary shelter and defense.[3] They were located "about sixty yards from the river,"[4] something over two hundred yards southwest of the lick,[5] and constituted what was immediately named "Fort Boone."[6] This so-called "fort" was neglected from the start. The road-makers were so much engrossed with securing land and in the wholesale destruction of animals for their skins that

[1] Henderson.
[2] Boone.
[3] "Daniel Boone had prevailed upon fifteen men to assist him in erecting some small huts for defense," says an extract from a manuscript fragment of William Cocke. (Copy in Wis. H. Library.)
[4] Boone's own words.
[5] Compare distances given by Henderson, W. B. Smith, and Bowman.
[6] It seems to have received that name as soon as erected, and is so called familiarly in both Henderson's and Calk's journals, under date of April 20, 1775. The "borough" termination was added later on.

even the killing of one of their comrades by the Indians on the 4th of April[1] did not move them to complete it. It is plain, though, that only the coolness and intrepidity of Boone prevented the country from being entirely abandoned, as it was the year before. Henderson afterward declared "it was owing to Boone's confidence in us and the people's in him that a stand was ever attempted."[2] The whole panic subsided as quickly as it had started when it was found that the attacks came from a ridiculously small number of adventurous Indians. Fortunately for the settlers, all such violent acts of bad faith were strongly condemned by the chivalric and influential Cornstalk.[3] The treaty of Point Pleasant was, for a time at least, observed, and for more than a year from the date of this last murder no regular party of Indians visited Kentucky, and no skulker did mischief at Boone's settlement, except in one solitary instance.[3] It was a blessed season of peace, and so when Captain Cocke arrived the savages were almost forgotten, and he, greatly to his surprise, found that his plucky adventure and the letters he brought excited as much interest as the news of reinforcements which he had risked his life to bring.

[1] Boone's Nar.
[2] Henderson's letter of July 12, 1775, Appendix. The Company, at its September meeting, granted Boone two thousand acres of land for his services.
[3] Williams' letter, Appendix.

Judge Henderson and party, which now included Robert and Samuel McAfee,[1] reached the unfinished and only half-watched little fort on the 20th of April, the Judge's fortieth birthday. They were welcomed with a discharge of rifles and with much rejoicing, and were all seated down forthwith to a dinner of cold water and lean buffalo beef, which the Judge declared was the most joyful banquet he ever saw. Of that there could not be the shadow of a doubt, for with it ended the most intense and protracted strain of care and anxiety he had ever experienced. The immense region of incalculable value for which he and his Company had risked so much, and which day after day for many days seemed about to slip from their grasp, was still safe, and a journey of a solid month, which, to one used to inns, offices, and court-rooms, seemed a solid year of hardships, aggravations, and miseries, was over. To such a man, worn out and disgusted, the lifting of such a burden changed the poorest hunter's meal into a banquet fit for the gods. And to the negroes, who saw an "Ingin," bloody-handed and awful, behind every rock and tree on the route, the sight of the little log huts was as a sight of heaven itself, and their loud laughter, merry songs, and exclamations of delight echoed

[1] Henderson's journal. Henderson met them returning to Virginia and persuaded them to go back.

along the river and among the very hill-tops. But with eighty persons in the united companies, including boys and negroes, the food question was a serious one, and especially since the improvident woodsmen had quickly driven away the but lately abounding multitudes of big game. Even this early in the action squads of hunters, detailed from the sixty-five riflemen,[1] had to range fifteen, twenty, and even thirty miles away for the wild meat that was almost the sole dependence of the settlers, for bread was already becoming a rarity and promised to give out altogether long before the corn crop[2] could mature. Fortunately some of Boone's men had planted corn a few days after they arrived. More was now planted, and companies were organized to work it in common — the members signing an agreement to appear every morning at the blast of a horn or sound of a drum and labor in the fields or stand guard while others worked, as the "captain" required.[3]

Henderson saw as soon as he came that his men, stores, and especially his gunpowder, would require much more commodious and substantial shelter than either his tents or Boone's little cabins could afford. It is also

[1] Cocke.

[2] Of course we refer here only to maize or Indian corn, the accepted meaning of the word in America.

[3] United States Register.

intimated that Boone's position was exposed to rifle fire from the over-topping hills on the other side of the river, which is doubtful, considering the distance, but especially the fact that the forests on both sides were then so dense as to completely shut off observation. But it might be that danger from very probable overflow of the river was considered. Be that as it may, Henderson decided at once to erect a fort that would be large enough and strong enough to accommodate and protect the stores and present settlers, and be capable of easy future extension. He selected a site for it on the opposite side of the lick from Boone's quarters and about three hundred yards from them,[1] but staked off the line of its front wall within less than a hundred yards of the lick itself, from which it was reached by a hilly ascent. The chosen spot, therefore, was much higher than the camp-ground it overlooked, which soon became known as "The Hollow"—the "Sycamore Hollow" of to-day—which was much deeper in pioneer times than it is now. The fort site was on a plateau, and was probably as close to the river as the log "huts," but though it was many feet above the water, it could hardly be said to have extended along a cliff, as it has sometimes been represented. At any rate, as far back as the memory of the oldest residents of the neigh-

[1] Henderson and Cocke.

SITE OF FORT BOONESBOROUGH.
(A Cornfield.)

As it appeared in November, 1900, looking toward the River.

borhood goes, the southern bank of the river has always fallen away from the spot, as it does now, in a succession of little ridges, and the site does not appear nearly as elevated as it really is, and especially when viewed from the river itself or from the opposite shore. The selected ground was occupied by Henderson and most of the last comers on Saturday, April 22d, the third day after they reached the settlement.[1] Nearly a week was consumed in making a "clearing," felling trees, shaping and notching logs, and splitting clapboards, but on the 29th the fort was begun, under the supervision of Daniel Boone, with the building of a small log magazine, which seems to have been half under ground, with a shed roof covered with clay to protect it from sparks that would surely come from chimneys and snapping flints, from "live chunks" that settlers were always borrowing from each other to start fires with, and from possible torches that attacking Indians might use. One of the earliest cabins, one story high, erected after this was made especially commodious to accommodate the Company's supplies, which were thrown open to an eager crowd of rangers, hunters, and road-makers, to whom the Company was indebted for services.[2]

[1] Henderson's Manuscript Journal, Appendix.
[2] In one item of the Company's ledger Michael Stoner is charged with "£7 3s 6d for powder, lead, and osnaburgs," and credited with "£10 10s for work making roads to Cantucke." (Nat. Hart, junior, in Frankfort Commonwealth.)

This was the first store ever opened in Kentucky. Judge Henderson took up his quarters in a block-house, erected at this time. It formed an angle of the defense — the angle nearest the river. A number of other cabins had also been built, when it was discovered that Indian signs had ceased, and forthwith the workmen relaxed their exertions, and, much to the disgust of the leading spirits, the completion of the fort was postponed. The error has been carelessly perpetuated that Boonesborough Station was entirely finished at this time, and it is even pictured with the stars and stripes flying over the front gate in 1775, in spite of the fact that the flag was not adopted by Congress until 1777. It is gratifying to know that the shape and general outline of this famous wooden stronghold are not matters of mere conjecture. A plan of the fort, designed at this very time and in the handwriting of Judge Henderson himself, was long preserved,[1] and a copy of it is herewith given. The building of the station, as far as it was prosecuted in the spring of 1775, was done in accordance with this plan, which was fully carried out later on. Fortunately the clearing was extensive and ultimately cut no small figure as a defensive feature of the place. A few trees were left standing inside

[1] It was in the possession of James Hall, the historical author, as late as 1835, and was copied by him.

the stockade, and the tops of several others that grew down on the rugged slope to the river projected above the bank back of the fort, but, though stumps were plentiful, the long rifles of the pioneers had a pretty clear sweep of the ground in the rear of the defense, along the descent to the springs in "the hollow," and for a considerable stretch toward a long ridge that extended at quite a distance off in front of the fort. This continuous hill soon received the name of "Hackberry Ridge."

On the 26th of this month, while the woodsmen on the banks of the Kentucky were busy at their clearing, the representatives of the Company in distant North Carolina sought, through a skillful letter [1] that reflects the uncertain condition of the times, to secure for their enterprise the influence and support of two already conspicuous lights of the opening Revolution — Patrick Henry and Thomas Jefferson. Shortly after this Judge Henderson formulated "a plan of government by popular representation" for the Company's wilderness domain, and on the 8th of May, in behalf of the proprietors, ordered an election of members of a "House of Delegates of the Colony of Transylvania" to meet on the 23d of that month at Boonesborough.[2] In this call of the 8th of May the Colony and its "capital" are formally and for the first time given the

[1] For letter, see Appendix M.
[2] See Journal of the House, Appendix N.

names respectively of "Transylvania" and "Boonesborough," which they bore from that date. Elections were duly held at the four little settlements[1] south of the Kentucky River, and on Tuesday, the 23d of May, 1775, the chosen representatives of the Colony, rifles in hand, rode up to the log quarters of the Chief Proprietor, Judge Henderson. But while a few absolutely necessary cabins had been built, the fort was so incomplete and encumbered that the "divine elm" in the hollow was selected as the temporary forum of the capital. Here the delegates did their preliminary work, and the next day, the 24th, under the spreading dome that the Immortal Architect himself had fashioned, and which overshadowed what an eye-witness called "a heavenly green" of fine white native clover, was attempted for the first time in the vast region west of the Alleghanies the founding of an independent State which proclaimed that sublime axiom that "all power is originally in the people"[2]—a proprietary government built largely on the lines of a republic. A House of Delegates for the Colony was there and then organized, and was formally opened by Judge Henderson in behalf of the Proprietors with a carefully written and statesmanlike speech,[2] in which the independence of "the newborn

[1] Boonesborough, Harrodsburg, Boiling Spring, six miles southeast of Harrodsburg, and St. Asaph's, a mile west of the present Stanford.
[2] House Journal, Appendix.

country" is asserted in the declaration, "We have the right to make laws for the regulation of our conduct without giving offense to Great Britain or any of the American Colonies." The House was in session three days, during which nine bills were passed, and its business, conducted though it was in the open air, was transacted with all the dignity, regularity, and ability that marked the Colonial legislatures of the time. The laborers employed by Boone to cut the first regular road to Kentucky were of the usual woodchopping type, but the men who participated in the effort to establish the Transylvania government distinguished it with a moral and intellectual force that utterly refuted the published assertions of Martin and Dunmore. A striking incident of Saturday, the last day of the session, was the formal and public observance before the House of the ancient feudal ceremony, "Livery of Seisin,"[1] the final act in the transfer of the immense portion of the territory sold by the Cherokees to Henderson and Company. Standing under the great elm, the attorney employed by the Indians, John Farrar, handed to Judge Henderson a piece of the luxuriant turf cut from the soil that extended beneath them, and, while they both held it, Farrar declared his delivery of seisin and possession of the land, according to the terms of the title deed which

[1] House Journal, Appendix; Butler in Western Journal.

Henderson displayed, and the immediate reading of which completed a legal requirement now long since obsolete and almost forgotten. The session closed with the execution of its most important feature, the signing of a compact between the Proprietors and the People,[1] which, crude as it is, takes historical precedence as the constitution of the first representative government ever attempted west of the Alleghany Mountains.

The House adjourned, but the delegates met once more before they dispersed, for, the next day being Sunday, the entire settlement assembled under the grand old elm, where "divine service for the first time" in Kentucky was performed by Reverend John Lythe,[2] of the Church of England, a minister from Virginia and a member of the delegation from Harrodsburg. It was a religious event absolutely unique. Most of the usual accessories of the service were wanting, from echoing church bell and "long drawn aisle" to pealing organ. No woman was there to join in litany or hymn, no child to lisp "amen." Only men were present—Dissenters as well as Episcopalians—for common dangers had drawn them together, and this one chance for public worship was eagerly seized by

[1] House Journal, Appendix.
[2] Henderson, who spelt proper names to suit himself, gives this one in his journal as "Lyth," but in the proceedings of the Convention it is spelt as above.

MEETING OF THE TRANSYLVANIA HOUSE OF DELEGATES

At Boonesborough, May, 1775. (Design from Historical Data by the Author.)

Boonesborough

pioneers who were as strong in simple faith as stout in heart, for there were others in the Colony of Transylvania besides the reckless few among the woodmen from Powell's Valley. And so, cut off from the whole civilized world, the forerunners of a mighty West of many States knelt together in the sweet white clover, under that magnificent tree, the sole cathedral in a wilderness as vast and as solitary as the illimitable ocean. This was the first and last time that prayers were ever publicly recited on Kentucky soil for the King and royal family of England.[1] In less than a week the news, so long on the road, of the battle of Lexington[2] threw the settlements into a fever of excitement, and minister and people not only sided at once with "the rebels," but the pastor, like some he had preached to under the elm, ultimately sealed his devotion to liberty with his blood.[3] The Transylvanians would have been even more excited if they had known that Governor Martin, who had proclaimed them outlaws, had fled from

---

[1] The very next spring the Virginia Convention expunged from the liturgy the words relating to the royal family.

[2] The news was a little more than six weeks getting to Boonesborough, and did not reach the site of Lexington (Kentucky) until the 5th of June. (See page 19, History of Lexington, Kentucky.)

[3] John Lythe was with the Virginia Militia, presumably as Chaplain, in the campaign of the next year against the Cherokees, and certainly served in that capacity with the Virginia troops in 1777. (See Payments of Militia in Virginia Records.) According to Morehead, Lythe was killed by the Indians.

his "palace"[1] while their legislature was in session, and that, while they were responding to the slogan of the Revolution, Lord Dunmore also was preparing to fly to a British vessel.[2]

On the 8th of June, a few days after the arrival of the great news, the notorious Dr. John F. D. Smythe rode into Boonesborough. He said he was touring the Colonies for material for a book of travels, which he did publish after the Revolution,[3] but the wily Scotchman kept religiously to himself the rather dangerous fact that he was also a spying emissary of Lord Dunmore to aid in uniting the Indians and frontier Tories in a scheme to sweep Virginia and her Kentucky territory clean of "rebels." It was skimpy times at the executive cabin just then, for bread was not to be had, and the salt was expected every day to give out. Even "big" meat was none too easy to get, but Judge Henderson's black Dan managed to keep a supply, and with some vegetables from the fort garden, "cats" from the river, and milk punches — for "the capital" was not without cows — the plotting guest was entertained. Smythe had his own reasons for enduring pioneer fare for several weeks, for

---

[1] Volume X, Colonial Records of North Carolina.
[2] He escaped to the Fowey June 8, 1775.
[3] In London in 1784.

during this time he openly and very innocently visited the Shawanese and other Ohio Indians, all then at peace with the whites. He doubtless made a diagram of "the works" at Boonesborough. In his notes, which the unsuspecting settlers did not get a chance to see, he mentions Henderson as "a man of vast and enterprising genius, but void of military talents," and says, in the disgust of his loyal soul at the outrageous independence of the Transylvanians, "such is the insolence, folly, and ridiculous pride of these ignorant backwoodsmen that they would conceive it an indelible disgrace and infamy to be styled servants even of His Majesty." The doctor was still more disgusted before he left the country, for shortly after this he barely escaped being tarred and feathered in a Virginia town, and later on was arrested, imprisoned, and the plan nipped in the bud.

Early in this same month of June, while the American troops were girding themselves for the approaching contest at Bunker Hill, every thing was quiet enough in the Kentucky wilderness, and Boone, who wanted to bring out his wife and children to Boonesborough, was concerned to have them safely lodged, and again urged his men, as he had often done before, to complete their little log shelter in the hollow. This time he was successful, and the cabins which, though they required no great attention, had been so long neglected, were easily finished.[1] They seem never to have been used except for residence and domestic purposes.

It was about this time, too, that reports of Dunmore's efforts to inflame the Indians began to reach and arouse Boonesborough, and it is probable that Henderson and Boone seized the chance to impel the self-confident woodsmen to further defensive exertions, for the "big fort" on the rise overlooking the Lick was then almost but not entirely completed, much to the satisfaction of the resident proprietors, who had been exceedingly uneasy over their unprotected condition.[2] This was the

---

[1] It is the usual thing for writers of Western history to confuse these little defensive cabins commenced in "the hollow" on the 1st of April with the fort begun by Henderson on the the 22d of the same month, though they were so different in location and importance. Even so late a writer as Roosevelt makes the two defenses identical, as Marshall did. The mistake dates from 1784, when Filson wrote his valuable but high-flown account of Boone, in which he fails to distinguish between the two, and makes the plain old hunter speak of the cabins begun April 1st as "works," and has him "busily employed" on them until the 14th of June. Filson wrote nine years after the event. Henderson, in his journal and in his letters written on the ground, says the log affair in the hollow was "a small fort," and that it was persistently neglected in spite of repeated efforts of both himself and Boone to get the men to finish it. The large fort completed later on was the only one that could aspire to such a title as "works," or that men would be "busily employed" on for weeks. Writers followed Filson without investigation, and hence the perpetuation of the error. (See Boone's Narrative, Henderson's letter of June 12, 1775, William Cocke, etc.)

[2] Henderson's letter of June 12, 1775, Appendix X, and letter of July 18, 1775, to the Company. (See Frankfort Commonwealth, May 26, 1840.)

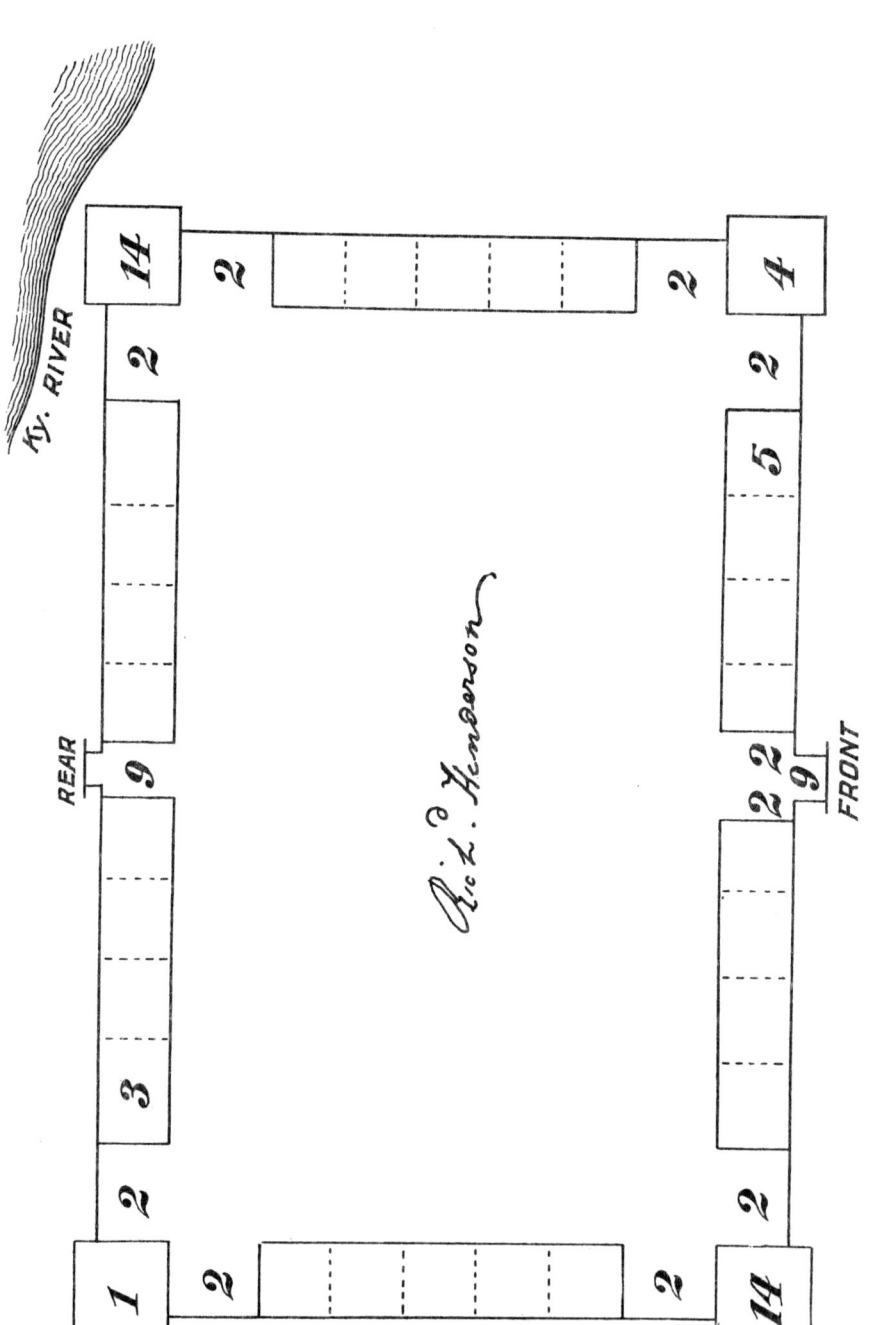

PLAN OF FORT BOONESBOROUGH.

From the Original in the Handwriting of Richard Henderson. Copied by James Hall. Henderson's Autograph from Original in possession of Wisconsin Historical Library.

1—Henderson's Cabin. 2—Stockades. 3—Henderson's Kitchen. 4—Luttrell's Cabin. 5—His Kitchen.

only real fortification Boonesborough ever had, and the only one that figured in the Revolution. Fortunately, a plan of this celebrated station, drawn by Judge Henderson himself, was preserved,[1] and other information about it from some of its actual defenders is still extant. In the summer of 1775 it consisted of twenty-six one-story log cabins and four block-houses, arranged after the usual pioneer style, in a hollow square estimated as two hundred and sixty feet long and one hundred and eighty feet broad.[2] The block-houses, with their projecting second stories, formed the angles or bastions of the fort, and the roofs of the cabins, which were shed-shaped, sloped inwardly. Spaces between the block-houses and the cabins nearest them were intended to be stockaded, but as pickets were the least needed features of the fort in time of peace, it is probable that these were the parts neglected at this time, which afterward had to be supplied to "finish the fort."[3] Both cabins and stockades were provided with little portholes for the rifles. The back of the station, so to speak, or back row of cabins comprising one of its longest sides, was substantially parallel with the river,[4] though one of the angles on the river was nearer the bank than the other,

[1] Copied by James Hall in 1835.
[2] Estimated by Hall from original documents.
[3] John Floyd's letter of July 21, 1776.
[4] Henderson and Draper manuscripts.

while the front commanded the open space in the hollow below the fort, in which were the lick and the two springs. There were two gates — generally forgotten except in time of danger — one in the front and the other in the back wall facing the river. At Boonesborough, as at nearly all the pioneer stations in Kentucky, no provision whatever was made to insure a supply of drinking-water inside the stockade, plain as was the danger of the garrison being cut off from the springs in case of siege. All the cabins of the fort were not continuously occupied, for some of the settlers lived on their variously-located lands nearby, and some even had farms across the river; but the cabins were often filled by newly-arrived immigrants, and all were crowded to overflowing whenever an Indian alarm was given. Then all the settlers in the neighborhood rushed in. It is certain, however, that in 1775 Judge Henderson lived in the block-house in the angle nearest the river; that he used for his kitchen the nearest cabin to him in the back row, and that old Dan, his negro cook, presided over it.[1] Colonel Nat. Hart's quarters were nominally in the other angle near the river, but really with Colonel Callaway, it is believed, in one of the cabins in the hollow,[2] when not at his White Oak clear-

---

[1] Diagram of the fort and Draper manuscripts.
[2] Diagram of the fort and Nat. Hart, junior's, notes.

Boonesborough

ing, which he had already made about a mile above the fort. Luttrell's house was in the corner to the right of the front gate, and the angle that overlooked the lick was subsequently inhabited by John Williams, the Company's Agent. The cabins of Floyd and others have not been located, but "the store" is supposed to have formed part of the end of the station adjoining "the block-house," as Judge Henderson's rough residence was curiously called, considering that there were three other block-houses.

Toward the middle of June Captain Cocke left Boonesborough for Black's Fort (Abingdon), to which his wife had returned, under the impression from his long absence that he was dead. On the way — following a gentle habit that had been observed in most of the colonies — he scalped an Indian[1] who had been killed and overlooked by some immigrants after the savage and his party had attacked them in Powell's Valley. It was not long after this that he commenced a career that became distinguished.[2]

On the 13th of June, after superintending the work on the fort, Boone set out for his family, which was still

---

[1] Henderson and Luttrell. (See Frankfort Commonwealth, May 26, 1840.)

[2] He figured gallantly the very next summer as an officer in the victory over the Cherokees at Long Island of the Holston, and ultimately became one of the first United States Senators from Tennessee. He died August 22, 1828, at Columbus, Mississippi, and was there buried.

at Snoddy's Station,[1] the stockaded home of his comrade, John Snoddy, located on the margin of the Clinch River, on the site of the present town of Castlewood, Russell County, Virginia. His old neighbor, Richard Callaway, went along with him for a like purpose, his family, too, being in a frontier fort of Virginia at this time.[2] They had the company, as far as Powell's Valley, of Thomas Hart, who was *en route* to North Carolina. With Boone was a detail of men engaged to bring back the salt[3] which had been left behind at Martin's cabin by Henderson when the wagons were abandoned there. When the party set out Boonesborough was on the eve of a salt famine, which was in full force by the middle of the succeeding month, increasing the scarcity of provisions through the extreme difficulty of preserving wild meat, and especially big game, which now had to be brought

[1] The exact location of Boone's family "on Clinch" at this period is now given for the first time, thanks to Judge W. B. Wood, of Bristol, Virginia, who obtained the information from T. W. Carter, of Scott County, Virginia, a descendant of Samuel Porter, who was with Boone in 1773 when driven back by the Indians from Wallen's Gap. (See Appendix.) Castlewood has a population of about five hundred, and the Clinch Valley Division of the Norfolk & Western Railroad runs through the place.

[2] Callaway evidently moved from Virginia to the Yadkin region of North Carolina after the French and Indian War, but returned to Virginia just before the Revolution.

[3] The salt had, doubtless, been originally secured from the primitive works then existing on the North Fork of the Holston, at the place now known as Saltville, Smyth County, Virginia.

in from quite a distance through the heat. The men, after securing the salt, evidently waited in Powell's Valley for Boone to arrive there on his return from Snoddy's, for Henderson dolefully says, in his letter of July 18th: "Our salt is exhausted, and the men who went with Colonel Boone for that article have not returned, and until he comes the devil could not drive the others this way." Tradition says that before the party got back the distressed settlers exerted themselves to the utmost to make salt from the sulphur water in the hollow, but the results were too small to encourage any repetition of the experiment. Henderson and Luttrell were both anxious to make a visit to North Carolina, where pressing business demanded their presence, but delayed their start until assured that Boone was well advanced on his return trip and would soon be back. They seem to have left about the latter part of August. Henderson hardly dreamed when he set out from the proprietary capital that fateful circumstances would make his absence from it one of years, nor did Luttrell imagine that he would see it no more forever.[1] When Boone started back to

[1] He was ultimately swept into the Revolution, was active against the Tories, and met death at their hands. He was shot through the body at Cane Creek, North Carolina, September 14, 1781. in an engagement with the notorious David Fanning, the Tory partisan leader, and died the following day. (Draper.) Colonel Luttrell was a native of Westmoreland County, Virginia. He left a widow, but no children.

Kentucky he was joined, not only by the salt men, but by quite a number of immigrants, including several families from North Carolina, that of the reckless Hugh McGary being one, who were bound for Harrod's Station. When these families left the company at "the hazel patch,"[1] in the present Laurel County, Kentucky, for their new home, about thirty persons were still left in Boone's party, which, with its cattle and dogs, its pack-horses loaded with the precious salt, provisions, and household "traps," arrived on the 8th of September at delighted and excited Boonesborough, which turned out *en masse* to welcome it. Boone's was the only family[2] in the party, and his wife and grown daughter, Jemima, were not only the first white women to set foot upon the margin of the picturesque Kentucky,[3] but they remained for nearly three weeks the only women there. The Boones immediately occupied a cabin in the hollow, but soon exchanged it for better quarters in "the big fort," and the influence of sunbonnets, though there was but a solitary couple of them, was soon seen. The men, and

[1] Hazel Patch is eight miles north of London, Kentucky.
[2] This party is said to have consisted of Boone, his wife and children, and twenty-one men, and as — according to Peck — Boone had eight children, not including the son killed two years before at Wallen's Gap, the above estimate is substantially correct.
[3] Boone to Filson. The other families mentioned reached their destination the same day the Boones arrived at theirs, but Harrodsburg is on Salt River, which runs within a mile of the town.

SITE OF FORT BOONESBOROUGH.

(Marked by Corn Stacks.) As seen from the opposite side of the River in 1900.

especially the younger ones, immediately improved in appearance, for there was a sudden craze for shaving and hair-cutting. An ash-hopper, soap kettle, and clothes line were set up. Hickory brooms and home-made washboards multiplied. The sound of the spinning-wheel was heard in the land, and an occasional sight could be had of a little looking-glass, a patch-work quilt, knitting-needles, and a turkey-tail fan. Cut off entirely from the companionship of females of their own race, great was the relief of Mrs. Boone and Miss Jemima when on the 26th of the month (September) Colonel Callaway returned with his family and a party which included William Pogue and Barney Stagner and their families, adding three matrons and several young women to the social life of the station. Pogue, being "an ingenius contriver," blessed the settlement by making piggins and noggins, washtubs and churns, and provisions were more plentiful now that there was salt to preserve the game, and the fields for the first time brought forth their increase. Times were better at Boonesborough.

The Transylvania Legislature did not convene at Boonesborough this September according to adjournment. The spread of revolutionary sentiments was not confined to the seaboard, and before the summer of 1775 had ended the idea of a proprietary government had become obnoxious to the Kentucky settlers. But a meeting of a majority of the Company's members was held on the twenty-fifth of the month[1] at the little town of Oxford, Granville County, North Carolina, about which several of them resided, and immediately steps were taken to secure the recognition of Transylvania as the fourteenth member of the United Colonies by the adoption of a memorial to the Continental Congress, then in session at Philadelphia, and the election of James Hogg as a delegate to that body. Mr. Hogg reached Philadelphia on the 22d of October, and, though not received as a delegate, he labored faithfully among the great spirits of that great assembly, and one of them, Silas Deane, thought so seriously of the new colony as to draw up a paper (which is herewith appended)[2] to aid in the proper shaping of its economy and government, but advised him to sound the Virginia delegates, "as they would not *chuse* to do any thing in it without their consent." Other Connecticut men besides Mr. Deane were thinking of Transylvania at this time, but in a different way. The prospect of securing generous slices of its rich domain at a trifling cost was so enticing to his constituents that two thousand of them, it is said, were considering the matter of settling

[1] See Proceedings of Meeting, Appendix O.
[2] Appendix P.

there.[1] Of the Virginia members of the Congress, Thomas Jefferson said it was his wish to see a free government established back of theirs, "but would consent to no congressional acknowledgment of the colony until it was approved by the Virginia Convention"; so to that convention the matter went. It is plain that none of the Congressmen that Hogg consulted countenanced a proprietary government. In what Hogg styles "an account of my embassy,"[2] he says, "You would be amazed to see how much in earnest all these speculative gentlemen are about the plan to be adopted by the Transylvanians. They entreat, they pray that we may make it a free government, and beg that no mercenary or ambitious views in the proprietors may prevent it. Quit rents, they say, is a mark of vassalage, and hope they shall not be established in Transylvania. They even threaten us with their opposition if we do not act upon liberal principles." In this same report to Judge Henderson, Mr. Hogg significantly adds, "Enclosed I send you a copy of a sketch by John Adams,[3] which I had from Richard Henry Lee." In this

[1] Letter of Governor Martin, of North Carolina, November 12, 1775, to Lord Dorchester, in Canadian Archives for 1890, pages 103–156.
[2] Appendix Q.
[3] This sketch was in the shape of a letter to George Wythe, of Virginia, and was entitled, "Thoughts on Government Applicable to the Present State of the American Colonies." At this time "there was much discussion," says Mr. Adams, "concerning the necessity of independence, and the

document Mr. Adams, like Jefferson and Deane, urged the adoption of full and complete republican constitutions by all the colonies. It must have been plain to Henderson and Company, even six or eight months before the Declaration of Independence, that the prospects of an American colony with a proprietary form of government were not encouraging.

At the before-mentioned September meeting of the Proprietors they advanced the price of land in Transylvania from twenty shillings to fifty shillings per hundred acres, which had much to do with raising a storm that was already threatened.

On the first of December John Williams, uncle of Judge Henderson and recently elected general agent of the colony, arrived at Boonesborough, accompanied by some immigrants, and opened a land office. John Floyd, who had returned from a trip made in the summer, was appointed surveyor, Nathaniel Henderson entry officer, and Richard Harrison secretary. Williams soon found

---

several States were advised to institute governments for themselves under the immediate authority and original power of the people." But the contemplated transition from a royal to a republican form of government presented difficulties. The important question was how to overcome these difficulties, and Mr. Wythe, in seeking more light upon it, requested Mr. Adams "to advise a plan for a colony to pursue in order to get out of the old government and into the new." This essay was in answer to that request. It can be found on page 189 of Volume IV of Life and Works of John Adams, by Charles Francis Adams.

that the rise in the price of the land was causing great dissatisfaction to the Transylvanians, which some of them at Harrodsburg soon exhibited in a formal remonstrance delivered to him by a special committee. His reply[1] was not satisfactory, and the trouble grew.

On the 23d of this month Boonesborough was amazed as well as exasperated by an Indian outrage,[2] for the Western savages were still neutral in the Revolutionary struggle. On that day two boys, McQuinney and Sanders, left the place without their rifles — a common thing with the long undisturbed settlers — crossed the river, climbed the hills opposite the fort, and fell into the hands of some lurking Shawanese, who fired on another member of the garrison who was also on that side. At first it was feared that quite a body of Indians had arrived, and, as the boys did not return, great anxiety was added to alarm, but on the 27th McQuinney, killed and scalped, was discovered in a cornfield about three miles north of the river, and it was evident that his slayers had decamped. A party of rangers under Jesse Benton,[3] father of the afterward famous Thomas H. Benton, scoured the woods with an offer of the Colony before their eyes of £5 for the scalp of each of the fleeing

[1] Appendix R.
[2] Williams' Report of January 3, 1776, Appendix S.
[3] Transylvania Company's books.

murderers, but no such gruesome trophy was secured, and Sanders, killed or a prisoner, never returned. It was soon learned that there were only about a half-dozen of the Shawanese, and that they were the unauthorized marauders alluded to by Cornstalk at the October conference at Fort Pitt between the American commissioners and the chiefs of the Western tribes. That noble Indian gentleman informed the commissioners that such a party had left for Kentucky just before the conference; that he could not be responsible for them, and that if any of them got killed he would take no notice of it whatever.[1] The settlers were relieved to know that the outrage was not yet the beginning of Indian hostilities, but all the same the first Christmas at Boonesborough was one of grief, anxiety, and tears.

The New Year, 1776, opened peacefully enough at the station, business at the "land office" went on,[2] and the spring was uneventful, but immigration was checked by the tragedy just related, unauthorized though it was, and by fears for the future. The English and the Americans were both working for an Indian alliance, but it was evident already that the savages, as usual, would side with the strongest, and the outlook was gloomy for the pioneers.

[1] Williams' letter.
[2] See Appendix T for specimen of the Company's land survey warrant.

In May a petition[1] embodying the substance of the December remonstrance was received by the Virginia Convention from "the inhabitants and some of settlers of that part of North America now denominated Transylvania." It was the last time that Transylvania was formally recognized as the name of the colony. Henderson, who was at Williamsburg watching the interests of the Company, filed an answering petition,[2] and feeling waxed hotter in the Kentucky wilderness. The rise in the price of its land, the uncertainty of its title, and its feudal features were not the only objections to the Proprietary government. It was not countenanced by any of the old colonies, and had no organized militia, and these deficiencies grew suddenly momentous when a warning came to the settlers from friendly Indians that some of the Western tribes were leaguing against the Long Knives. The people realized at once the importance of an open and decided recognition of their territory as a part of Virginia; steps were taken to effect this, and an eight-day election held at Harrodsburg, and commencing June 6th, resulted in the choice of two representatives, George Rogers Clark and John Gabriel Jones, from "West Fincastle," as the colony was newly called, to the Con-

[1] Appendix U. This petition to the Convention (not to the Assembly, as some authors have it) was received May 18, 1776.
[2] Filed June 15th. See Journal Virginia Convention.

vention of Virginia, and of an Executive Committee to voice the wishes of the people, which was done on the 20th of the month by the adoption of a petition[1] to the Convention, which in its own unique way prays for the incorporation of West Fincastle as a county of Virginia. This was not what the high-spirited and adventurous Clark was after, but the people had settled the matter and he acquiesced. He declares in his Memoirs :[2] "I wanted deputies elected at Harrodsburg to treat with the Virginia Assembly. If valuable considerations were procured we would declare ourselves citizens of the State, otherwise we would establish an independent government." The Convention adjourned before these proceedings could be submitted to it, but not before it had made provision to accurately determine Virginia's chartered interests in the Kentucky territory, and for an inquiry into alleged illegal purchases from the Indians,[3] both of which were ominous for the Transylvania Company, and brought from it a warning proclamation as to settlement on disputed lands.[4]

[1] Appendix V.
[2] Dillon's Indiana, Volume I, page 128.
[3] See journal of Virginia Convention, pages 63 and 83, for resolution adopted June 24, 1776, against purchase of land from the Indians without authority from the State, and for act of July 3, 1776, appointing Commissioners to examine into such illegal purchases.
[4] See Appendix W.

The summary action at Harrodsburg against the Proprietary government made but little stir in a region that was by this time constantly exercised about threatened Indian hostilities, and from which many an apprehensive soul had already departed. The tribes still claimed to be friends of the "Long Knives," but all the same Indian "signs" and alarming rumors increased, and early in July the significant fact was noted that several of the men who had left the settlement on hunting trips had never returned. Boonesborough was anxious, but more than six quiet months had elapsed since the murder of McQuinney, and no enemy had threatened the station yet.

It was as quiet as ever on the afternoon of Sunday, July 14th, and the customary Bible reading was over, when Elizabeth and Frances Callaway, daughters of Richard Callaway, and Jemima Boone,[1] daughter of Daniel Boone, started in one of the rough canoes of the settlement to visit a family located on the other side of the river, and only a short distance from Boonesborough. They had crossed and were only a few yards from a landing when the canoe struck a little sandbar nearly opposite a spot on the shore which tradition says is the same now known as "The Four Sycamores," from the four trees

[1] Boone's Narrative and W. B. Smith. Floyd's letter of July 21, 1776. See extract, Appendix X.

of that kind which afterward grew there, and which still designate the place. And here, when neither the faintest sight nor sound had intimated the presence of an enemy, the little boat was suddenly seized by five Indians — four Shawanese and one Cherokee — who darted from the thick cane that bordered the river. The eldest of the girls, "Miss Betsey," though startled and terrified, instinctively dealt one of the savages a blow on the head with a paddle, while her younger companions, paralyzed with fear, covered their blanched faces with their hands. In a moment, while too breathless and bewildered to give an alarm, they were rushed through the shallow water to shore and then up a densely wooded ravine to the summit of the high and lonely hills that stretched along that side of the river. From there, made dumb by a threat of the tomahawk, they were marched in silence through streams and canebrakes and woods toward the ancient "Warriors' Trace" that led to the Ohio. So cleverly had the savages managed that it was hours before the girls were missed — for it was not until milking time that the alarm was sounded by a hunter who had gone out to meet them. In the midst of the grief and excitement that ensued, and after exasperating delays, one band of riflemen under Daniel Boone and another under Colonel Callaway, comprising about twenty men in all, started in pursuit. This force

THE HILLS OF CLARK, ON THE KENTUCKY RIVER OPPOSITE BOONESBOROUGH,

Showing on the extreme right the traditional locality, now designated by "The Four Sycamores," where the three girls were captured by the Indians July 14, 1776.

included,[1] besides the leaders, John Holder, Samuel Henderson, Flanders Callaway, William Bailey Smith, John Floyd, Nathaniel Hart, David Hart, Nathan Reid, John Gess, David Gess, and others, from Boonesborough; and John Martin, John McMillan, and William Bush, who had recently built improvers' cabins across the river in easy distance from the fort. The outcome of this romantic incident is familiar to every reader of early Western history. The savages were surprised, routed, and two of them killed as they halted three miles south of the Upper Blue Licks, the tattered, torn, and despairing girls were rescued unharmed, and, after a torrent of happy tears and exclamations, were caught up on horseback and brought back worn out but safe to the rejoicing settlement.

But the event was a prophecy of evil. It was the beginning of days and years of trouble, and the rescuing party did not return a whit too soon. In fact, some mischief was done before they did return, for Indian stragglers went to Nathaniel Hart's clearing,[2] burned his cabin, and ruined his young apple trees, while the force left behind was too small to punish them. The news brought in by scouts and messengers was plain enough. Small parties of hostile Shawanese were haunting all the stations. The Indians had dug up the hatchet. Such of the neighbor-

[1] Names from John Floyd, John Bradford, and Draper manuscripts.
[2] United States Historical Register.

ing settlers, including those across the river, as had families brought them into the fort, which was now provided with cumbersome but substantial gates, and all the open gaps in the walls were filled in either with more cabins or with sharpened posts that stood ten feet above the ground. "The works" were finished at last[1] according to the original plans, and now another panic set in. Numbers left the country. On the 20th the discouraged settlers of Hinkston's Station[2] camped inside the stockade while *en route* to Virginia, and ten of the Boonesborough people went with them when they departed, leaving less than thirty riflemen to defend the place.[3]

Fortunately the Indians made no formidable movement this year, and though murders and depredations by skulkers and petty bands were incessant, all was not dark among the undaunted holders of the wilderness forts. On the 7th of August, three weeks after the capture of the girls, there was a wedding in one of the cabins at Boonesborough, when Squire Boone, Baptist Elder as well as Indian fighter, officiated, and Elizabeth Callaway, the oldest of the heroines of that adventure, and Samuel Henderson, a brother of Judge Henderson, were made

---

[1] Floyd's letter.

[2] One of the earliest settlements in Central Kentucky, located in the present Harrison County, and afterward called "Ruddles."

[3] Floyd's letter.

husband and wife.[1] At this, the first marriage that took place in Kentucky, there was dancing to fiddle-music by the light of tallow "dips," and legend says the guests were treated to home-grown watermelons, of which the whole station was proud. A few days later a returning settler brought in the first news of the Declaration of Independence and a copy of the Virginia Gazette containing the text of it. The immortal document was read out to the assembled garrison, was concluded amidst cheers and war-whoops, and was given the endorsement of a big bonfire that night. There were Sons of Liberty in the Kentucky wilderness as well as on the Seaboard, and some of them were right in Boonesborough at this time.

In September the station lost two more officers of the Proprietary government, John Williams and John Floyd, who left for the old settlements in the interest of the jeopardized Company. Their plans were soon changed by the action of Virginia in the Transylvania matter. Williams returned to North Carolina, became one of her leading citizens,[2] and saw the backwoods capital no more. Floyd, who was not destitute of love of adventure,

---

[1] Alfred Henderson to R. H. Collins.

[2] Williams was elected judge the next year, 1777, and was afterward a member of Congress. He died in October, 1799, on his farm a mile west of Williamsboro, in what is now Vance County, North Carolina, and was buried on the place.

embarked in the Revolution as a privateersman.[1] Isaac Shelby acted as surveyor for a short time at Boonesborough in his place, but the uncertain fare with its lack of salt injured his health, and he, too, departed.[2]

During the first session of the newly created State Legislature of Virginia, which began at Williamsburg in October, Henderson and his colleagues fought hard and long for the recognition of the claims of their Company,[3] but the battle ended in the assumption by the Commonwealth itself of jurisdiction over the disputed territory. On the 7th of December an act was passed creating the county of Kentucky out of the domain which was destined to be rechristened the State of Kentucky, and the new county included the Henderson purchase. The Proprietary government of Transylvania now ceased to exist, and Boonesborough suddenly found herself figuring unequivocally as a wilderness settlement of the extremest western county of the State of Virginia. The splendid and promising scheme of the Transylvania Company to possess an empire of territory and garner the magnificent revenues

---

[1] Floyd was captured by the British, and after an imprisonment of about a year returned to Kentucky.

[2] Wheeler's History of North Carolina.

[3] See Appendix T for deposition of Charles Robertson, a sample of the evidence taken by the Commissioners appointed by the Convention to investigate the purchase from the Cherokees. (Volume II, Cal. Virginia State papers.

it was to yield ended in a struggle for mere compensation for the expenses, labor, and trouble incurred in the enterprise. Much of the documentary history of that struggle is herewith appended.[1] Certain features of the Company's plan of government deserved the condemnation they received, but for the great work it did in opening up a continuous path to the banks of the Kentucky, in planting the strongest early barrier against the Indians, inspiring the desperate people with hope, and insuring the permanent occupation of the soil, it fully merited all the compensation it received, and will ever hold a prominent place in the history of the Commonwealth. And such a place will certainly be held by the master spirit of the Company, Richard Henderson, one of the ablest and boldest of the American colonizers of his day. The name of Transylvania was stricken from the map of "the country on the western waters," but his own name is justly perpetuated by one of the most fertile counties[2] of the Commonwealth he unwittingly but powerfully helped to plant. Henderson's brilliant hopes were

[1] See sundry documents in Appendix, including above deposition.

[2] It was mainly through Henderson's exertion that Virginia, in December, 1778, granted the Company by way of compensation two hundred thousand acres of land in Kentucky below the mouth of Green River. The present city and county of Henderson are on this tract, where William Bailey Smith and heirs of Luttrell, Hogg, and other associates of Henderson finally settled.

blasted, but the future proved him undaunted. He was to visit Boonesborough once more.[1]

On the 1st of January, 1777, about half a dozen refugees from McClelland's fort (Georgetown) reached Boonesborough, which meant that the Indians, contrary to their usual custom, had been active in the winter, and that the last station north of the Kentucky River had been abandoned. Early in March, just after Boone had been regularly appointed to the command of the fort, and before the feeble militia of Kentucky County had been organized a week, a number of Shawanese were lurking unseen about Boonesborough. They were under the distinguished Black Fish, who was to be heard of in this locality again. Some one else was hiding near the fort at this time. It was Simon Kenton, known then by his assumed name of "Simon Butler," who was waiting for a chance to warn its inmates of their danger. But the stalwart adventurer, then only twenty-one but six feet tall, already understood Indians too well to attempt to enter the station in the daytime. He got safely in at nightfall, but not in time to avert a tragedy, for two of the garrison who had not waited for the darkness, as he had, were waylaid and killed as they openly went toward the stockade.[2] Incursions of small parties of the enemy

[1] See *infra*.
[2] Collins.

now constantly occurred, and Kenton and Thomas Brooks, who were appointed by Boone as special scouts, had a perilous task, and a bigger one than two men could always perform.

The first time "the big fort" was actually attacked was about sunrise on the 24th of April,[1] while the scouts were in. The Indians, numbering from fifty to a hundred,[2] arrived without their advance being either suspected or announced, and the station, with its poor little force of twenty-two riflemen,[3] barely escaped capture. During a successful maneuver to draw out the garrison an Indian tomahawked and scalped Daniel Goodman, when Kenton, who was at the fort gate with his loaded gun, killed the exulting savage. The garrison, in pursuing the apparently retreating enemy, was cut off from the fort and only regained it after a desperate fight, in which Boone, Isaac Hite, John Todd, and Michael Stoner[4] were wounded and a number of Indians killed — three of them, it is said, by Kenton alone. It was on this occasion that Kenton saved the life of Boone, carried him into the fort, and was knighted in backwoods fashion when his leader, of

---

[1] Boone says April 15th in his Narrative, dictated seven years after the event. We accept the date given in Clark's journal, as it was written at the time.

[2] Boone says "above a hundred;" Clark says "from forty to fifty."

[3] Boone.

[4] Clark's journal.

few words and fewer compliments, called Kenton "a fine fellow." After the failure of their familiar stratagem the Indians, who were never prepared for a protracted siege, retreated, carrying their dead off with them. Threatened as Boonesborough now continually was, her defenders, true to the pioneer trait that more than once brought disaster, would risk much to gratify their love of adventure. One day in June Captain William Bailey Smith started after some retiring marauders with a force that left the station almost unprotected. The riflemen ventured clear to the Ohio River, killed one of the Indians, and in returning had the gratification of surprising and scattering another party. Fortunately the fort was not attacked in their absence, and they got back uninjured except John Martin, a scout, who was wounded.[1]

About two weeks after this the Indians made another and more serious attempt than the April one to capture Boonesborough. After a swift descent to the Kentucky they sent detachments to threaten the other stations and prevent the march of reinforcements, and early on the morning of the Fourth of July they suddenly encompassed the fort with two hundred warriors,[2] who swarmed up from the river bank and hid themselves in the now deserted hollow, and behind trees and stumps, and in such patches

[1] Bradford.
[2] Boone's Narrative.

Boonesborough

of corn as their predecessors had spared. But this time the scouts had warned the garrison, and there was not only no surprise, but no rushing out after retreating decoy parties. For two days and two nights the savages, by their persistent firing and repeated attempts to burn the fort,[1] kept the handful of men in the station incessantly employed while the weary and anxious women loaded the extra rifles, passed the precious water from the rain-barrels, distributed food, and attended to the horses, cows, and other live-stock that had been hastily gathered in. Failing in surprise and stratagem, the Indians left before sunrise on the 6th, carrying off—to hide away—seven dead comrades whose bodies had been seen and counted from the portholes by the garrison, which had one man killed and two wounded. As soon as the scouts reported the enemy as certainly gone the cumbersome gates of the fort were dragged open with a will, when the live-stock delightedly rushed out to the green grass and to the river, while the settlers as eagerly sought the cool, fresh water of the lick spring. A small party immediately set out to scour the country for wild meat, a mounted messenger was soon hurrying over Boone's Trace on his way to the old settlements to implore aid for the sorely tried and diminishing people, the wounded now were given full

[1] Clark's journal and Marshall.

attention, and there was a mournful burial in the graveyard adjoining the station.

Boonesborough was not besieged again this year, but life was made almost a burden to its inmates all the same, for Indians either as skulkers or in small bands haunted the locality until freezing weather. Pent up, stagnant, half-starved, exposed to sudden death whenever they ventured from the station, the settlers wearily waited for the relief they had sent for. It came at last on the 25th of July,[1] when forty-five riflemen from North Carolina rode in among the wornout but rejoicing people. A week after these men were succeeded by a detachment from a force of a hundred Virginia militia, which Colonel John Bowman[2] brought to the aid of the county, and these in turn were replaced by a smaller body commanded by the adventurous pioneer, Captain John Montgomery.[3] While each of these militia reliefs, being under short enlistment, soon returned home, they were nevertheless such a strength and encouragement that the settlers were often enabled to take the offensive, while hunters were at least given a chance to seek big game, for ammunition was too scarce to use, except in cases of extreme necessity, on squirrels, rabbits, and birds. Often the danger

---

[1] Boone.
[2] Clark's Memoirs.
[3] From Botetourt County, Virginia.

was such that no game of any kind could be sought, and the sole dependence was such corn, potatoes, and turnips as could be raised so close to the station as to be almost under the rifle barrels of its defenders. Late in the fall pawpaws and wild grapes were a blessing, and big stores of walnuts and hickory nuts were laid in. Once the gunpowder was entirely exhausted, and the whole garrison got heartsick, when a little hoarded store was remembered of the brimstone and saltpetre that Henderson brought in. Some charcoal was made, and Boone and a couple of frontiersmen, who, like himself, had taken lessons from dire necessity, soon manufactured enough powder,[1] scant as that was, to tide the settlement over the emergency. But salt, almost as great a need as ammunition and to secure which the pioneers often risked captivity and death, was again distressingly low. The dwellers in the log cabins of Boonesborough always remembered the year 1777 for its varied and long-continued trials. It was a year of sieges, minor engagements, and single combats, of tragedies, romantic adventures, and great suffering, but the men and women of Boonesborough were too busy

[1] Gunpowder was manufactured several times at Boonesborough. A few months after this when Boone was a prisoner at Detroit he surprised Hamilton by making his own powder, and the fact did not encourage the governor as to the capabilities and resources of the Kentucky settlers. (Howe's Ohio, page 191.)

struggling for existence to make more than a casual record of the events that crowded it, and what should have been one of the richest pages of pioneer history is a blank. But through it all the settlers listened with the keenest interest for every echo of the Revolution that might penetrate the wilderness. About the middle of November they heard with exultation and renewed hope of the surrender of Burgoyne. That night a bonfire of dry cane was made in the center of the spacious stockade, where a crowd of rejoicing men, women, and children, singing negroes, and capering dogs was gathered. Every cabin door was open, and from each came the feeble light of a tallow dip or rude bear's oil lamp, or the brightness of blazing logs in a yawning fireplace. It was all that the patriotic but hard-pressed settlers could do in the way of celebrating, and they did that with the fort gates securely barred, with their horses and cattle all penned inside the pickets, and with scouts continually on the watch.

Among the pioneer conveniences and features that had gradually accumulated at Boonesborough by this time were sheds for corn and fodder and for the storing of peltry, rough but indispensable hand-mills or mortars, stock troughs made from hollow logs, skins of wild animals pegged to the palisades to be cured, hulled walnuts and hickory nuts spread out to dry, a bare but all-important blacksmith shop, the usual assortment of packsaddles, ploughs made up with irons "brought through the wilderness" and of wood fashioned in the fort, and the home-made rain barrels fed by bark gutters from the cabin roofs, for neither well nor cistern had yet been made inside the log walls by the strangely negligent garrison, and the springs and the river were still the main dependence for water. Most of the cabins were provided with a slab table, either a feather bed or a buffalo one, hickory chairs with deerskin seats, iron pots, ovens, and skillets, and gourds, big and little, that were used for every thing, from dippers to egg baskets, and to hold every thing, from cornmeal and soft soap to maple sugar. Bucks' antlers and wooden pegs held rifles, powder-horns, and fishing-poles, sun-bonnets and saddle-bags, bundles of dried herbs, strings of red pepper, and "hands" of tobacco. A shelf over the fireplace was reserved for medicine, the whisky jug, tinder box, ink bottle, and quill pens, the Bible, almanac, and a few other books, which, in some cabins, included The Pilgrim's Progress and Shakespeare.

Before December ended the stock of salt was exhausted at Boonesborough and the other stations also, and the slim rations of cornbread, turnips, and venison were not only insipid, but sickness was threatened. The long trip to the North Holston wells was not to be thought of, and, as the Indians seldom went on the warpath in midwinter, the pioneers determined to make their own salt at the ancient springs now known as the Blue Licks, to which the buffaloes, ages before, had guided the red men as they afterward guided their pale-faced foes.[1] A Captain Watkins arrived at Boonesborough about this time from Virginia with a few militia to aid in the defense of the county, and it was arranged for his force to alternate with another under Daniel Boone in making the desired salt,[2] and on the 1st of January, 1778, Boone, with a party of thirty men made up from the three forts, started on a long, cold ride for the "Lower Salt Spring," with a few pack-horses carrying the crudest of manufacturing outfits in the shape of the largest iron kettles then in domestic use in the settlements, together with meal, fodder, and axes. As for meat, they relied solely on their rifles for that. The work at the salt camp, which was slow and difficult[3] enough, was made more so by the cold

---

[1] One of the principal buffalo traces of the Kentucky wilds led to the Blue Licks, in what is now Nicholas County.

[2] McDonald's Kenton.

[3] As from five hundred to eight hundred gallons of this water was required for a bushel of salt, one can fancy the time consumed in making even a moderate supply of it with such a makeshift as cooking kettles. One bushel of salt at this time was worth a cow and calf in barter, and no telling how much in depreciated Continental currency. It was sold by measure — a half-bushel measure being used. Two bushels, with a few light

weather and the constant efforts to secure game, so that many days elapsed before any salt was sent back to the settlements, but it went at last on pack-horses and in charge of three of the men, who got through safely. The work had dragged on for five weeks, when, on the 7th of February, it was suddenly ended by a band of a little over a hundred Indians,[1] which included the Shawanese Chiefs Black Fish and Munseka, and two of Governor Hamilton's French employes, Lorimer and Charles Baubin. The weather was very severe, and Boone, who was several miles from camp hunting game for the men, and who was helpless from cold, was easily secured. He soon discovered that the object of the expedition was the capture of Boonesborough. To save the fort, which he was convinced could, under the circumstances, be taken, he pretended great loyalty to the Crown, offered to prove it by the surrender of his men already surrounded, expressed deep regret that Boonesborough was too strongly garrisoned for so small a body to expect any thing but defeat, and suggested its capture a little later by a larger force. The stratagem was a desperate one, but it succeeded.[2]

articles, was the usual load of a led pack-horse. For years after peace was declared there were extensive salt-works at both "the Upper and the Lower Spring" on the Licking.

[1] Haldimand manuscripts, April, 1778; Boone and Marshall.

[2] Hamilton says in Haldimand manuscript: "The savages could not be prevailed upon to attempt the fort, which, by means of their prisoners, might have been easily done with success."

Boone obtained good terms for his men, whose surrender the next day so convinced the Indians of his friendship and sincerity that the attempt on Boonesborough was abandoned, and the greatly elated savages retired with their prisoners across the Ohio. Later on some of the captives were ransomed and some escaped,[1] but a few were heard of no more. Boone was adopted as a son by Black Fish, who gave him the name of "Big Turtle,"[2] and he seems to have been kept with the Shawanese during his entire captivity. The disaster was almost immediately discovered by Brooks[3] and another scout in advance of the Watkins force that had started to relieve the salt-makers. They found a deserted camp and so many significant Indian signs that they hastily gave warning to the advancing men, and all turned back with heavy hearts. This loss of twenty-seven men, including such a leader, out of so small a fighting force was by far the greatest calamity that had yet befallen the pioneers, and caused consternation, grief, and discouragement at all the stations, and especially at Boonesborough. As days went by without bringing news from the ill-fated men the discouragement increased, and when spring had fairly opened and still no

---

[1] One of them at least, Joseph Jackson, it is known was still a prisoner in the spring of 1780.

[2] Lossing, and Thwaits in Withers' Chronicles.

[3] McDonald's Kenton.

RELICS OF DANIEL BOONE.

tidings came they were given up for dead, and Mrs. Boone and all of her immediate family except Jemima, who remained with the family of her uncle, Squire Boone, together with some of the relatives of the other missing settlers, loaded up their pack-horses and made their weary and dangerous way back to North Carolina.

The veteran Indian fighter, Richard Calloway, was now the leading spirit at Boonesborough, and did his best to cheer up its inmates, but it was no easy task, for not only was Boone, their tower of strength, gone, but W. B. Smith was absent doing imaginary recruiting for Clark in Holston, the rollicking and adventurous "Butler"[1] was scouting for the same leader, and many old friends had gone back across the mountains. In addition to the pent-up and isolated life of the fort, which was hard enough of itself, skulking savages waylaid the hunters so persistently when they went for game that the people were at times reduced almost to starvation, and it was well indeed for the Kentucky settlements that an Indian army did not swoop down upon them during the gloomy spring of 1778.

Summer commenced dolefully enough, enlivened only by the preparations of Clark at the Falls of the Ohio for the expedition to Kaskaskia. It was the first summer

[1] He did not resume his real name — Kenton — until 1782.

that had opened yet at Boonesborough without Daniel Boone. But the great woodsman, though missed and duly mourned, was far from dead. For four months he had been forced to lead the wild and uncertain life of his self-constituted Shawanese kinsmen, who, in their varied wanderings, had carried him along to Detroit, headquarters of the British for the Northwest, on one of their trips to get rewards for scalps and to dispose of some of their prisoners. There he won the friendship of Governor Hamilton,[1] who tried to ransom him, and who treated him with a kindness and consideration that Boone, steadfast and grateful, never forgot. But, unfortunately for Boone, the Indians were too much charmed with him to let him go at any price, and when they turned their faces again toward the Ohio country he knew his only hope was in the desperate chance of escape. But the chance did not come, and the beginning of summer found him apparently contented but exceedingly watchful and patiently boiling salt for the Black Fish family at a secret spring[2] a few miles from the favorite old Indian haunt, Chillicothe.[3] It was to this familiar region that the fighting force of the Shawanese returned on the 15th of June, exasperated over an unsuccessful foray against Donelly's

[1] Boone's Nar. Peck *et al.*
[2] Said to be located in the present Fayette County, Ohio.
[3] Old Chillicothe.

Fort,[1] on the Greenbrier River, and determined to avenge its insulted dignity by an immediate surprise and capture of Boonesborough. Keenly observant as he was, and familiar with the Indian tongue, Boone quickly scented the impending danger, determined to escape at once at all hazards and warn his friends, and before another sunrise he had left the salt spring far in the rear. On a horse that Hamilton had given him he moved swiftly down the silent channel of track-obliterating streams, forced his way through dense reaches of encompassing cane, and, with face turned toward the Ohio River, entered a leafy wilderness as vast as the ocean itself. On the 20th of the month, after an almost incredible journey, which left him emaciated and starving, he arrived at Boonesborough, which greeted him as one just risen from the dead. The whole population rushed up to him with astonishment and delight. There was an eager ministering to his wants, a thousand questions asked, sympathy in his bitter disappointment at the absence of his family, and no little alarm and consternation at his news. For about ten days there was great anxiety and activity. The posterns and bastions were strengthened, badly needed repairs were made, and the garrison actually began to dig

[1] Campbell's Virginia, and Volume I, American Pioneer. This fort was about ten miles north of Lewisburg, in what is now West Virginia.

a well,[1] but when the scouts reported no signs of an advance of the enemy the pioneers, with their usual strange but characteristic carelessness, abandoned the effort to secure a regular supply of water inside the stockade. In the meanwhile Clark's little force had left Kentucky for the Illinois country, and Boone, anxious as he was about his family, would not abandon the settlements, now weaker than ever in riflemen and threatened with an invasion which he was sure would sooner or later occur.

Early in July a party of riflemen made a venturesome march to that camp-ground on the Licking that seemed ever to be a fatal spot to the pioneers, and recovered the kettles that were so sadly needed. Later on "Simon Butler" returned with the inspiring news of the capture of Kaskaskia, to which was soon added the tidings of the arrival of the French fleet, causing the rejoicing garrison to almost forget its danger, when another prisoner of Black Fish — Stephen Hancock — reached the fort, after six months of privations, bringing the depressing information that the savage movement against Boonesborough was liable to occur at any time, and had only been temporarily delayed by the flight and warning of Boone.

---

[1] Western Review, Volume I. This stupidity in failing to provide wells *inside* of stations was not monopolized by the Kentucky pioneers. It was a common omission. Even Vincennes had no well within its walls at this time. See Haldimand manuscripts.

After this, in August, the scouts reported that the war parties of the Shawanese were again concentrating at Chillicothe, and the settlers were on the lookout for the invasion, but for some reason it did not occur, and about the middle of the month hearts were made lighter by intelligence of the capture of Vincennes and of the friendly feeling so plainly exhibited to Americans, since the French alliance, by the unstable French residents of the Northwest, who were especially noted for their intimacy with the Indians.

But the fall of Vincennes was the very thing that precipitated the long-deferred invasion, for Hamilton, terribly mortified and exasperated by Clark's success, energetically urged on the lagging Ohio savages to action against the "rebels of Kentuck."

Boone, who had already sent a messenger to the Holston settlements[1] announcing the threatened danger and asking for aid, determined, though no reinforcements had yet arrived, to acquaint himself clearly with the movements of the enemy. Heading a party, which subsisted on parched corn and such provisions as were secured on the way, he crossed the Ohio, scouted about the familiar spring and town of his captivity, and after a skirmish, in

---

[1] Colonel Arthur Campbell, Washington County, Virginia, was the military commandant.

which one savage was killed, discovered that the Indians had not only concentrated but had actually begun their march. He at once ordered a rapid retreat, evaded the advancing enemy, and, with all his men except Butler and Alexander Montgomery, who expected to catch up after one more adventure, reached Boonesborough in safety.

The invading expedition, which was the largest that had yet threatened the Kentucky settlements, consisted, according to the conservative Boone, of four hundred and forty-four Indians and twelve Frenchmen.[1] The savages, with a few exceptions, were Shawanese, and the whole force was under the command of one of the ablest and most eloquent chiefs of that tribe, the veteran Black Fish,[2] son of Puckashinwa, who fell at Kanawha in

[1] Several imaginative writers make the force number six hundred, and two aged pioneers, many years after the event, ran the figures up to a thousand. We give Boone's estimate because he was personally familiar, from recent captivity, with the fighting strength of the Shawanese, and because his statement is substantially confirmed by contemporary evidence, viz: Hamilton's own letter of September 5, 1778, in Haldimand manuscripts.

[2] See Nathaniel Hart, in Shane's Collection; Captain John Carr, in "Indian Battles;" John Bradford's "Notes," and Lossing. Boone's Narrative only says, in a vague and general way, that "the Indian army was commanded by Captain DuQuesne(?), eleven other Frenchmen, and some of their chiefs," but J. M. Peck, who subsequently wrote an accurate and valuable life of Boone from data given him by the old pioneer himself, makes Black Fish the commander. Doctor L. C. Draper, who was backed by much manuscript contemporary information on this point, says positively in his manuscript on Boone that the French and Indians were "all under the command of Black Fish."

1774. As already related, Black Fish had participated in Kentucky expeditions twice, if not oftener, before this. His principal aide and adviser was Lieutenant Antoine Dagnieau DeQuindre, a French Canadian of the Detroit Militia, and the leader of the above-mentioned squad of his countrymen, which Hamilton had detailed to carry a stock of ammunition to the Indians and to otherwise assist them in this expedition.[1] DeQuindre was thirty-five years of age, and, though a resident of Detroit, was a native of Montreal. He is the same person who, through some error, was mentioned in Boone's Narrative as "DuQuesne," a misspelling of the name and a confusion of the identity of DeChaine (Isadore), who was a member of the squad, but who was conspicuous only in his usual capacity of interpreter.[2] The mistake was perpetuated for more than a century. Peter Douiller, a trader well known at Detroit, was also connected with the French contingent. Each of the principal Indian colleagues of Black Fish was, like himself, a veteran. One was Black Bird,[3] called by Governor Patrick Henry "the great Chip-

---

[1] Haldimand manuscripts.

[2] The mythical name, "DuQuesne," used for the first time in Filson's Boone of 1784, was accepted for more than a hundred years as the correct name of the leader of the French squad. The real name, DeQuindre, was established beyond a doubt by the publication, only a few years ago, by the Canadian Government of the exceedingly interesting and valuable Haldimand manuscripts.

[3] This chief's name is correctly given as above in Clark's Diary.

pewa Chief," and who very shortly after this changed to the American side. Another was Moluntha, a leader of the Shawanese in all the serious movements against the Kentucky posts, and still another was the sagacious and distinguished Catahecassa, or Black Hoof, who was already a mature warrior when he participated in Braddock's defeat of 1755, and who was probably the only Indian who could claim to be a native of Kentucky,[1] as he was born on the margin of what was afterward known as Lulbegrud Creek, in Clark County, where his Shawanese parents had a temporary hunting-camp. One negro was along, a man named Pompey, captured, doubtless, from some settlement, but none the less a slave, and mainly useful to the Indians because he could speak English.[2] As usual, the savages were scantily equipped, with a view only to a short campaign. No warrior carried any thing heavier than a flint-lock rifle and a buckskin wallet of parched corn,[3] for wild game was depended on for meat,

[1] Harvey's History of the Shawanese. History of the Indian Tribes. Black Hoof revisited his birthplace in 1816. He died in 1831, after attaining a wonderful age, estimated at one hundred and twelve to one hundred and twenty years.

[2] Some of the Indians kept negro slaves, and frequently sold them. Of the population of Detroit at this time, one hundred and twenty-seven were slaves worth each from £180 to £260 in New York currency, says Haldimand's manuscripts.

[3] They did not expect to secure corn in Kentucky, where they had made it almost impossible for the settlers to cultivate it that season.

Boonesborough 75

but a train of pack-horses was along devoted mainly to the carriage of extra ammunition and of such provisions and conveniences as were absolutely necessary to the simple-habited but less seasoned militia. But, as will be seen later on, the pack-horses were expected to do still more important service.

And so, with scalp-locks befeathered and their more than half-naked bodies streaked with the war-paint they so delighted in,[1] the savages moved swiftly to the Ohio, crossed it near the mouth of Cabin Creek,[2] from whence they followed the ancient war road of their race to a point beyond the Upper Blue Licks, where they entered a great buffalo trace which extended toward and far beyond the stockaded posts of their enemies. The Indians made a rapid march, and Boone and his scouting party made a narrow escape. The hunters galloped into the fort some time before sunset on the afternoon of the 6th of September, and that night the savages camped on the north bank of the Kentucky.

Early on the morning of the next day, Monday, September 7, 1778, the dusky crowd crossed the river about

---

[1] The savages used immense quantities of paint in the decoration of their persons. Hamilton, in a report for this very month (September) of goods on hand at Detroit for the Indian department, mentions "eighty pounds of rose pink and five hundred pounds of vermilion."

[2] Near the present Maysville, Kentucky.

half a mile below the present ferry,[1] at a point still known as "Blackfish Ford," climbed the steep southern bank, passed to the rear of "Hackberry Ridge," marched along its base until nearly opposite Boonesborough, and then crossing it, came down to a cover of trees and undergrowth within rifle shot of the fort. The position was gained without the firing of a gun. The settlers were too utterly weak for any contest outside of their wooden

[1] We give September 7th as the date of the commencement of this siege, because it is the only date supported by contemporary evidence, that is, documents written at the time. Colonel John Bowman, in his letter (see Appendix Y) of October 14, 1778, less than a month after the siege, forwarded from Harrodsburg to Colonel George Rogers Clark, says that the Indians and French appeared at Boonesborough September 7th. The British contemporary account points the same way, for before Bowman wrote, Governor Hamilton, in a letter of September 16, 1778, reports to Sir Frederick Haldimand that the Shawanese, with DeQuindre, had gone to attack the forts on the "Kentucke," and on September 26th, before he could have heard of the outcome of the expedition, says "the Shawanese have not yet broke up their little siege." (See Haldimand manuscripts.) Two, at least, of the leading participants in the siege afterward stated the time of its commencement, viz: Daniel Boone, who gave it as the 8th of August in his Narrative, dictated six years after the event, and William Bailey Smith, who (in Volume III of Western Review), after a still longer interval, gave the same date as Bowman. Boone may be said to have substantially corrected his date when, some years after the publication of his Narrative, he and another eye-witness of the siege, Flanders Calloway, furnished Reverend Mr. Peck the facts for his Life of Boone, which gives the time as September 7th, but Marshall, Bradford, and other historians, who did not have the benefit of the Bowman, Hamilton, and Peck data, adopted and long perpetuated the date as given in the first life of Boone. The evidence quoted fixes the date as September 7th, the date also given by the late Lyman C. Draper, after a full and careful investigation.

stronghold, for, according to one of its defenders,[1] its whole fighting force then amounted to but thirty men and twenty boys.[2] One may well believe it after the loss of the salt-makers, the return home of the militia and discouraged immigrants, and the absence of a few of the riflemen with Clark. The women,[3] though, should have been reckoned in — they certainly deserved to be — for in courage and marksmanship they were not to be despised. Neither concealment nor surprise was attempted by the Indians, not only because they knew that the garrison was already warned, but for other reasons. They were hopeful of capturing the place without a fight. They were greatly attached to Boone,[4] who understood them so well, and who certainly was not a vindictive enemy, and in spite of his desertion they were confident that he was equally attached to them and could be persuaded to return to his adopted home. They evidently believed that the garrison was so favorably impressed with their

---

[1] William Bailey Smith.

[2] In addition to the boys who lived in the fort were several who were there temporarily, having come in as pack-horse drivers.

[3] Jemima Boone and the wives and daughters of the few families still remaining in the fort, including Richard Calloway's and Squire Boone's, comprised almost the entire white female population during the siege.

[4] There is nothing more plainly expressed in Boone's Narrative than this. He declares that he had the "entire friendship" of the Shawanese King; that he "had a great share in the affections of his new parents, brothers, sisters, and friends," and that the Indians refused a ransom of five hundred dollars for him.

good faith at the Blue Licks surrender, and their really humane treatment[1] of the captured salt-makers, and that the settlers had suffered such long and terrible privations that all that was needed to insure a capitulation was the appearance of an overwhelming force, an assurance of honorable terms, of a safe conduct to the tempting flesh-pots of Detroit, and of a comfortable refuge there from the certain miseries of the approaching winter. It is a matter of record that Hamilton himself labored for a while under the same delusion,[2] and this belief of the savages, strange as it may sound to civilized ears, cut no small figure in this event, partly accounts for their remarkable forbearance at the beginning of the siege, and resulted in great advantage to the garrison. There is no contemporary evidence to support the time-honored but fanciful assertion that the enemy marched up to Boonesborough "brandishing their rifles and with fearful yells." The truth is that they made no hostile demonstrations whatever when they first appeared, but, on the contrary, they immediately sent forward an unarmed English-speaking messenger with a flag of truce, and as he passed over

---

[1] It is only fair to the much-abused Hamilton to say that the conduct of the Ohio Indians at this time tallied with the declaration in his report of July 6, 1781, that he then, at least, tried to carry out the orders of Lord George Germain to restrain the Indians from barbarities. (See Haldimand manuscripts.)

[2] See Hamilton to Carleton in Haldimand manuscripts.

FORT BOONESBOROUGH

the cleared ground that intervened between the sheltered Indians and the fort there were no more alarming tokens of a martial host than the neighing and stamping of a multitude of pack-horses and ponies.

In its shape and outlines, at least, Boonesborough at this time was substantially what it had always been, but instead of but one double bastion, as formerly, another story had been added to each of the three single ones, so that now all four of the corners were provided with regular block-houses, and cabins occupied some of the spaces guarded before only by the pickets of the stockade.

The lonely station never looked more peaceful than it did in the cool of this early summer-like morning, for it was determined before the Indians arrived to conceal as much as possible the feebleness of its force by keeping close within the stockade and out of sight of the enemy. The lumbering gates were closed, and the sounds of life were so faint and few that but for the smoke that ascended from the rude kitchen chimneys the inexperienced might have imagined that the garrison slept. But all the same every soul within the station was keenly alive to the magnitude and the imminence of the danger, and hearts were beating painfully, eyes were glued to port-holes, and ears were strained to catch the slightest sound as the messenger of the savages advanced.

Mounting a stump within easy calling distance of the fort, and keeping his white flag conspicuously displayed, he gave notice of his presence by the usual prolonged and peculiar "hello" of the woodsman. There was no reply and no sign that he was even seen. The leaders of Boonesborough understood Indian nature too well to betray their weakness by either hurry or excitement, and it was only after the call was repeated that an answering "hello" came from the block-house nearest to him. He then announced himself as a messenger from a British force, with instructions to say that its commander was the bearer of letters from Governor Hamilton[1] to Captain Boone, and desired a meeting of the opposing chiefs to consider their contents. The garrison, secretly delighted with this chance to open negotiations with the hope of gaining time for the arrival of the Holston men, consented, after a deliberate silence and apparent reluctance, to receive the letters, but only under the guns of the fort and at the hands of three unarmed leaders of the enemy. These conditions were agreed to, and the bearer of the flag of truce not only quickly announced the presence of Black Fish, DeQuindre, and Moluntha, but, as a token of their good faith, brought from them a present of seven roasted buffalo tongues,[2] which had a

[1] Bradford and McAfee.
[2] Bradford.

welcome from the half-starved settlers that the enemy little dreamed of. The two chiefs and the Canadian were met by Captain Boone, Colonel Calloway, and Major W. B. Smith,[1] carrying only a pipe and a white handkerchief tied to a ramrod, and the messenger acted as interpreter. This meeting with his adopted father was embarrassing enough to the runaway Boone, for Black Fish had in truth made him a member of his family, but even more was he troubled at meeting Moluntha, "the Shawanese King," who had been particularly kind to him,[2] for that chief sorrowfully reproached him for killing his son "the other day over the Ohio," but Boone assured him that that act was not his. Hamilton's letters, which were delivered by Black Fish, evidently contained a demand for the surrender of the post on terms that both the Governor and the Indians thought too seductive to be resisted, for the old chief, with neighborly consideration, assured the Boonesborough delegation that "he had come to take the people away easily; that he had brought along forty horses for the old folks, the women, and the children to ride."[3] The pioneers, apparently pleased, but intent on delay, proposed a truce of two days to enable

---

[1] Some writers on this subject hopelessly confuse the actions of the messenger and the proceedings of this meeting with the subsequent treaty conference, observing neither order nor the sequence of the events.

[2] Boone's Narrative.

[3] Bradford.

all the garrison to consider the Governor's terms. To this the complacent savages, blinded by the bloodless capitulation at the Blue Licks, immediately consented, and the meeting closed. After an astonishingly free and friendly stroll together about the exterior of the still silent fort, the parties separated, and each retired in high good humor to its own camp, from which neither side was to make a hostile movement until the expiration of the truce.

Great as were the odds against them, and desperate as the situation seemed, the men and women of Boonesborough made short work of Hamilton's proposition. Convinced by this time that the enemy had no artillery, confident from the statement about the "forty horses" that the savages were ignorant of the weakness of the garrison, protected by walls that laughed at rifles — walls which the benumbed salt-makers had so fatally lacked — and hoping still for the Virginia militia who had made no sign, they unanimously decided against a surrender and proceeded at once to make every arrangement that the emergency permitted to withstand a siege. Fortunately the fort had already been repaired, and the horses of the scouting party at least were within the stockade, but, alas, the well had been neglected until every soul was needed for the work of defense alone, and all suddenly realized that they were to be cut off from their regular water-supply when the weather was hottest and when the very fate of the garrison might depend upon it. But, to the surprise and delight of the settlers, there were no hostile movements whatever from the Indians when trips were made to and from the fort to the Lick Spring, and all the water was secured that could possibly be obtained without exciting their suspicions. There was a general cleaning of rifles and picking of flints, powder was distributed, an extra stock of bullets moulded, and the women and children, as well as the men, though intensely excited, resolutely pushed on the preparations. Toward sunset there was another striking exhibition of the forbearance of the singularly friendly savages, for the cows and other live stock were unmolested by them and came up to the back of the fort as usual, and they were not only brought in and penned, but as soon as darkness permitted the garden that had been possible only under the very guns of the fort was gleaned of such of its scant store of vegetables as could be used by man or beast. That night a sentinel was on the lookout in every block-house, and every man in the station, whether watching or dozing, held on to his rifle, but no shot was fired either then or the next day, for the painted warriors honorably observed the truce to its close, and then in the cool of the second evening the white flag was seen again, and Black Fish and his little party soon arrived in front of the fort and confidently awaited the announcement of its surrender. The answer from Boone himself that the garrison had "determined to defend the fort while a man was living," and the sudden realization that their favorite and enforced kinsman had no intention of returning to his adopted tribe, astonished, disappointed, and exasperated the Indians, who, in this matter, seem to have indeed been "children of the forest." But they were as grave and impassive as ever when they heard the news, when they stepped aside to deliberate, and when, after the speedy adoption of a new plan of action, they returned to the meeting-place. They were convinced that there was no chance for either a complete surprise or a peaceful surrender of the place. To attempt to storm it with no appliances whatever for that purpose was not to be thought of and would be not only directly contrary to their usual wily and cautious course, but especially dangerous and unadvisable in view of the recent report of reinforcements,[1] which the conduct of the garrison seemed

---

[1] Before they started on this expedition the Shawanese had captured a Kentucky prisoner who, for his own purposes, no doubt, gave out the news that the forts there "had lately been reinforced with three companies each of seventy men." (See Hamilton to Haldimand about September 1, 1778, in Haldimand manuscripts.)

to confirm. The decision was for stratagem, and the settlers, who expected an immediate opening of hostilities, were in turn astonished when conciliatory overtures were made by DeQuindre through the interpreter, DeChaine. The Canadian said they had come to talk of peace, not of war; that they had not contemplated war even if a surrender was declined; if they had, they never would have allowed the cattle to enter the stockade; that Governor Hamilton's orders were to avoid bloodshed, and that, therefore, he suggested that a meeting be held to frame a treaty of peace, and that if nine representative men from the garrison would sign such a treaty, the Indians would withdraw.[1] Ordinarily such a proposition from such a greatly superior force would have been regarded at once as sinister and absurd, but the circumstances were far from being ordinary. The pioneers had the same strong reason as ever for wanting to gain time. They hoped a little from the genuine friendship of Hamilton for Boone, more from the affection of the Shawanese for their adopted

[1] Speaking of this proposition of DeQuindre, Colonel Bowman says in his letter to Clark of October 14, 1778 (see Appendix): "Hearing that the Indians gladly treated with you at the Illinois gave them (the Boonesborough men) reason to think that the Indians were sincere." In a letter of September 5, 1778, Hamilton says: "For the French inhabitants at all the outposts, I firmly believe, there is not one in twenty whose oath of allegiance would have force enough to bind him to his duty; added to this, that the greatest part of the traders among them, who are called English, are rebels in their hearts." (Haldimand manuscripts.)

kinsman, but above all they were encouraged to treat by the wonderful transformation that Clark had brought about in "the Illinois." They knew that there the French Canadians had not only become enthusiastic adherents of the American cause, but had strongly influenced the savages the same way. The settlers had heard of the gratifying change of front of the Indians at Cahokia, and rumors were rife that even the British traders and interpreters were secretly working against the King, and that he had enemies inside the very walls of Detroit itself. These rumors were subsequently verified, and, with the light we now have from British sources, one can imagine without much effort the possibility of a repetition of the Cahokia transaction at Boonesborough at this time if another Clark had then confronted the Indians and Canadians.[1] Hopeful, but especially intent on gaining time, the Kentuckians consented to the conference to be held the next morning; but, suspicious ever of the savages, they took care to do so only on condition that it be held

[1] The united influence of the French Alliance and Clark's success on the Indians and Canadians of the West was great. One of the most important leaders of the Boonesborough expedition, Black Bird, went over to the Americans immediately after this siege, as did, later on, one of the officers, Baubin, who had aided in the capture of the salt-makers at the Blue Licks. Some of LaMothe's company of Detroit militia deserted Hamilton, and so many others—Indians, officers, and men—proved false, that Hamilton afterward declared that "the secret treason" of such had ruined him. (See Haldimand manuscripts.)

in the hollow at the Lick Spring,[1] which could be easily swept by riflemen from the bastion nearest to it. Black Fish and his colleagues retired to their camp, and the garrison selected its peace commissioners. As far as known, they were Daniel Boone, Richard Calloway, William Bailey Smith, and William Buchanan, with their "subalterns," Squire Boone, Flanders Calloway, Stephen Hancock, and William Hancock.[2] Instructions were given for every woman and child, white and black, in the fort to make a showing at the pickets the next morning, as men, to impress the enemy with the strength of the garrison, and for that purpose every old hat and hunting-shirt in the station was gathered up, and some new ones even were hastily manufactured.[3]

The next morning, Wednesday, the 9th, when Black Fish, DeQuindre, the older chiefs, interpreters, and attendants filed down to the meeting-place they did not fail to note the large number of hatted heads that bobbed up at the top of the stockade to see them pass, and were doubtless disgusted at the apparent confirmation of the report as to the strength of the garrison. What they

---

[1] John Bowman and R. B. McAfee manuscripts.
[2] John Bowman, Peck, and records Circuit Court Clerk's office, Madison County, Kentucky. Boone is indefinite and gives no names. According to Judge William Chenault, Buchanan was from Virginia, where he had been a captain of militia.
[3] Daniel Trabue.

did not see when Boone and his companions joined them was the little band of sharpshooters that moved at once to the block-house that commanded the rendezvous. Both parties, unarmed, sought the shade of the great sycamores near the Lick Spring, where the pioneers were invited to seat themselves on deerskins and panther-skins spread on the ground by their hospitable enemies, who passed around the pipe and the whisky. The day was spent in pow-wows, which the settlers protracted, and in feasting — the besiegers seeking, with suspicious generosity, to beguile the half-starved "rebels" with eatables and drinkables from the British commissary department at Detroit, such as most of them had not seen, much less tasted, in many a long month. By sunset a compact, inscrutable to this day, was agreed to, which was to be signed the next morning. The settlers seemed completely hoodwinked, hilarity reigned, and DeQuindre was confident that the royal standard of England would quickly float over the wooden walls of Boonesborough. Neither party was sincere. That night, unseen, a strong detachment of the Indian army, detailed to assist in a surprise, hid itself in the weeds and underbrush that skirted the hollow. The next morning when Black Fish led the way toward a rude table under the great elm, the watchful settlers were struck by the fact that stalwart young bucks had taken

CLIMAX OF THE TREATY.

Treachery of the British and Indians. (Designed from Historical Data by the Author, with copies of Autographs of Boone and DeQuindre, referred to on pages 103 and 168.)

Boonesborough

the place of most of the old Indians who had figured as attendants the day before,[1] and they mentioned it, but Black Fish coolly and unblushingly declared that his party was unchanged. Be that as it may, every rifleman in the fort was ordered to keep his eye on the hollow and to fire on the redskins at the waving of a hat. The sham treaty was signed, and Black Fish then declared that it must be confirmed by what he said was the Indian custom — a hand-shake all around, two braves to each white brother.[2] It was the signal for treachery. The young Indians, in apparently high good-humor, seized the hands of the pioneers, but in the very act they betrayed their purpose by too tight a grasp and by a sudden movement toward the underbrush. Suspicious, alert, and quick, with the quickness of desperation the hunters freed themselves almost as soon as touched, and in the same thrilling moment, as they sprang aside and waved their hats, came the deadly crack of the ready rifles from the block-house, and the unarmed savages vanished in the surrounding thickets.[3] Then up the steep hill dashed the fleeing pioneers, bounding from tree to tree and from stump to stump to protect themselves from the hail of bullets sent after them by the enraged ambuscaders, whose carefully

[1] Bradford.
[2] Bowman.
[3] Bowman, Smith, Boone, and Trabue.

planned rush on the fort was summarily defeated, as they were far too wise to expose themselves in the open to the fire of such a force as they believed defended the rough but formidable stockade. At least two hundred guns were fired by the invisible combatants, but the leaden storm was mainly spent on the logs of the block-house and on the sycamores at the lick, for all the "rebels" but one gained the fort at last unhurt. Squire Boone was wounded in the left shoulder, and another "commissioner," caught within range of the Indian rifles, remained for many weary hours flat on his face behind a stump, and only reached the fort when night came down and hid him from savage view. But the firing, the swift-running, and the "treeing" that followed the treachery at the elm were succeeded with surprising suddenness by totally different sounds and movements in the camp of the enemy. All during the afternoon there was a bustle that indicated the gathering up and gearing of ponies and the loading of pack-horses, and many orders that were given with suspicious loudness were understood by members of the garrison familiar with the Indian tongue. The Shawanese evidently meant it to be known that they were disgusted with their luck and were preparing to leave. That night — Thursday — a heavy detail of Indians was again concealed as close to the fort as possible, and the next morning just before day, when it was still too dark for the watching settlers to distinguish any thing clearly, what seemed the whole force of the enemy noisily retreated.[1] Their horses were heard splashing and clattering as they crossed the river. The calls of DeQuindre's bugle resounded through the neighboring hills, and then grew fainter and fainter, and died away at last in the dark and wooded distance. Then the marching Indians quickly and noiselessly retraced their steps and posted themselves in ambush near the buffalo road and close to the north bank of the river. And so another trap was set for the pioneers, but it was set in vain. When the sun rose that Friday morning it was on a quiet and peaceful scene. There was neither sight nor sound of the enemy, nor the faintest hint of an ambuscade. The savages seemed of a certainty to have left the station far behind them, but all the same no settler stepped foot outside its walls. How the pioneers detected their danger is not now known, but detect it they did, and the gates of the fort remained as securely barred as ever. This convinced the impatient Indians that their trick had failed, and inside of an hour they were as thick about Boonesborough as before. All that day, protected by trees and stumps and prostrate behind logs and hillocks,

[1] R. B. McAfee.

the savages directed their rifle balls at every crack and port-hole of the station that might possibly have life behind it. The deep gorge of the Kentucky echoed and re-echoed with the shots of the contending forces, and at night the surrounding forests, the solemn cliffs, and the everlasting hills were doubly sublime in the red glow of a multitude of savage camp-fires. The siege was now prosecuted in earnest, and every effort short of direct assault was made to reduce the wooden stronghold. Such an assault up and over no small area of cleared and open ground, that could be swept by such a force of sharpshooters as the Indians believed the fort contained, was not a part of the cautious savage programme. This was made still more evident the very day the enemy returned from the pretended retreat. Between the spells of firing new sounds like those of woodchoppers at work were heard coming up from the river bank back of the fort, and shortly after a broad muddy streak was noticed to commence in the water at the same locality and extend further and further down the stream. The curiosity these suspicious signs awakened inside the station grew at once into lively alarm, when, after no little exposure and risk, one of the garrison reported that he had caught a glimpse over the cliff of a pole moving as if it was being used to loosen[1] dirt. All jumped to the conclusion that DeQuindre,

[1] Trabue, McAfee, and Draper.

concealed and protected by the cliff, was trying to push a mine from the river bank up to or under the back wall of the fort, and that the incessant firing of the Indians was mainly intended to hide his design by drowning the sounds of the work and diverting attention from its location. As it was important to determine as quickly as possible whether this surmise was correct, the settlers erected of thick lumber a rough but bullet-proof attempt at a watch-tower.[1] It was built on top of the cabin which three years before had served Henderson as a kitchen, and which was evidently nearest to the scene of the suspected mischief. The fears of the garrison were now confirmed, for the watchers saw the fresh earth as it was thrown from the excavation into the river. It was a thrilling discovery. Great and unexpected dangers threatened them. The allies certainly designed either to blow up the fort or to suddenly capture it by throwing their force into it through this underground passage. But the garrison faced these new perils as resolutely as it had confronted the others. The tower was made still stronger to serve as a sort of "battery," and day and night it was occupied by scant details of riflemen, who wearily watched with ready guns for any suspicious thing that might spring up outside the wall from the now danger-charged earth. Inside the fort little relays of its defenders

[1] Draper.

were set to work on a countermine[1] or trench which would expose and cut off the tunnel of the enemy, and which would require only a few men to balk a whole subterranean force. This countermine, which was about three feet wide and of considerable depth, and which cost days of excessive labor, was commenced inside of Henderson's kitchen, and extended up the river through several other cabins that helped to form the back wall of the station. A spell of cloudy, drizzly weather which set in about this time and reduced the fierce September heat was especially grateful to the weary diggers, while the whole garrison rejoiced that it lessened the demands on the fast-diminishing supply of water.

Every morning at daybreak both sides resumed their efforts to pick off the unwary. In this petty warfare the pioneers took by far the most careful part in the effort to save precious ammunition;[2] but desultory as the firing was, and at long range, no day went by without one side or the other adding its little quota to the list of either killed or wounded. A notable shot, attributed of course to Daniel Boone, and fired probably from the "battery," killed Pompey,[3] the only negro man, as afore-

---

[1] Trabue, McAfee, and W. B. Smith.

[2] The Indians, according to Boone, wasted one hundred and twenty-five pounds of bullets, which were afterward picked up about the fort.

[3] Peck.

said, known to have been with the savages. He was sheltered by a tree, from which he was trying to pick off imprudent settlers, when he exposed himself for an instant, and that instant was a fatal one to him. Once, indeed, the pioneers ambitiously ventured beyond the use of the rifle, and prompted, it is said, by Colonel Callaway, emulated the artillery of another era by making a wooden cannon,[1] which was banded with such strap iron as the station afforded, and loaded with musket balls. Its first shot was directed against a knot of Indians who, thinking they were fully protected, both by distance and location, amused themselves by yelling taunts and curses at the garrison. With one quick yell the savages vanished, but whether they sustained any loss is now unknown. The gun was a terror to them while it lasted, but unfortunately the next time it was used it went to pieces, and the Indians, suspecting what had happened, repeatedly dared the disgusted artillerymen, from a safe distance, to "shoot the big gun again."

On the night of Sunday, the thirteenth of the month, the seventh night after the arrival of the enemy, the settlers had the most frightful experience of the siege, for suddenly, when such a movement was entirely unsuspected, the Indians succeeded in hurling lighted torches

[1] Trabue.

against a side of the stockade, and in lodging blazing arrows on the roofs of the cabins in that quarter,[1] and then to prevent the extinguishment of the fiery implements, swept the locality with bullets. As both torches and arrows were wrapped with flax stolen from an outside cabin, and with the inner oily fiber of the shell-bark hickory, they burned rapidly and fiercely. The garrison was terrorized, for the water-supply was about exhausted. The arrows could be battled with, but only with inflammable brooms and while exposed to savage rifles, but the torches blazed on. The fort seemed doomed, and for a few terrible moments all was black despair within it, when directly the whole watching, heart-sick settlement saw with unspeakable relief that the arrows and torches were dying out, that the cabins were too damp after the recent drizzles to be ignited by them, and that the danger of a conflagration was over. Little was said, but the thanksgiving was deep and fervent. Boonesborough had escaped by the skin of its teeth.

In the meanwhile the mining and countermining continued, and as the siege dragged on the suffering of the settlers and the live stock from thirst was great and would have been unbearable but for timely showers that enabled the garrison to gather supplies of water from the

[1] McAfee and Bradford.

Boonesborough

cabin roofs.[1] Strange to say, the well, for some reason, seems never to have been completed. While digging his trench, Boone, to discourage the enemy by plain evidence of a countermine, contrived to have much of the excavated dirt hoisted up and thrown over the stockade,[2] but the Indians, with a persistency in manual labor that was remarkable if not unexampled in their history, continued their underground approach. It was a curious siege, and not less curious from some of the courtesies that each side indulged in. "What are you red rascals doing down there?" an old hunter would yell in Shawanese from the "battery" to the unseen Indians on the river bank below. "Digging!" would be the return yell. "Blow you all to devil soon; what you do?" "Oh!" would be the cheerful reply, "we are digging to meet you, and intend to bury five hundred of you."[3] The banter was rough, but seems not to have been at all hostile; at the same time the beleaguered riflemen conscientiously fired at every Indian who exposed himself in going to and from the tunnel and the camp. In fact, it was in this way that the besiegers suffered the most.

By the fifteenth of the month the savages had pushed their mine so close to the fort that the guards in the

[1] McAfee.
[2] Kenton to James.
[3] Trabue's Memoir.

station trench could hear the sound of their implements,[1] and the settlers felt that the crisis was at hand. The outlook was black indeed. It was raining, and the pent-up people could slake their thirst, but they were worn out by labor, the heat, and incessant watching and by privations, for the long-drawn-out provisions were about exhausted, and though some of the miserably reduced live stock remained, the pioneers had already reached the starvation point. There were dissensions among the principal officers of the garrison,[1] possibly over conflicting claims to the leadership. Colonel Callaway was the ranking officer; Major W. B. Smith, however, according to what is apparently his own statement,[2] had been appointed commandant of the fort by Clark after the capture of Boone at the Blue Licks, while the actual leadership during the siege seems, by common consent of the settlers, to have fallen to Captain Daniel Boone from his special gifts and experience in Indian ways and warfare. The methods of Boone at this time were strongly disapproved by the venerable Callaway, but all were united in the face of the enemy, and especially now when the fate of Boonesborough was trembling in the balance. All day long the rain poured down in torrents upon ground already deeply soaked, and all day

[1] Trabue.
[2] Hunt's Review, Volume III.

long the harassed and weary little garrison waited to meet, as best they could, the unknown event which they feared would herald the sudden onrush of the enemy. But the long and gloomy day was uneventful, ending in a night that wrought the apprehensions of all up to the highest pitch, for the darkness was so thick that the keenest watchers had no chance, except the poor one the flashes of lightning gave, to detect an advance of the enemy above the ground, while the tumult of the pouring rain and wind-swept forests drowned all other sounds and favored every movement of the mining force. Would the enemy blow up the postern gate and seek to capture the fort by a rush from the outside, or would they penetrate to the countermine and try that way to flood the interior of the station with warriors, or was all the mining a mere trick to cover a deeper and more deadly plan? Miserably uncertain and terribly anxious, and only hoping now for the Holston militia, with that "hope deferred" which "maketh the heart sick," the men, women, and boys of Boonesborough watched and waited, with many a prayer, through the long, lagging hours for the quick and bloody incident that would signalize the attack. Even in this, the season of their greatest extremity, there was no thought of surrender. Encompassed overwhelmingly by the savage power of England, cut off from the world in the depths of a solitude vast and obscure, forgotten by the overburdened Continental Congress, unaided by hard-pressed Virginia, worn out by privations and sorely tempted, the feeble little handful of "rebels" at Boonesborough were true to the last to the principles of the Revolution, and battled as valiantly and suffered as nobly for freedom and for country as did the men of Bunker Hill or the shivering heroes of Valley Forge.

The weary night dragged to an end at last, the rain ceased, and the vigilant settlers were surprised to discover that no sounds whatever came from the mysterious mine, that no dreaded disaster of any kind had happened, and the bright and beautiful Wednesday of September[1] the 16th, 1778, found all Boonesborough hopeful again and devoutly thankful but immeasurably bewildered. Why was the big tunnel so strangely silent, and why all that commotion on the river trace? Directly the blessed truth dawned upon them that the whole savage army was in full but leisurely retreat, but not till high noon, when wary scouts returned with the glad tidings that the enemy was certainly gone and no new trick was being practiced, did they throw open the gates, release the starving, half-mad cattle, give way to rejoicing, and indulge in the luxury of a rest. The wet weather had done more to balk the Indians than rifles or wooden walls. The rain had not

[1] See note on page 76 and Bowman's letter, which gives length of siege.

only strengthened the thirsty garrison and saved the fort from destruction by fire, but, as the settlers soon discovered, it had caused such quantities of the saturated earth to cave in and obstruct the mine as to effectually ruin it, and the fickle savages, who never willingly engaged at all at any manual labor, had abandoned the siege in inexpressible disgust.[1] It is probable from the collection of huge torches and other inflammable articles that the Indians had prepared and abandoned, that they intended to emerge from the mine just outside the back wall of the station and burn a passage through it for the entrance of their army.[2] It goes without saying that no pursuit of the savages was possible by a garrison so feeble, so much exhausted, and whose necessities were so great. Though closely invested for nine days and nights, such was the protection afforded by the simple but effective defenses of Boonesborough that its garrison had only two killed and four wounded, while the enemy had "thirty-seven killed and a great many wounded."[3] The dead

[1] Boone was under the impression that it was the discovery of the countermine that caused the Indians to raise the siege. That certainly discouraged them, but it is plain from the statement of "Drewyer" (Douiller) to Kenton at Detroit that the caving in of the tunnel was the crushing blow to the Indians.

[2] Pioneer statements in Draper manuscript. (See Judge James' Notes.)

[3] We give the figures of Boone himself, who was singularly calm and unprejudiced. Another "eye-witness" of the siege says that two hundred Indians were killed, and no telling how many more were wounded. Not a few of the statements of the pioneers are fanciful, conflicting, and

settlers were, of necessity, buried inside the stockade. The Indians, as usual, hid away their slain and obliterated every sign that might betray their resting-places. It is said that the only body they did not remove was that of the negro already alluded to.[1] They had no use for negroes except as slaves, and always regarded them with lofty and contemptuous indifference. The most serious damage inflicted outside of the station was in the loss of cattle which the settlers failed to secure during the truce, and which furnished the fresh meat supply of the savages.

And so ended the last investment that Boonesborough was to experience, one which Boone characterized as "a dreadful siege which threatened death in every form," one of the longest that the unstable and impatient Indians ever attempted, and one of the most curious of the military episodes of the American Revolution. If DeQuindre was in earnest, why was no attempt made by such a force to scale the stockade? Why was the work of many days devoted to a mine, when scaling-ladders for a ten-foot wall could have been made of

exaggerated, especially those made in old age, and must be estimated accordingly. The British story that the besiegers, exposed as they frequently were, had only two killed and three wounded (see Haldimand manuscript) sounds like some of the above-mentioned inflated statements.

[1] Peck.

young saplings and deer or cattle thongs in one afternoon? How much were the French-Canadian colleagues of the Indians influenced in the conduct of this siege by that sympathy for the Americans which was then so strong in Hamilton's department? The records of the time afford no answer. Neither of the principal leaders of the Indians long survived this famous siege. Black Fish, as we will see, closed his career the following May. DeQuindre barely survived the Revolutionary struggle, dying in the spring of 1784, at the age of forty-one. He was a trusted adherent of the British to the end of the war.[1]

The backs of the besieging Indians were hardly turned on Boonesborough before Montgomery and the young dare-devil "Butler" (Kenton) popped into it, their horse-stealing expedition almost forgotten after their long waiting spell in the rear of the savage army. But Kenton

[1] Dagniaux DeQuindre, as he signed himself, was a son of Colonel Louis C. DeQuindre, and was born in Montreal, Canada, in 1743. He was married, and his son Antoine and other descendants lived in Detroit. He was a Lieutenant in the Indian Department at Detroit, and was employed mainly among the Lake tribes. He died April 18, 1784, and was buried in the graveyard of the parish of Saint Anne. See Tanguay, records of Saint Anne, and Haldimand manuscript. We are indebted to the accomplished investigator, C. M. Burton, Esquire, of Detroit, for data and for the copy of DeQuindre's autograph used in this publication, and which was taken from an original written only a few months before the Boonesborough siege.

was gone again in a few days—gone to get captured—and did not see the fort again until the next summer. He was fortunate enough to be purchased from the Indians by Peter Douiller, who did not let bad luck at Boonesborough keep him from being kind to the prisoner from "Kentuck."

A few days after the siege the news came to Boonesborough that the Holston company of eighty men, which had been looked for with such intense anxiety, was at last approaching, and a runner met it at Rockcastle River and conducted it to the station.[1] The cause of its heart-sickening delay is not of record. The men remained in Kentucky several weeks, and doubtless had something to do with hastening the final departure of the Indian force, which did not leave the country until its scattered detachments had ravaged and pillaged about the other stations.[2]

A sad echo of the siege shows that poor human nature is about the same in the rough log fort as in the luxurious palace. Captain Boone just had time to get fairly rested from his exhaustive service when he had a

---

[1] Carr's Narrative in "Indian Battles," and Colonel John Bowman.

[2] Bowman's letter to Clark. It seems probable that Black Fish's warriors did not recross the Ohio until about the last of September, 1778, as Hamilton does not mention DeQuindre's return until October 14th of that year. (See Haldimand manuscript.)

PRESENT APPEARANCE OF SYCAMORE HOLLOW, BOONESBOROUGH,

Where the Springs, the Lick, and the Famous Trees were located. Here the First Huts were erected, the Transylvania Legislature met, the First Sermon in Kentucky was delivered, and the Treaty made with the Indians and British.

Boonesborough

summons served on him to attend a court-martial[1] at Logan's Station, at which Colonel Callaway and, apparently, Captain Ben Logan charged him with treasonable attempts to aid the British—in surrendering the salt-makers, in undertaking the Paint Lick expedition, and in favoring the peace negotiations at Boonesborough. Boone showed to the entire satisfaction of the court that all the acts mentioned were patriotic, and that his conduct at both the salt-camp and the treaty conference were deceptions and stratagems necessitated by the emergencies of war, and practiced solely for the advantage of the settlers and in defense of the fort. He was not only completely exonerated by the court, but his conduct was further endorsed, for shortly after he was commissioned a Major. A competent authority,[2] who thoroughly investigated this matter, attributes the charges to "some unfounded prejudice." Boone now seized the opportunity, while no unusual danger threatened the settlements and while the weather was fine, to start back to North Carolina for his family. He left Boonesbor-

[1] Manuscript Narrative of Daniel Trabue, who was present at the trial, and who is the only authority for the statement. Trabue was a native of Virginia, and a man of intelligence and character. He came to Kentucky in the spring of 1778, and first settled at Logan's Station, but afterward was a well-known resident of Adair County, Kentucky, where he died in 1840 at the age of eighty. His Narrative was written in 1827.

[2] The late Lyman C. Draper.

ough early in October, expecting soon to return, but the train of sorrows and misfortunes that had already begun to sadden his life greatly delayed him. He seems to have made a short business trip to Kentucky the next year, but it is certain that he did not come back to stay until the second summer after the siege.

Late this fall there came to the settlement a reminder of its so-called Colonial days in the shape of news that the General Assembly had again, and this time formally and definitely, declared void the Henderson purchases from the Cherokees,[1] and also in compensation for its efforts and expense in the settlement of the same had granted to the Company an extensive tract of land on the waters of the Ohio and Green rivers in the County of Kentucky.[2] But to the settlers, so tried and troubled, the formal announcement of the dissolution of even so grand a scheme as that of Transylvania, long practically accomplished anyhow, caused no sensation.

After this last siege Boonesborough but slowly recuperated. Never in any one season yet had the Indians inflicted so much damage on the Kentucky settlements[3] as in 1778. It was the hardest year Boonesborough had experienced.

[1] See Resolutions, Appendix Z.
[2] See Act, Appendix I.
[3] Bowman's letter.

But the battle-scarred station was now to be a little shielded from the savage storm. Clark's wonderful march, which resulted, on the 24th of February, 1779, in the surrender of the astonished Hamilton and the recapture of Vincennes, inspired immigration anew, and before the spring of that year was over settlers had planted themselves once more on the north side of the Kentucky River, and block-houses and stockaded cabins had arisen between Boonesborough and the Indian country beyond the Ohio. Patterson and his men, who established Lexington, went from Harrodsburg, but the founders of Bryan's Station, the company under John Grant and William Ellis, who settled Grant's Station, and the bands for Strode's, Martin's, and Ruddle's all seem to have gone by way of Boonesborough. It was about this time, too, that Squire Boone, who had recovered from the wound in his shoulder, set out with a little company and established his station on Clear Creek, near the present town of Shelbyville. Urged by their necessities and encouraged by a prospect of at least temporary immunity from invasion, the settlers about Boonesborough made unusual efforts to clear and cultivate the land, devoting by far the greatest part of it to corn. The crops, as often before, were in many cases made in common by companies organized for the purpose. A contract was signed, directors elected, and the members appeared every morning at the sound of a conch or beat of a drum, some to work in the field and others to guard those who did work. A member failing to comply with the contract forfeited his claim to the crop. A list of the members of one of these companies is preserved.[1]

If Boonesborough had a regular commandant at this time it was probably Captain John Holder, who had been one of its leading spirits since early in 1776, when he came in from Stafford County, Virginia. He certainly commanded the company which constituted Boonesborough's quota this year (1779) to the unfortunate expedition of Colonel John Bowman against the Shawanese. Fortunately the roll of his company is still extant.[2] Holder's men left Boonesborough about the middle of May[3] and camped *en route* at Lexington, then only a block-house six weeks old.[4] They were destined to feel again the quality of their persistent foeman, Black Fish,

---

[1] The list includes Benjamin White, Jesse Peake, James Anthony, Nathaniel Hart, John Cartwright, Robert Cartwright, George Maddern, Nicholas Anderson, John Harper, Peter Harper, William Johnson, Whitson George, Edward Hall, William Hall, John Kelley, Edward Williams, and Jesse Oldham. (U. S. Hist. Register.)

[2] See Appendix II.

[3] That Marshall and other early historians plainly err in giving the month as July is shown by Captain Henry Bird's letter of June 9, 1779, in Haldimand manuscript, and by depositions of members of the expedition.

[4] Located on southwest corner of Main and Mill streets. Butler, note, page 101, and statements of its founders to William Leavy.

who smote the outnumbered Kentuckians hip and thigh. But it was the old chief's last campaign. He was badly wounded, and, though successful, surrendered to get the benefit of a white surgeon, which, owing to the confusion and exigencies of the retreat, he failed to receive, causing the wound to prove fatal.[1] After the manner of his people, he gloried that he was allowed to yield up his soul to the Great Spirit in a time of victory.

Education was not forgotten even in these perilous days, and while the pioneers were fighting the Shawanese, pioneer children were at their lessons in a log cabin of Boonesborough fort, where one of the earliest schools of the troubled wilderness was conducted by Joseph Doniphan.[2] The young teacher had come out only a few months before from Stafford County, Virginia, from whence other Boonesborough settlers had migrated, so that he felt at home. He had an average attendance of seventeen pupils during this summer. One of the McAfees, who had now returned to Kentucky, seems also to have taught in Boonesborough a while this season before the erection of their permanent station.[3]

[1] Bradford.
[2] This pioneer teacher died in 1813. He was the father of Colonel A. W. Doniphan, who made the famous march to Chihuahua during the Mexican War.
[3] McAfee's Station was established in November, 1779.

The stream of immigrants that began to pour into the country in the spring of 1779 steadily increased, and Boonesborough became, for a while at least, the busiest post in Virginia's remotest county. It was a stopping-place not only of constantly arriving companies of settlers, traders, and land speculators, who came in with their long trains of loaded pack-horses over the Wilderness Road, but of many such as returned after coming by water, going back from necessity by the land route, as a struggle against the current of the Ohio in the "dugouts" and other rude floating craft of the day was not to be thought of. The old fort was too small to accommodate the newcomers, a municipal government was needed, immigrants clamored for a better way of crossing the river than the risky and uncertain one of fording, which often occasioned long and expensive delays, and the inhabitants, strengthened and encouraged, proceeded to enlarge their borders, to lay off additional lots, to name contemplated streets, and to petition the Virginia Assembly to duly incorporate the place and grant it a ferry. The petition was complied with in October, when the Assembly passed "An Act for establishing the town of Boonsborough in the County of Kentuckey,"[1] and one is

[1] Henning's Statutes at Large, Volume X, page 134. See Appendix III. Several of the names in the Act are doubtless improperly spelt — "Boonsborough" certainly is.

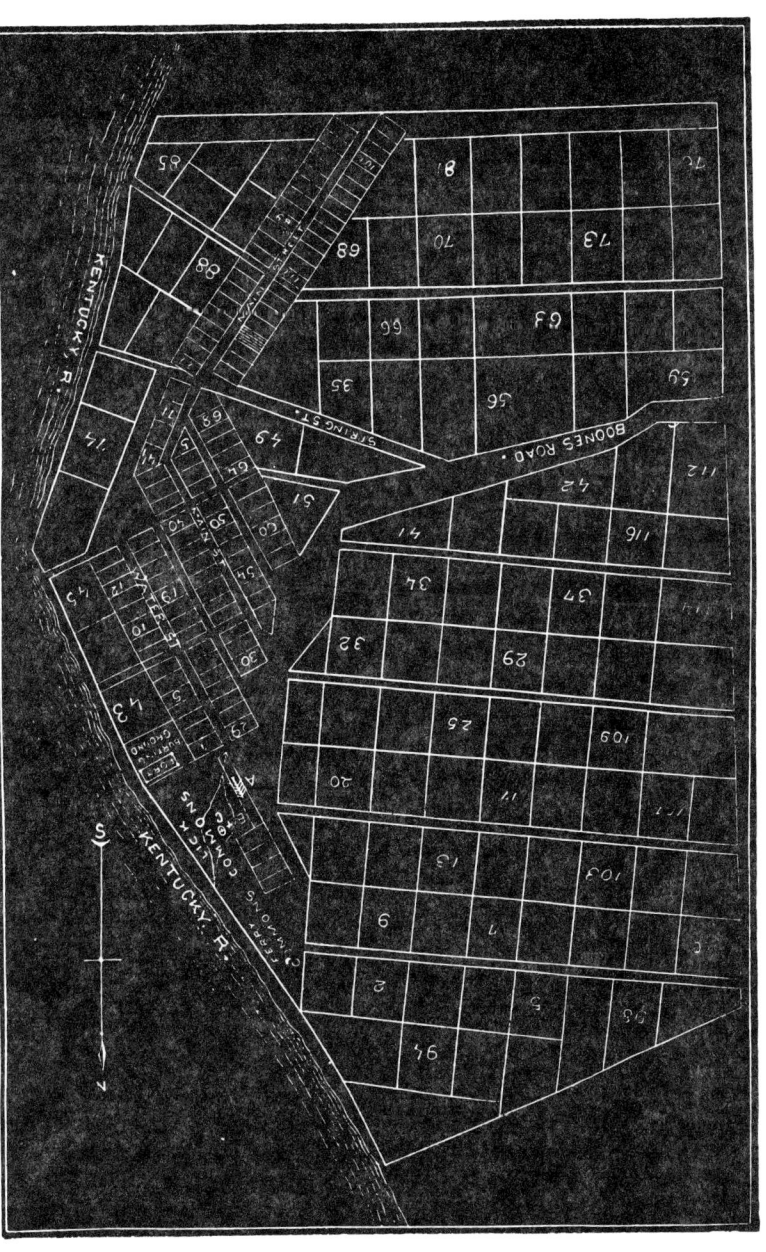

THE TOWN OF BOONESBOROUGH IN 1787.

Showing Plan Adopted During the Revolution. (From the Collins Drawing.)

reminded of the great increase of immigration to the new country by the statement in the bill that the town is established "for the reception of traders." In addition to the land included in the town site, six hundred and forty acres adjoining it were allowed for "a common." The trustees appointed were "Richard Callaway, Charles Mims Thruston, Levin Powell, Edmund Taylor, James Estre, Edward Bradley, John Kennedy, David Gist, Pemberton Rollins, and Daniel Boon."[1] The keeping of the ferry, from the newly incorporated town across "Kentucky" River to the land opposite, now in Clark County, was granted with its emoluments to Richard Callaway, and the toll was set at "three shillings each for man or horse." Quite a number of log cabins were erected outside the stockade at Boonesborough this year, but the fort itself was unchanged and kept up as usual.

Thanks partly to the inactivity of the Indians, by far the largest crop of corn yet raised in the region about the station was made this season, fortunately for the immigrants who continued to push into the country until winter weather blockaded the routes. One of the

[1] Boone's name is incorrectly given in this charter, just as it was afterward by a strange oversight by Filson. The signature to Boone's letter of April 1, 1775, to Henderson, which was long in the possession of James Hall, the historical author, gives his name plainly as "Boone," and all the original autographs of the famous woodsman or *fac-similes* of them that the writer has ever seen show the name with the final "e."

late trains was headed by Colonel Callaway, who had been serving as a representative of Kentucky County in the General Assembly of Virginia. He brought in a good supply of lead and plenty of gun-flints for the garrison, but only a small quantity of powder, as that material was badly needed just then by the Continental troops of the seaboard. His company consisted of forty mounted men, with as many pack-horses. Since the passage the preceding May of the famous land law there had been no trouble in getting an escort through the wilderness for immigrants or stores, as the fever was raging in the old communities, in spite of the war, to secure some of the fertile acres of Kentucky, and every opportunity, including escort duty, was seized to get to them. After a short rest at Boonesborough the home-hunters scattered out on the lonely trails and were swallowed up in the vast expanse of leafless woods. But some of them were back at the station by the 18th of December, increasing the crowd of settlers and speculators who had eagerly gathered to attend the land court which opened there on that day.[1] The crowd that "cabined" or camped by the river while the court was in session included many a veteran of the French and Indian War, and claims on military bounties were frequent among the

[1] Marshall.

numerous ones for settlement and pre-emption rights. Boone, who seems to have hurried back to attend this court, probably reached the settlement the last of December, after the court had adjourned, for he is quoted as entering land on the Commissioners' books a few days after, while the court was being held at Bryan's Station.[1] He left for Richmond[2] to buy land warrants just as soon as he could raise some money on his little property.

The gunpowder that Colonel Callaway had brought in was spun out as long and as carefully as possible, but it was nearly exhausted before the spring of 1780 opened, and there was no Daniel Boone present to make more. The garrison was getting nervous when "Uncle" Monk, an intelligent negro slave who belonged at Estill's Station, a few miles away, came over to Boonesborough to visit his wife, whose owner lived there. Monk not only volunteered to make a supply of powder, but to the relief of everybody he did it,[3] and was highly regarded and favored for it. Monk had learned the art at an exposed settlement in the valley of Virginia. He exercised it several times after this at the stations south of the Kentucky.

The unusual amount of corn that had been raised about Boonesborough not only prevented much suffering and

---

[1] Depositions.
[2] The capital of Virginia had been removed from Williamsburg to Richmond the preceding October.
[3] N. Hart, junior.

anxiety during the winter, but was a source of no little profit to the inhabitants in the spring of 1780, for the demand for grain was then urgent. It was partly to secure a supply of this indispensable staple that, about the first of March,[1] brought back to the station once more its former official head and *de facto* Governor of Transylvania, Judge Richard Henderson. The affairs of the Company had energetically engaged him ever since he had left Boonesborough, and it was mainly through his efforts that the Virginia Assembly had granted to the Company the great tract of Kentucky land below the mouth of Green River. He was now by recent appointment a commissioner on the part of North Carolina to run the boundary line between that State and Virginia, and was promoting the settlement of the Company's lands on the Lower Cumberland, which were within the supposed boundary of North Carolina. Just now breadstuff was badly needed at half-starving French Lick,[2] the future Nashville — the stockaded nucleus of Henderson's second colony. His stay at Boonesborough lasted but five days, and his trip through Kentucky was necessarily a hurried one; but he saw enough of settlements and population to convince him that he had not overestimated the future value of

[1] Haywood.
[2] James Robertson seems to have made this settlement in the interest of the Transylvania Company.

OLD REVOLUTIONARY RESIDENCE OF RICHARD HENDERSON

At Williamsboro, North Carolina. (See foot note, page 115.)

the great prize that had slipped from the Company's grasp. The corn he bought cost two hundred dollars per bushel[1] in Continental currency, and was shipped the entire distance by water in log perogues,[1] which made their long and crooked way down the Indian-haunted Kentucky and the Ohio and up the Cumberland to French Lick Station. The unique little fleet was in charge of Major W. B. Smith, whose connection with Boonesborough now ceased.[2] This visit of Henderson's was the last he ever made to his famous log "capital." His years thereafter were few,[3]

[1] Nat. Hart, junior.

[2] After his arrival at French Lick, Smith assisted Henderson in the interstate survey. He finally settled about sixteen miles from the site of the present city of Henderson, Kentucky, on a tract of land which he received from John Luttrell, of the Transylvania Company, in payment for services. His residence was near what was afterward known as "Smith's Ferry," mouth of Green River, and there he died in October, 1818, at the age of eighty. He never married. (Draper.)

[3] Soon after this visit to Boonesborough Henderson opened an office at French Lick for the sale of the Company's lands. In 1781 he was a member of the North Carolina House of Commons, and in 1783 his Company received from that State two hundred thousand acres of land in Powell's Valley in compensation for settlement and expenses of 1775. About that time (1783) he retired to his farm, located in the fork of Anderson Swamp and Big Nut Bush Creeks, about seven miles northeast of Williamsboro, in Granville (now Vance) County, North Carolina. Much of the farm is now owned by a connection, W. G. B. Snead, Esquire. Here Judge Henderson died January 30, 1785, in his fiftieth year, and here he was buried in the family lot about a quarter of a mile southeast of his residence, and only a few steps from the burial-place of the adjoining (Stamper) farm. No stone or memorial of any kind marks the grave of one of the most enlightened and enterprising characters of colonial North Carolina and pioneer Kentucky, and no portrait of him exists. Fortunately

and they were saddened by the failure of his great plans. Even as late as ten years after his death the Transylvania Company made an ineffectual appeal to Congress for redress of alleged wrongs.[1]

In this spring of 1780 the Indians made up for lost time. Their scouts and man-hunters were in Kentucky before the snow was fairly gone, and tragedies commenced again. Early in March Colonel Callaway began preparations to establish his ferry, and on the 8th of the month while he, Pemberton Rawlings (or Rollins), and three negro men were building a ferryboat on Canoe Ridge, about a mile above Boonesborough, a volley of rifle shots was heard, and shortly after one of the negroes rushed, panting and terrified, into the settlement with the news that the boat-builders had been attacked by Indians. A party of riflemen, headed by Captain Holder, and including young Bland Ballard, then just commencing his career as a scout and spy,[2] galloped to the rescue, but were too late. Colonel Callaway had been instantly killed,[3] scalped, and robbed of most of his clothing. Rawlings had been

his residence is preserved. Some years after his death it was removed to Williamsboro, and now, though modernized, stands as a historic personal reminder of the head of the most unique of the Colonial Governments of America.

[1] See Appendix IV for the Company's Memorial to Congress in 1795.

[2] Ballard was then about nineteen, and had been in Kentucky but a few months.

[3] N. Hart, junior, and Draper.

shot down, tomahawked in the back of the neck, and scalped, but, though mortally wounded, was still alive, and the two negroes were prisoners, destined for savage slavery. They were heard of no more. The Indians who, almost as a matter of course, were Shawanese, and who successfully eluded pursuit, had evidently watched the movements of the boat-builders, and fired with impunity from a nearby place of concealment. There was sudden, crushing grief in two homes, and sorrow throughout the settlement as the stricken forms were tenderly brought in, and there was even deeper gloom soon after, for the terribly wounded Rawlings died before the setting of the sun. The gallant old leader and his brave lieutenant were buried in one grave back of the fort they had helped to defend, and where the soil they loved overlooks the beautiful river that is consecrated to the memory of the pioneers. Colonel Callaway's hair was noticeable both for its length and for its peculiar shade of gray, and when the scalp was carried by the exulting savages to their town across the Ohio it was recognized with horror and sadness by Joseph Jackson, one of Boone's unfortunate party of salt-boilers of the Blue Licks, who was still a captive.

Anxieties were added to griefs as the days went by at Boonesborough, but the greatest of them all was occasioned by the news brought by Abraham Chaplain and one Hendricks, who had escaped from Wyandot captivity about the middle of May, and tattered and famished had been welcomed by the pitying settlers. They reported that the Indians and Canadians were assembling in unusual force to attack Boonesborough; that they would certainly move in about four weeks, and that this time they would come with cannon, against which the wooden forts would be utterly helpless. The information, reliable as it was startling, was dispatched at once to Colonel John Bowman in a letter signed by E. Worthington, Ben Roberts, James Patton, and Edward Bulger,[1] who, in earnestly requesting more militia to repel the invasion, declared, with patriotic fervor, that such was "the humble prayer of this garrison and of every other son of liberty." Heavy as this news was, there is no data now extant to show that any steps were taken to meet this the greatest danger that had yet threatened the Kentucky settlements. In the absence of such data it looks like there was the same remarkable failure on the part of the authorities as to scout service and ordinary military precautions that in another invasion, two years after this, brought such scathing rebukes and stinging sarcasms from George Rogers

[1] The original letter was in the possession of the late John B. Bowman, of Kentucky University. The fact that this warning was given is strangely omitted in all accounts of this invasion by Kentucky historians.

Boonesborough

Clark.[1] One little colony—that under Grant and Ellis at Grant's Station—did make a wise and timely withdrawal,[2] but it was the only one to do so. In spite of the warning a month in advance, the invading force under Captain Bird[3] was allowed to reach the heart of Kentucky not only unresisted but undiscovered, and, on the 22d of June, Ruddle's and Martin's Stations succumbed to the enemy's artillery. The swift tidings of the actual presence of cannon, even more than the report of the disaster itself, was almost a forecast of doom to Boonesborough. The once redoubtable fort looked suddenly weak to the settlers, but in spite of that there was a quick and instinctive rush for it by all outsiders near it. Only once—when the blazing arrows of Black Fish struck the station— had the pioneers felt so hopeless, and the panic reached its height when marauders from the Indian army surrounded Strode's Station,[4] across the river and only a few

[1] The Girty and Caldwell expedition of August, 1782. (See Virginia State Papers, Volume III, page 385.)

[2] Grant and Ellis both returned home by way of Boonesborough and re-entered the Continental Army, but both located permanently in Kentucky in the winter of 1781. (See The Traveling Church.)

[3] McBride says (page 190) that Bird was from Virginia originally; that his father returned to England when the Revolution broke out and obtained a commission for his son in the British army. Captain Bird's retreat seems to have been due to his humanity. Kentuckians of that day could thank their stars that his American training had given him a horror of savage barbarity.

[4] Strode's Station was about two miles from what is now Winchester, Clark County, Kentucky.

miles away. But they came without field pieces, mainly to steal horses, and soon disappeared, and the relief at Boonesborough was inexpressible when it was discovered that the entire invading force had strangely retreated without striking another blow, when the whole interior of the country was at its mercy.

It was about this time that the simple-hearted and uncomplaining Boone returned to Boonesborough[1] from North Carolina with his wife and family, bereft of his little fortune[2] and saddened by domestic troubles. The population of the station had greatly changed during his absence, most of his old friends were missing, and the settlement was becoming entirely too crowded for the inveterate hunter and lover of the free and lonely woods. But he made his home at Boonesborough until shortly after another misfortune overtook him, the killing of his brother Edward by the Indians in October at fateful Blue Licks, when he moved out with his family, a few loaded pack-horses, and his dogs, crossed the river and located in what is now Fayette County, at a spot about five miles

---

[1] He had been in Kentucky probably less than two weeks when he was summoned to serve on the Jury of Escheat at Lexington Station (July 1, 1780), when lands of certain British subjects were confiscated.

[2] He had been robbed of his own money and of funds entrusted to him the preceding February while *en route* to Richmond to purchase land warrants. See Morehead's Address for Thomas Hart's letter exonerating him, and page 136 of Marshall, Volume I.

northwest of Boonesborough, near where several buffalo traces conveniently crossed each other, and on a stream that has ever since been known as Boone's Creek. Boone inherited the tract on which he now settled from his eldest brother, Israel Boone,[1] then recently deceased, and who seems to have briefly "adventured" to that neighborhood about 1776, shortly after the establishment of Boonesborough. Boone's Station,[2] as the new log and stockaded home of Daniel Boone was immediately known, stood, it is claimed, on the land at the junction of Boone's Creek and Boffman's Creek, still called on that account "the station pasture," and from this little wooden fort he sallied forth on many a hunting and surveying trip, to many an adventure with the Indians, and to the disastrous conflict in which he lost another son.

Thanks to the confidence restored by Clark's Piqua expedition, the number of settlers so increased that in

[1] Deed Book "D," page 143, Fayette Circuit Court and History of Fayette County, Kentucky.

[2] The site of Boone's Station is now included in the Garrett Watts farm. Boffman's Creek was named after Captain John Boffman, who raised corn in that locality in 1776. The company of immigrants he came out with was defeated by the Indians on Skaggs' trace. We use the name as given by one of his descendants (see 1810 edition of Hardin's Reports, page 348), but it is also spelt "Baughman" in Fayette County records. Boone's Station was succeeded, so to speak, by a little settlement that sprang up near it at the crossing of the buffalo traces, which fact gave it the name of "Cross Plains," but it lost its identity shortly after 1826, when the present town of Athens was started about half a mile away.

November of this year (1780) Kentucky County was divided by the Virginia Legislature into three counties, which were given the names of shining lights of the heroic struggle then in progress—Jefferson, Fayette, and Lincoln. Boonesborough now found itself in the most populous of the new counties, Lincoln, and Daniel Boone became the lieutenant-colonel of the county in which he then resided, Fayette.[1]

The Indians now gave the people a rest, but the winter that followed was as terrible as the savages. It commenced unusually soon with a succession of snow-storms, followed by the coldest weather the settlers had ever experienced. The snow that banked the ground was locked in ice, the trees seemed made of marble and glass. The streams were solid. The Kentucky River was lost in snow, and the transformed hills opposite the fort were as white, as desolate, and as beautiful as the towering ice-packs of the Polar Sea. The very firewood had to be chopped out of encircling ice, and every thing that wild animals could eat was hidden in snow and shut in by ice. And this desperate and apparently interminable weather continued without a thaw until the spring of 1781, and with all the suffering that such an experience comprehends. Not only did forest animals freeze

[1] Calendar Virginia State Papers.

to death, but cattle and hogs about the station, and many that did not die in that way perished of starvation. The settlers did manage with great exertions and misery to keep from freezing, but food was so scarce that they barely succeeded in keeping life in their bodies, for the corn gave out, and for weeks they had to exist on wild game, as in 1776, except that now it was so wretchedly poor as to be almost useless. The name given this unprecedented season, "The Hard Winter,"[1] but mildly expresses the terrors of it.

Miserable, however, as were the cooped-up settlers during this memorable time, they did not forget to sympathize with the distant Continentals, and they especially exulted in the signal success at King's Mountain of their old friends and neighbors of Watauga and the Holston. Time and again at night, as they huddled close to their cabin fires, did the subject come up, and it was only supplanted at last by the news of the Battle of the Cowpens, which did not reach them until nearly a month after that British defeat.

[1] Authors differ as to the date of "The Hard Winter," some, with apparent correctness, placing it the season before this. We follow Boone mainly because he seems to have been the only authority actually in Kentucky at the time who gave any thing like contemporary testimony about it. If The Hard Winter occurred the preceding season, one is puzzled to account for the evident abundance of corn, at Boonesborough at least, in March, 1780.

The patriots of the backwoods were now more hopeful of their country, and they were encouraged both by the auspicious opening of the spring of 1781 and the influx of immigrants that distinguished it; but the gloom of Indian prospect brightened not at all, for savage war bands, generally small, but occasionally important, were striking somewhere in Kentucky in 1781 from the time they attacked McAfee's Station in May until winter came again. Boonesborough barely escaped a visit about the middle of September from probably the strongest and certainly the most successful of these parties, comprising Hurons and Miamis, who, under the noted Brant, had just defeated Floyd at Long Run.[1] The Indians were urged by Alexander McKee, who accompanied them, to march against the hated fort "on the Kentuck," but the fickle and elated savages were so anxious to celebrate their victories that they scattered at once to their villages. Boonesborough was unassailed this time in force, but few indeed were the weeks that followed when minor tragedies did not bring sorrow to some dweller within her gates or to some family within sound of her rifles. All through this fall, and especially at the gathering in of the crops, the avenging or marauding Indian was at

[1] Haldimand manuscripts. Letters of McKee and Thompson of September, 1781.

BOONESBOROUGH FERRY, ESTABLISHED IN 1779.
(As it now appears.)

his deadly work, and the very Christmas-tide was ushered in with mortal combats and savage murders, for it was in December that some of the Pennsylvanians, who had located so close to Boonesborough,[1] were ambuscaded, and that the heroic Mrs. Duree took the place of her fallen husband and defended both the living and the dead of her desolated cabin. Absorbed utterly in the desperate struggle for the possession of a home and for life itself, the Kentucky pioneer had but little time to give to the preservation of the deeds of daring and of blood that were almost commonplace in their perpetual occurrence, and this is especially true of the year 1781. There is no record extant that conveys any adequate idea of the trials and the tragedies of that eventful season. Even the surrender of Cornwallis, which made the whole Atlantic seaboard exult in the certainty of peace, seemed only to incite the British and the savages of the Northwest to still greater exertions to sweep the "rebels" of the frontier from the face of the earth, and the spring of 1782 found the Kentucky settlers penned up as closely as ever in their cramped, crowded, and monotonous forts.

On the 19th of March of this year all Boonesborough was stirred up at the sight of two or three logs, united

[1] At White Oak Station, about a mile away.

in the crudest way, drifting down the Kentucky and past the station. To the inexperienced the incident was too trifling for a second thought, but to the veteran woodsman the little raft betrayed the presence of Indians, from whom it had accidentally slipped away as they were crossing the river. It was, in fact, the first announcement of that incursion of Wyandots which resulted in Estill's defeat, which was probably the most equal, the most stubbornly contested, and the most desperate of the minor engagements of pioneer Kentucky.[1] And there was more grief at Boonesborough and at every station in the region about it.

The season of 1782 had opened, as it was to close, in blood. All during the planting-time the fields were haunted by straggling Indians, and such crops as were raised were made while contending both with them and with a drouth that extended from the last of April until late in July. But none of these things kept back the land-hungry immigrants, who came on in rapidly increasing numbers. The savages were now not only more seriously alarmed than ever, but they were incited with redoubled energy by the despairing British, who sought at once to regain their lost advantages and thus, if not already too late, to prevent the vast and magnificent

[1] Marshall's Reports, page 304, and Cists' Miscellany for 1845.

Boonesborough

domain of the West from passing, by a pending treaty,[1] forever from the British Crown. Once more a formidable force of Indians and Canadians was called together, and in August, under the leadership of Girty and Caldwell, they swarmed across the Ohio in a last, supreme effort to destroy the Kentucky forts.[2] Aiming first at the capture of the two principal ones on the "frontier," Bryan's Station and Lexington, by strategy they sought to draw away their garrisons to the south side of the Kentucky River through demonstrations of decoy parties sent in advance of the main body to the neighborhood of Boonesborough.

It was at this time that Hoy's Station,[3] only a few miles south of Boonesborough, was threatened, and the Indians, both in coming and going, left bloody tracks. Two at least of their victims were identified with Boonesborough. One was Captain William Buchanan,[4] killed while with Holder's men in pursuit of one of the decoy bands, and the other was Colonel Nathaniel Hart, way-

[1] The Treaty of Paris. England would have welcomed any pretext during the consideration of this much-delayed instrument to prevent the absolute cession to the United States of the territory conquered by Clark. Influences were at work in Paris at this very time to that end.

[2] The writer has given an account of this invasion in his "Story of Bryan's Station."

[3] Located close to the present village of Foxtown, Madison County, Kentucky.

[4] Judge William Chenault.

laid in the vicinity of White Oak Station while out hunting for his horse, unconscious of the presence of an enemy. The savages in an attempt to take him prisoner broke his thigh, and finding that it would be impossible on that account to take him along with them they shot the helpless sufferer through the heart with a rifle that was placed so close to his breast that the powder burned his skin. In addition to this he was tomahawked and scalped, and in the turmoil of the incursion it was two days before his poor mutilated body was found.[1]

Holder was defeated, and another and an apparently serious demonstration was made against Hoy's Station. Boone hurried across the river to Boonesborough to assume command of the riflemen ordered to the relief of the threatened post; William Ellis[2] was just about to join him with mounted men that had assembled at Boone's Station; the Lexington garrison was well on its way to the Kentucky River, and the ruse of the Indian leaders was almost a success when their real object was discovered, and soon the entire fighting force of all the settlements was on the march to the relief of Bryan's Station. Boone led off a company that had gathered at Boonesborough. It was

[1] Jesse Benton's letter of December 4, 1782, to Thomas Hart.
[2] Ellis' Station was convenient to Boone's, being located near the present Pine Grove. A few hours after this, Captain Ellis led the cavalry charge at Bryan's Station.

the last time that "the knight errant of the wood" sallied forth with men at arms from the pioneer castle he had done so much to render famous. During the next few days the only defenders of Boonesborough were one or two of its oldest men, the women and the children, and, with the exception of a little cooking, domestic employments ceased. Details of women, rifle in hand, did guard duty day and night, and during that memorable period none of the inmates of the stockade ever slept except as they had watched, fully clothed and ready for any emergency. The anxious days only ended in darkness, for then came the crowning disaster of that year of pioneer defeats, the Battle of the Blue Licks, the last battle of the American Revolution,[1] when Boonesborough, with all Kentucky, was overwhelmed with grief. And the consternation was as great as the grief, for it was feared that the savages "would bring another campaign into the country," and that, said Boone in an appealing letter to the Governor of Virginia, written at Boone's Sta-

[1] Collins, by a singular error, places Loughry's defeat after the Battle of the Blue Licks; but it has been plainly shown to have occurred on the 24th of August, 1781 (see Anderson's Diary in Indiana H. S., Pamphlet No. 4), and the fight at Combahee Ferry, South Carolina, which took place August 27, 1782, General Greene himself called "a paltry little skirmish." Whatever may be said as to "the last blood shed in the field," the fact is evident that the engagement at the Blue Licks on the 19th of August, 1782, was the last *battle* of the Revolution.

tion a few days after the defeat, "would break up these settlements." Never since the spring of 1775 had the pioneers come so near to abandoning Kentucky. They were in the depths of despair until electrified by a bugle-call from the indomitable Clark to invade the enemy's country. Two months were devoted to careful preparations and to the march, and when at last, on the 10th of November, they descended upon the haunts of the Miamis, the astonished savages fled without a fight; their towns were burned to ashes, all their corn and winter stores were utterly destroyed, and the pioneers became their confident and defiant selves again.

This blow and the progress of negotiations at Paris brought a quiet winter to the harassed frontier. But early in the spring of 1783, in spite of the assurances of peace, minor Indian outrages began again and continued, and among them, and of especial interest to Boonesborough, were the killing of its former resident, John Floyd,[1] and the attempted capture of Boone, but no

---

[1] Colonel Floyd had acted as Surveyor for the Transylvania Company. He was killed on the 12th of April, 1783, a short distance from his station on Beargrass. The settlements were not without their own superstitions at that time, for, according to Shane's pioneer notes, Floyd's wife did not want him to leave home, because the day before he started "a bird flew round his head seven times and flew off in the very direction he had to go, and that night a chunk of fire popped out and went by Samuel Aikin's gate." She said that if a personal enemy did not kill him the Indians would.

serious expedition of the savages into Kentucky was ever again attempted. Boone's adventure was long recounted at his old stamping-ground. It seems the Shawanese still sighed for the companionship of their adopted brother, and four of them undertook to bring him back to his former Indian home. They haunted Boone's Station and caught him at last outside of it at work, says Peck, in his log tobacco barn. Boone submitted so good-naturedly that his delighted red kinfolks allowed him to go up into the loft of the barn, as he requested, "to get some fine tobacco to carry along." In a twinkling he sprang down upon them with an armful of dry tobacco that he scattered as he fell, and before the blinded and sputtering savages could recover themselves he was safe within his stockade.[1]

The preliminary articles of the Treaty of Paris had been signed at the beginning of the year,[2] but it took two months for the news to creep to America, and then nearly another month for it to penetrate the Western wilderness. In the meanwhile Virginia's three terribly tried frontier counties had been erected into a separate district, per-

[1] Boone's Station, near what is now Athens, was still the home of Boone in 1784, when he related the story of his life to Filson, and continued to be his home until he left the State, ten or twelve years thereafter.

[2] The preliminary treaty was signed January 20, 1783; a cessation of hostilities was formally declared by Congress the 19th of the following April, and the final, definitive treaty was signed the 3d of the succeeding September.

petuating the ancient Indian name Kentucky, and an unprecedented flood of hopeful settlers was pouring into the country. In April the long-looked-for tidings of the signing of the treaty reached Kentucky, and when at Boonesborough a mounted messenger rode into the stockade with the word "Peace" displayed upon his coonskin cap the welkin rang with the sounds of rejoicing, with hurrahs for "Washington and the Continental Congress," and with the songs of the Sons of Liberty, and far into the night a great bonfire blazed and volley after volley rang out from horse-pistols and flint-lock rifles. But the peace so ardently celebrated was far from coming at once in its fulness to the District of Kentucky as it came to the seaboard States, for the British posts located in the great Northwest, and whose surrender had been guaranteed, were long withheld and as long exerted a baleful influence upon the former savage allies of the Crown. But in spite of every obstacle the "wilderness blossomed as the rose," and henceforth from that day of rejoicing in April, 1783, the ponderous gates of the battle-scarred fort of Boonesborough were closed no more. Soon the great pickets between the cabins gave way to progress; streets were opened, log houses increased, and the one-time stockaded little capital of the Colony of Transylvania became an open town.

Boonesborough

The War of the Revolution was over, and with it ended the tragic and romantic part of the story of Boonesborough that will be forever identified with the history of that struggle, and is of itself almost a history of the permanent settlement of Kentucky.

In 1792, when Kentucky was admitted into the Union, Boonesborough was one of the largest towns in the State,[1] was conspicuous for its shipments of the great tobacco crops[2] that were produced in the region surrounding it, and contested for the location there of the capital of the new Commonwealth. But it was soon left behind in the march of population and events. By 1810 it had declined to an obscure hamlet; a little later on even its decreasing cabins had disappeared, the town site had become only a lonely part of a river farm, and Boonesborough was

---

[1] Even in 1789, according to a report on "The Colony of Kentucky," made to Lord Dorchester at Quebec, a report slightly mixed in its topography, the statement was made that "Boonsburg, upon Red River, comprehends upwards of a hundred and twenty houses." (See volume Canadian Archives published in 1890.)

[2] The cultivation of tobacco, which began almost with the permanent settlement of Kentucky, was wonderfully increased when the Revolution ended, and had much to do with the close and wholesale clearing away of the timber in certain sections of the State. One flood in the Kentucky, that of 1817, carried off more than three hundred thousand dollars' worth of the tobacco of the counties of Madison, Clark, and Jessamine that was warehoused on the river banks.

reckoned among the towns of Kentucky that once had been.[1]

One and only one institution survives that was established by the settlers of the place, and that figured familiarly in their lives. It is the picturesque old ferry, the oldest in Kentucky, and consecrated by the blood of its founders. The ferryboat is fashioned still exactly like its quaint and simple predecessors of the Revolution, and is polled across the river yet in the same primitive style as in the fighting days of Boone. No remnant of the battle-scared old fort remains. For nearly a century the plow has been busy where it stood, and year after year the tall corn has rustled and ripened above its site. Elevated as the fort ground is, it has not always, it is said, escaped the obliterating effects of great overflows of the Kentucky River,[2] and now the graves of such of the founders and defenders of the old stronghold as were buried within or near its wooden walls have long been leveled and lost to sight. The famous "Hollow," owing

[1] Among the extinct or projected towns of Kentucky may be mentioned Leestown, a mile below Frankfort; Saltsburg, at Bullitt's Lick; Transylvania, at the mouth of Harrod's Creek; Port William, merged into Carrollton; Granville, named for the North Carolina county, and Lystra. Another was "Ohiopiomingo," whose title was to honor a beautiful river and a noble Indian; but the name, though musical, ingenious, and magnificent, was about all there ever was of the town.

[2] There was a great overflow of the river in the spring of 1894, and the water then is said to have risen twenty-five feet in Sycamore Hollow.

THE FAMOUS OLD SYCAMORE.

The only Surviving Witness of the Rise and Fall of Boonesborough.
(As it appeared in the Autumn of 1900.)

to successive deposits from river floods,[1] is not nearly so deep as it was in the days of the pioneers, and, long undisturbed, it is thick with sycamores that have sprung up since the settlement died out, and once again the ancient haunt of the buffalo and the elk is a romantic and luxuriant wild. The mighty elm, whose majestic dome sheltered the first legislature and the first worshiping assembly of a wilderness empire, and which witnessed one of the strangest episodes of the American Revolution, fell under the axe in 1828, and fell in all its stateliness and splendor. It was the most unique and precious historical monument in the whole domain of Kentucky, and was invested with a charm that the loftiest sculptured column could not possess. But hedged about and obscured as it has been by deposits from river floods, the sulphur water[2] is there around which the wild animals of the wilderness gathered for unnumbered generations; the Lick

[1] The descriptions here given were written in November, 1900, when the writer made his last visit to Boonesborough, at which time also most of the views of its scenery and historic sites included in this volume were secured.

[2] Owing to the partial filling of the hollow, as already mentioned, the sulphur spring had to be surrounded by a wall, and, in time, it virtually became a well, in which shape it still exists. Many years ago an old musket barrel, unearthed on the place and a relic of the days of Indian investments, was fitted into this spring as a drinking tube, says Mr. H. S. Halley, whose boyhood was spent at Boonesborough, and to whom the writer is indebted for facts and courtesies.

Spring still exists which refreshed alike the Indian and the pioneer, and near it stands the last of the great sycamores[1] that were there when the white men first invaded the vast solitude in which they grew. Its hoary old trunk, hollowed by time, decay, and the leaden storm of a Revolutionary conflict, is now a mere shell, within which four or five men could stand. It is the one solitary living thing still at Boonesborough that has felt the familiar touch of Boone and Henderson and Kenton; that stood while the vanished fort was standing; that participated in the remarkable siege of 1778, and that has survived the throngs of sturdy pioneers and painted savages that have gone the way of all the earth. An age has passed since Boonesborough echoed with the appalling war-cry of the Indian and the crack of the settlers' flintlock, and few sounds disturb it now but the dying clatter of railway trains that pass it by in the distance, the sighing of the wind as it bends the tall tops of a thousand sycamores, and the noises of a crossing at the ferry which come up indistinctly from the deep-down beautiful river, which once knew no other traveler but the red man and no other craft but his bark canoe. The whole place, upland

[1] Of the three great sycamores that graced this spot a century and a quarter ago, one fell in 1873 and another in 1885. Both might have been preserved by timely efforts of the Commonwealth.

Boonesborough

and hollow, has all the sadness of a deserted village,[1] the melancholy charm of lonely nature, and the eloquence of an historic past. It thrills the soul with a suggestion of that untouched wilderness that was as sublime as the ocean, of a hunting-ground that has never been surpassed, of that quickly shattered dream of Colonial wealth and feudal power, and of the heroic men and the heroic women who, unaided and forgotten, laid the foundation of a free and independent State. Boonesborough clusters thick with memories of that solitary log fort that was pelted with lead, blackened by fire, and stained with blood. It is rich with the romance of the Revolution and the romance of Indian warfare. It is hallowed by the sufferings of her settlers. It is consecrated by the ashes of her dead. It is ground immortalized that

---

[1] Boonesborough, or, strictly speaking, the site of it, would now be described as being in Madison County, Kentucky, and located immediately on the south bank of the Kentucky River and between it and the close-by Richmond and Winchester turnpike. It is about two miles from the town of Ford, which is on the opposite side of the river in Clark County and on the Louisville & Nashville Railroad, and the site of the fort is reached from that place by a picturesque country road which leads to the historic river, which is crossed at a ferry so close to the old settlement that it may itself be called a part of it. Ford is only a short ride by rail from Richmond, Winchester, and Lexington, Ky. Boonesborough is by turnpike twelve miles from Richmond, nine miles from Winchester, and about twenty miles from Lexington. It is about sixty miles by land from the mouth of the Kentucky River, and about one hundred and thirty miles from it by water.

should be owned, honored, and eternally cherished by the Commonwealth[1] it cradled.

[1] The writer would respectfully suggest that Boonesborough could be strikingly and most appropriately marked if the work were done in accordance with the eternal fitness of things. A log fort, stockade and all, could be built almost exactly similar to that of Boone and Henderson, as the plan of their station still exists. Such a realistic reminder of the life, the times, and the heroism of the Kentucky pioneers would, if suitably cared for, last for generations. In the center of this enclosure, suitably inscribed, could be a giant boulder from the bed of the Kentucky or from the Rockcastle River, an object which the settlers themselves no doubt often saw, which was personally associated with them, and which would be virtually indestructible. A like great rock could mark the site of the famous elm in the famous hollow, and it would be about the only thing that could withstand the river floods. It strikes the writer that memorials of this kind would require but little attention, could be but little injured by relic hunters, and would be in harmony with the rugged virtues of the settlers and defenders of Boonesborough and with the solitude, the natural features, and the historic associations of the spot they immortalized. Of course these suggestions are based on the assumption that the ground would be the property either of the State or of some patriotic or memorial association.

AUTHOR'S

APPENDIX

NOTES, DATA,
AND
HISTORICAL DOCUMENTS
RELATING TO THE
SUBJECT OF THIS VOLUME

CONTENTS OF APPENDIX.

	PAGE
A—The Name "Kentucky"	143
B—Boone Before 1775	145
C—Boone's First Attempt to Colonize Kentucky	146
D—Proclamation of Governor Martin of North Carolina	147
E—The Cherokee Deed to Henderson and Company	151
F—Deposition of Charles Robertson	158
G—Felix Walker's Narrative	161
H—Boone's Letter of April 1, 1775	168
I—Henderson's Journal	169
J—Proclamation of Lord Dunmore	181
K—Extract from Henderson's Letter written *en route* to Kentucky	183
L—Henderson's Letter from Boonesborough, June 12, 1775	184
M—Letter to Patrick Henry from Henderson and Company	194
N—Journal of House of Delegates of Transylvania Colony	196
O—Proceedings of the Transylvania Proprietors	212
P—Silas Deane's Letter to James Hogg	219
Q—Hogg's Report of His Embassy to the Continental Congress	224
R—Reply of John Williams, Agent, to the Harrodsburg Remonstrance	230
S—Williams' Report of January, 1776, on Transylvania Affairs	232
T—Survey Warrant of Henderson and Company	240
U—Petition of Transylvanians to Virginia Convention	241
V—Petition of Committee of West Fincastle	244
W—Proclamation of Transylvania Company, June, 1776	248
X—Capture of the Girls in July, 1776 — Extract from Floyd's Letter	249
Y—The Bowman Letter on the Last Siege of Boonesborough	251
Z—The Transylvania Purchase Declared Void	253
I—Virginia's Land Grant to Henderson and Company	254
II—Roll of Holder's Company for June, 1779	255
III—Act Establishing Town of Boonesborough	256
IV—Memorial of the Transylvania Company to Congress in 1795	257

AUTHOR'S APPENDIX.

A

THE NAME "KENTUCKY."

Both the country and the river that now bear the beautiful name "Kentucky" were called so by the Indians ages before the coming of their white destroyers. The Indians also called the river "Chenoca," a word which still distinguishes a mountain spur in Bell County, Kentucky, but the name they used by far the most was Kentucky. In coming into use among the whites early in the eighteenth century the word varied as to form and pronunciation according to the user's knowledge of the Indian tongue. John Salling, who was a prisoner among the Cherokees for some years before 1736, and who must have been somewhat familiar with their language, gives the name as we now have it, when he says they took him "to the salt licks of Kentucky."[1] Alexander Maginty, who had also been held by the Indians, deposed in 1753 that they captured him "on the south bank of the Cantucky,"[2] and Colonel George Croghan (not the Major Croghan of Fort Stephenson), who was for so many years British Agent among the Six Nations and an authority in savage matters, speaks in his journal[3] of 1765 of "the River Kentucky." Doctor Thomas Walker (1749) ignores the Indian name, if he knew it.

[1] Withers' Border Warfare.
[2] Made in Philadelphia. Howe.
[3] Published in The American Journal of Geology and N. S. for December, 1831.

Christopher Gist (1751) gives it in a corrupted form as "Cuttaway," and Lewis Evans (1755), who only caught the name from traders, put it down on his map as "Cuttawa." Later on, after many vicissitudes among the whites as to spelling and pronunciation, the name came into permanent use as the Indians themselves pronounced it, "Kentucky."

Authors differ as to the meaning of the name. According to Darlington, in Archives Americana, it is a Mohawk word signifying "among the meadows." Johnson, in "Indian Tribes of Ohio," claims it is Shawanese, meaning "at the head of a river," and others give it still different definitions. Probably the earliest writer to give its meaning as "The Dark and Bloody Ground" was Filson (1784), who says the country was so denominated by the Indians when Findlay traveled through it about 1767. This statement was adopted by succeeding historians and came into use, though Filson gave no authority for it, and there is nothing extant that this writer knows of to sustain it — certainly nothing from the Indians themselves. There is a popular impression that this phrase, "The Dark and Bloody Ground," was used as the meaning of the word Kentucky by the Cherokees at the treaty of Watauga in 1775, but that is a mistake. On that occasion Dragging Canoe, who was strongly opposed to the treaty, said in that metaphorical style which distinguished his race, that there was a "dark cloud" over Kentucky,[1] meaning by that expression, as he himself explained, the hostility of the northern tribes to its occupancy by the whites. On the same occasion an Indian opposer of the treaty, hoping to arouse the superstitious fears of the whites, said that the land desired by Henderson and Company was a "bloody country,"[2] but in neither case was a reference made to

---

[1] Deposition of Charles Robertson. See Appendix F.
[2] Deposition of James Robertson, Volume I, Virginia State Papers.

the meaning of the word "Kentucky." What this last expression did mean is not clear. Certain writers assume that it referred to the supposed bloody extermination of the Mound Builders, but on that theory the phrase would apply with even more force to Ohio and other States of the Ohio and Mississippi valleys. One has as much authority, apparently, for calling it "The Meadow Land" as "The Dark and Bloody Ground."

B

DANIEL BOONE BEFORE 1775.

Some of the Watauga settlers had known Boone before this spring of 1775, for they had come themselves from the Yadkin Valley, to which his father had emigrated from Pennsylvania in 1753, when Daniel was nineteen and already an adventurous hunter. As early as 1760 he had crossed the Alleghanies and begun to explore the Watauga region, and in 1769 he had passed the Cumberland barrier and was hunting up and down the Kentucky River. He had long been familiar with the lonely country west of the Blue Ridge when the Regulators of North Carolina were defeated, and had guided some of those victims of royal oppression over the mountains when they fled to the obscurity and freedom of the Watauga wilderness. In 1773 he had been frustrated in his attempt to plant in Kentucky a colony of which his family was a part (see Appendix C), and the next year, while waiting for another chance to settle there, had been called into service in Dunmore's War, from which he had returned but a few months before this spring of 1775 more determined than ever to carry out his Kentucky project.

C

BOONE'S FIRST ATTEMPT TO COLONIZE KENTUCKY (1773) BARRED AT WALLEN'S GAP.

(Statement of M. B. Wood.[1] See Footnote on page 38.)

About the first of March, 1773, Daniel Boone started from North Carolina with his first colony for Kentucky. He crossed Clinch River at the old Neil ford, and went up the Devil's Race Path and crossed Powell Mountain near the head of Wallen Creek. On this trip there were with Boone eighteen men, besides women and children. They went down Wallen Creek to "the gap," where it breaks through Wallen Ridge. Just as the immigrants were entering the gap they were attacked by twenty-seven Indians, and at their first fire Boone's oldest son was killed, and there they buried him. Boone fired and killed an Indian, and before the savages could carry their comrade away Boone had reloaded his gun and wounded another. The Indians then fell back. Boone had intended to go through the gap and camp in the level country beyond, but it was late in the evening and he selected his camping-ground in the gap. There was a dry hollow which led up into a gorge of the ridge, and in the wet season the water running down this hollow had washed the dirt from under the roots of a beech tree, forming a fair shelter from the winds. Here Boone put the women and children, and posted sentinels all around his camp. These dispositions being made, with a few of his men he followed the Indians some distance in their retreat down the creek, but night coming on they returned to their camp.

About midnight it was discovered that the Indians were stealthily approaching the camp, and the riflemen were soon ready

[1] The initial "M" of this name is incorrectly given as "W" on page 38.

for them. They waited till the Indians got in range, when they suddenly fired on them. The Indians were not expecting this, and hastily fell back. The next morning Boone and his men followed their trail down the creek. They saw traces of blood, and it was evident that some of the Indians had been killed or wounded. The pioneers advanced cautiously until they came to the mouth of the creek, where it empties into Powell River. On a bluff or spur on the opposite side of the river they saw the Indians hovering over a fire. Boone's party shot at them with no apparent result, but the savages scampered away. The pioneers, believing that the Indians had collected a large force in their front to oppose their further advance, fell back to Snoddy's Fort. After resting there a few days, the entire party except Boone and his family returned to North Carolina.

D

PROCLAMATION OF GOVERNOR MARTIN OF NORTH CAROLINA (FEBRUARY 10, 1775) AGAINST "RICHARD HENDERSON AND HIS CONFEDERATES."

(From Volume IX, Colonial Records of North Carolina.)

Whereas his Majesty by his Royal Proclamation bearing Date at St. James's the seventh day of October 1763, did among other Regulations thereby made, declare his Royal Will and Pleasure with respect to his Territory claimed by the Indian Nations in North America in the following words: "And Whereas great Frauds and Abuses have been committed in the purchasing of Lands of the Indians to the great Prejudice of our Interests and to the great Dissatisfaction of the said Indians. In order to prevent such Irregularities for the future and to the end that the

Indians may be convinced of our justice and determined Resolution to remove all reasonable cause of Discontent, we do with the advice of our Privy Council strictly enjoin and require that no private person do presume to make any purchase from the said Indians of any Lands reserved to the said Indians within those parts of our Colonies where we have thought proper to allow Settlement; but that if at any time any of the said Indians should be inclined to dispose of the said Lands the same shall be purchased only for us in our name at some public Meeting Assembly of the said Indians, to be held for that purpose by the Governor or Commander in Chief of our Colony respectively within which they shall be: And in case they shall be within the limits of any Proprietary Government they shall be purchased only for the Use and in the Name of such Proprietaries conformable to such Directions or Instructions as we or they shall think proper to give for that Purpose."

And Whereas in and by an Act of the General Assembly of this Province entitled "An Act for restraining the Indians from molesting or injuring the Inhabitants of this Government and for securing to the Indians the Right and Property of their own Lands;" it is, among other things, "Enacted, That no white Man shall, for any consideration whatsoever, purchase or buy any Tract or Parcel of Land claimed or actually in possession of any Indian without Liberty for so doing from the Governor and Council first had and obtained under the Penalty of Twenty pounds for every hundred Acres of Land so bargained for and purchased; one half to the Informer, and the other Half to him or them that shall sue for the same."

And Whereas I have information that a certain Richard Henderson, late of the County of Granville in this Province, confederating with divers other Persons, hath, in open violation of his Majesty's said Royal Proclamation and of the said act of the

General Assembly of this Province, entered into Treaty with certain Indians of the Cherokee Nation for the Purchase and Cession of a very large Tract of Country, by some reported to be Two Hundred Miles Square, by others Three Hundred Miles Square, and said to be part of the hunting Grounds of the Cherokee Nation, and actually comprized within the limits of the Colony of Virginia and the Royal Grant to the Right Honorable the Earl Granville.

And whereas, this daring, unjust and unwarrantable Proceeding is of a most alarming and dangerous Tendency to the Peace and Welfare of this and the neighboring Colony inasmuch as it is represented to me that the said Richard Henderson and his Confederates have conditioned to pay the Indians for the Cession of Land before mentioned a considerable quantity of Gunpowder, whereby they will be furnished with the means of annoying his Majesty's subjects in this and the neighboring Colonies; and that he hath also invited many Debtors, and other persons in desperate circumstances, to desert this Province and become Settlers on the said Lands, to the great injury of Creditors.

And whereas, it is to be apprehended that if the said Richard Henderson is suffered to proceed in this his unwarrantable and lawless undertaking, a settlement may be formed that will become an Asylum to the most abandoned Fugitives from the several Colonies, to the great Molestation and Injury of his Majesty's subjects in this Province in particular and to the manifest Detriment of the Interest of Earl Granville, within whose proprietary District the Lands treated for as aforesaid by the said Richard Henderson with the Cherokee Indians are deemed and reported to be in part comprehended: I have thought proper to issue this Proclamation hereby in his Majesty's Name and also in Behalf of the Earl Granville, as his Agent and Attorney strictly to forbid the said Richard Henderson and his Confederates, on pain of his Majesty's highest displeasure, and of suffering the most rigorous Penalties of the Law, to prosecute so unlawful an Undertaking, as also to enjoin all his Majesty's liege subjects to use all lawful means in their Power to obstruct, hinder and prevent the Execution of his Design of settlement, so contrary to Law and Justice and so pregnant with ill consequences. And I do hereby forewarn all, and all manner of persons against taking any part or having any concern or dealings with the said Richard Henderson, touching the Lands for which he is said to have entered into Treaty with the Indians as aforesaid or with any other Person or Persons who have engaged or may engage in Projects of the like Nature, contrary to the Tenor of his Majesty's Royal Proclamation aforesaid, as every Treaty, Bargain and Agreement with the Indians repugnant thereto is illegal, null and void, to all Intents and Purposes, and that all partakers therein will expose themselves to the severest Penalties. And as it is necessary for the more effectual Prevention of such illicit and fraudulent dealings with the Indians, to advertise them of the Rules and Regulations established by his Majesty's Proclamation; it is hereby required of his Majesty's subjects having intercourse with the Indians and particularly of the Officers appointed to superintend Indian Affairs, that they do fully explain to them the beneficial Nature and Design of the said Royal Proclamation to themselves and that they do make the Indians sensible of the High Offence they commit against his Majesty in doing any thing contrary to the directions thereof.

Given under my Hand, and the Great Seal of the said Province, at Newbern, the 10th day of February, Anno Dom 1775, and in the 15th year of his Majesty's Reign.

God save the King.   Jo. MARTIN.

By His Excellency's command.

JAMES PARRATT, D. Sec.

Appendix

E

TREATY OF WATAUGA.

COPY OF THE DEED FROM THE CHEROKEES TO HENDERSON & CO. MARCH 17, 1775.

(Furnished by James Alves for Butler's History of Kentucky, 2d Edition.)

This indenture made this seventeenth day of March in the year of our Lord Christ one thousand seven hundred and seventy-five between Oconistoto chief warrior and first representative of the Cherokee Nation or tribe of Indians and Attacullacullah and Savanooko otherwise Coronoh for themselves and in behalf of the whole nation. Being the aborigines and sole owners by occupancy from the beginning of time of the lands on the waters of Ohio River from the mouth of the Tennessee River up the said Ohio to the mouth or emptying of the Great Canaway or New River and so across by a Southward line to the Virginia line by a direction that shall strike or hit the Holston River six English miles above or Eastward of the Long Island therein and other lands and territories thereunto adjoining, of the one part and Richard Henderson, Thomas Hart, Nathaniel Hart, John Williams, John Luttrell, William Johnston, James Hogg, David Hart and Leonard Hendley Bullock of the province of North Carolina of the other part; witnesseth that the said Oconistoto for himself and the rest of the said nation of Indians, for and in consideration of the sum of two thousand pounds of lawful money of Great Britain, to them in hand paid by the said Richard Henderson, Thomas Hart, Nathaniel Hart, John Williams, John Luttrell, William Johnston, James Hogg, David Hart and Leonard Hendley Bullock, the receipt whereof the said Oconistoto and his said whole nation, do and for themselves and their whole tribe of people have granted, bargained and sold, aliened, enfeoffed released and confirmed, by these presents do grant, bargain, sell, alien, enfeoff, release and confirm unto them the said Richard Henderson, Thomas Hart, Nathaniel Hart, John Williams, John Luttrell, William Johnston, David Hart, James Hogg, and Leonard Hendley Bullock their heirs and assigns forever all that tract, territory or parcel of land, situate lying and being in North America on the Ohio River, one of the eastern branches of the Mississippi beginning on the said Ohio River at the mouth of Kentucky, Chenoca, or what by the English is called Louisa River, from thence running up the said River and the most northwardly branch of the same to the head spring thereof, thence a southeast course to the top ridge of Powel's Mountain, thence westwardly along the ridge of said mountain unto a point from which a northwest course will hit or strike the head spring of the most southwardly branch of Cumberland River thence down the said River including all its waters to the Ohio River, thence up the said River as it meanders to the beginning, &c.

And also the reversion and reversions, remainder and remainders, rents and services thereof, and all the estate, right, title, interest, claim and demand whatsoever of them the said Oconistoto and the aforesaid whole band or tribe of people of, in and to the same premises and of, in and to, every part thereof. To have and to hold the said messuage and territory, and all and singular the premises above mentioned, with the appurtenances unto the said Richard Henderson, Thomas Hart, Nathaniel Hart, John Williams, John Luttrell, William Johnston, James Hogg, David Hart, and Leonard Hendley Bullock their heirs and assigns, in several and tenants in common, and not as joint tenants; that is to say, one eighth part to Richard

Appendix

Henderson his heirs and assigns forever; one eight part to Thomas Hart his heirs and assigns forever; one eighth part to Nathaniel Hart his heirs and assigns forever; one eighth part to John Williams his heirs and assigns forever; one eighth part to John Luttrell his heirs and assigns forever; one eighth part to William Johnston his heirs and assigns forever; one eighth part to James Hogg his heirs and assigns forever; one sixteenth part to David Hart his heirs and assigns forever; and one sixteenth part to Leonard Hendley Bullock his heirs and assigns forever; to the only proper use and behoof of them the said Richard Henderson, Thomas Hart, Nathaniel Hart, John Williams, John Luttrell, William Johnston, James Hogg, David Hart, and Leonard Hendley Bullock their heirs and assigns that, under the yearly rent of four pence or to be holden of the chief, lord or lords of the fee of the premises by the rent and services therefore due and of right accustomed; and the said Oconistoto and the said nation for themselves do covenant and grant to and with the said Richard Henderson, Thomas Hart, Nathaniel Hart, John Williams, John Luttrell, William Johnston, James Hogg, David Hart and Leonard Hendley Bullock their heirs and assigns that they the said Oconistoto and the rest of the said nation of people now are lawfully and rightfully siezed in their own right of a good, sure, perfect, absolute and indefeasible estate of inheritance in fee simple of and in all and singular the said messuage, territory and premises above mentioned and of all and every part and parcel thereof with the appurtenances, without any manner or condition mortgage, limitation, of use or uses, or other matter, cause or thing to alter, change, charge or determine the same and also that the said Oconistoto and the aforesaid nation now have good right, full power, and lawful authority in their own right to grant bargain or sell and convey the said messuage territory and premises above-mentioned with the appurtenances to the said Richard Henderson, Thomas Hart, Nathaniel Hart, John Williams, John Luttrell, William Johnston, James Hogg, David Hart and Leonard Hendley Bullock their heirs and assigns to the only proper use and behoof of the said Richard Henderson, Thomas Hart, Nathaniel Hart, John Williams, John Luttrell, William Johnston, James Hogg, David Hart and Leonard Hendley Bullock their heirs and assigns according to the true intent and meaning of these presents and also that they the said Richard Henderson, Thomas Hart, Nathaniel Hart, John Williams, John Luttrell, William Johnston, James Hogg, David Hart and Leonard Hendley Bullock their heirs and assigns shall and may from time to time and at all times hereafter peaceably and quietly have, hold, occupy possess and enjoy all and singular the said premises above mentioned to be hereby granted with the appurtenances without the let, trouble hindrance, molestation, interruption and denial of them the said Oconistoto and the rest or any of the said nation their heirs or assigns and of all and every other person and persons whatsoever, claiming or to claim by, from or under them or any of them and further that they the said Oconistoto, Attacullacullah, and Savanooko, otherwise Coronoh for themselves and in behalf of their whole nation and their heirs and all and every other person and persons and his and their heirs anything having and claiming in the said messuage territory and premises above mentioned or any part thereof by, from or under them shall and will at all times hereafter at the request and costs of the said Richard Henderson, Thomas Hart, Nathaniel Hart, John Williams, John Luttrell, Willian Johnston, James Hogg, David Hart, and Leonard Hendley Bullock their heirs and assigns, make, do and execute or cause or procure to be made, done and executed all and every further and other lawful and reasonable grants, acts and assurances in the law whatsoever for the further, better and more perfect granting, conveying and assuring of the said premises hereby granted with the appurtenances unto the said Richard Henderson, Thomas Hart, Nathaniel Hart, John Williams, John Luttrell, William Johnston, James Hogg, David Hart, and Leonard Hendley Bullock their heirs and assigns to the only proper use and behoof of the said Richard Henderson, Thomas Hart, Nathaniel Hart, John Williams, John Luttrell, William Johnston, James Hogg, David Hart and Leonard Hendley Bullock their heirs and assigns according to the true intent and meaning of these presents and to and for none other use, intent or purpose whatsoever, and lastly the said Oconistoto, Attacullacullah and Savanooko otherwise Coronoh for themselves and in behalf of their whole nation have made, ordained, constituted and appointed and by these presents do make, ordain, constitute and appoint Joseph Martin and John Farrow their true and lawful attornies jointly and either of them severally, for them and in their names into the said messuage, territory and premises with the appurtenances hereby granted and conveyed or mentioned to be granted and conveyed or into some part thereof in the name of the whole, to enter and full and peaceable possession and seizure thereof for them and in their names to take and to have and after such possession and seizure so thereof taken and had the like full and peaceable possession and seizure thereof or of some part thereof in the name of the whole, unto the said Richard Henderson, Thomas Hart, Nathaniel Hart, John Williams, John Luttrell, William Johnston, James Hogg, David Hart and Leonard Hendley Bullock as their certain attorney or attornies in their behalf to give and deliver, to hold to them the said Richard Henderson, Thomas Hart, Nathaniel

Hart, John Williams, John Luttrell, William Johnston, James Hogg, David Hart and Leonard Hendley Bullock their heirs and assigns forever according to the purpose and intent and meaning of these presents, ratifying, confirming, and allowing all and whatsoever their attornies or either of them shall do in the premises. In witness whereof the said Oconistoto, Attacullacullah and Savanooko otherwise Coronoh, the three chiefs appointed by the warriors and other head men to sign for and in behalf of the whole nation hath hereunto set their hands and seals this the day and year first above written.

      OCONISTOTO,
        × his mark.

      ATTACULLACULLAH,
        × his mark.

      SAVANOOKO, otherwise Coronoh,
        × his mark.

Signed, sealed and delivered in presence of

WILLIAM BAILEY SMITH,	GEORGE LUMKIN,
THOMAS HOUGHTON,	CASTLETON BROOKS,
J. P. BACON,	TILMAN DIXON,
VALENTINE TUREY,	THOMAS PRICE, *Linguist*.

F

DEPOSITION OF CHARLES ROBERTSON, OCTOBER 3, 1777.

FROM EVIDENCE BEFORE THE COMMISSIONERS APPOINTED BY THE VIRGINIA ASSEMBLY, JULY 3, 1776, TO INVESTIGATE LAND CLAIM OF HENDERSON AND COMPANY.

(Cal. Va. State Papers, Volume I, page 292.)

He the said Chas. Robertson, deposeth, and saith, That he was at the Treaty held at Watauga, between the said Richd. Henderson and Company and the Cherokee Indians, in March 1775, and believes he heard every Public Talk, that was delivered by the parties—That as to the Treaty Conferences being held fairly and openly the Deponent frequently took notice that both Col. Henderson and the Indians would always cause to be present the white men and Indian Half Breeds who understood both Languages as a check upon the Chief Interpreter, lest he should mistranslate, or leave out, through Forgetfulness any Part of what either Party should speak and saith that he believes the Treaty was held fairly and openly, but does not remember the whole of the Boundary altho' he believes the Indians understood all that was said by the said Henderson—That he does not remember the Bounds of the Lands proposed to be bought, only that it joined the Ohio, and in them was mentioned something about the Head Springs of Kentuckie, and he believes of Cumberland, and that tis his opinion it was to keep the dividing Ridge between Cumberland and Tenase. That there was eight or nine different pieces of writing signed by the Indians, who were told that the reason of their being so many, was that there was so many different

Partners in the Company, and that each must have one for fear one should be destroyed, and that every one might know where his Land was—That none but one of them was read to the Indians. Col. Henderson told the Indians, these writings were all alike word for word (and no one hindered from reading them but does not know that any person did read them) and that they might have them all read if they chose it: to which they said they did not want them read.

He does not know how many Indians signed these Papers, but he understood it was done by consent of the whole, as he did not hear any Particular one make an objection.

The deponent frequently tried to count the number of Indians which he could not do exactly but from his best observations, there was about one thousand in all counting big and little, and about half of them were men — He did not understand there was any more than one principal man behind called Judges Friend, who he understood had sent word that what the other Chiefs agreed to he would abide by — On the second day of the Treaty, the Dragging Canoe went out displeased on hearing the Proposals of the said Henderson as to what Lands he wanted to purchase, because (as the said Indian said) the white people wanted too much of their Hunting Grounds.

On the first Day of the Treaty the Indians offered to give up some Lands which they said Col. Donelson had agreed to give them five hundred Pounds for, and had not paid them, but Col. Henderson said it would not be worth his while to talk about buying that only, as he had a house full of Goods for them, and should be at yet greater Expence for Beares and Rum to entertain them upon.

That towards the close of the Treaty, when the Indians seemed like Complying with Col. Henderson's Proposals, the said Henderson told the Indians there was Land between them and his Country—He did not love to walk upon their land. That he had more Goods, Guns and Ammunition which they had not yet seen. —After this something was said concerning Carter's Books being destroyed.

The Dragging Canoe in some part of the Treaty said there was bad People both of his Nation and the Whites—that there was a dark cloud over that Country—He could vouch that his own Countrymen would not hurt him, but was afraid the Northern Indians would—that it was good to have the path clear and clean, but on hearing what Col. Henderson said about the Land between them and his, the said Hendersons Country he (the Dragging Canoe) said stamping his foot on the ground, we give you from this place, pointing towards the Kentuckie—at which the deponent was displeased, because he was acting as a trustee to purchase the Lands on Watauga, (in conjunction with the said Henderson as to the Expense of the Treaty) of the said Indians as he thought the said Company were then getting the Watauga Lands, which he then had a promise of from the Indians, and had the Goods ready to pay for it.

The Deponent saith he in no ways interfered in the said Hendersons Purchase—His Business at the Treaty was a Trustee from the Watauga People to buy the Country of them Indians.

When the Dragging Canoe stampt his foot on the Ground, and said he gave up all the Land from that Place, the Deponent understood that not only the Lands at Watauga which he was about purchasing, but the Lands in Carters Valley which borders on Clinch Mountain, quite to the Ohio, was then given up, and that if he ever obtained them, it must be of the said Henderson, which was the cause of his being displeased—He knew nothing of any Deed being signed for these last mentioned Lands, tho' he has understood since, that the said Henderson did take a Deed for the Land from Watauga quite to Ohio—The Deponent heard no discourse about a boundary for the Lands Northward of Holston, and on this side Cumberland Mountain, except only what the Dragging Canoe said, when he stampt on the Ground, as he was then speaking of the Nation—The Deponent never heard Col. Henderson promise them any more goods—The Indians appeared to be satisfied with what he had given them, and that previously he told them, if they did not choose to take them they would still be friends.

The Deponent saith he saw these last mentioned Goods as well as all the others delivered and divided and saw Papers destroyed, said to be Carters Book of accounts against the Indians which he was informed by Col. Carter amounted to more than 600—The Deponent never heard there was any other bounds read to the Indians, than what was in the Deed—The Deponent heard there had been some claim to his Country, by the Northward Indians, but that these Indians said it was their Land and what they would so sell it.

And further saith not.

Sworn to before us &C.

ARTHUR CAMPBELL.
DAN SMITH.

Appendix

G

FELIX WALKER'S NARRATIVE OF HIS TRIP WITH BOONE FROM LONG ISLAND TO BOONES-BOROUGH IN MARCH, 1775.

(Written about 1824. Published in DeBow's Review of February, 1854.)

In the month of February in that year (1775), Captain William Twetty, Samuel Coburn, James Bridges, Thomas Johnson, John Hart, William Hicks, James Peeke, and myself, set out from Rutherford County, North Carolina, to explore a country by the name of Leowvisay, greatly renowned and highly spoken of as the best quality of land, abounding in game, now the State of Kentucky.

We placed ourselves under the care and direction of Captain Twetty, an active and enterprising woodsman, of good original mind and great benevolence, and although a light habited man, in strength and agility of bodily powers was not surpassed by any of his day and time, well calculated for the enterprise.

We proceeded to Watawgo river, a tributary stream of Holsteen, to the residence of Colonel Charles Robertson, now in the State of Tennessee, where a treaty was held by Colonel Richard Henderson and his associates, with the Cherokee tribe of Indians, for the purchase of that section of country we were going to visit, then called the Bloody Ground, so named from the continual wars and quarrels of the hunting parties of Indians of different tribes who all claimed the ground as their own, and the privilege of hunting the game; who murdered and plundered each other, as opportunity offered.

We continued at Watawgo during the treaty, which lasted about twenty days. Among others, there was a distinguished chief called Atticulaculla, the Indian name, known to the white people by the name of the Little Carpenter — in allusion, say the Indians, to his deep, artful, and ingenious diplomatic abilities, ably demonstrated in negotiating treaties with the white people, and influence in their national councils; like as a white carpenter could make every notch and joint fit in wood, so he could bring all his views to fill and fit their places in the political machinery of his nation. He was the most celebrated and influential Indian among all the tribes then known; considered as the Solon of his day. He was said to be about ninety years of age, a very small man, and so lean and light habited, that I scarcely believe he would have exceeded more in weight than a pound for each year of his life. He was marked with two large scores or scars on each cheek, his ears cut and banded with silver, hanging nearly down on each shoulder, the ancient Indian mode of distinction in some tribes and fashion in others. In one of his public talks delivered to the whites, he spoke to this effect: he was an old man, had presided as chief in their council, and as president of his nation for more than half a century, had formerly been appointed agent and envoy extraordinary to the king of England on business of the first importance to his nation; he crossed the big river, arrived at his destination, was received with great distinction, had the honor of dining with his majesty and the nobility; had the utmost respect paid him by the great men among the white people; had accomplished his mission with success; and from the long standing in the highest dignities of his nation, he claimed the confidence and good faith in all and everything he would advance in support of the rightful claims of his people to the Bloody Ground, then in treaty to be sold to the white people. His name is mentioned in the life of General Marion, at a treaty held with the Cherokees at Kewee, in South Carolina, in the year 1762 or '63. The treaty being concluded and the purchase made, we proceeded on our journey to meet Col. Daniel Boon, with other adventurers, bound to the same country; accordingly we met and rendezvoused at the Long Island on Holsteen river, united our small force with Colonel Boon and his associates, his brother, Squire Boon, and Col. Richard Callaway, of Virginia. Our company, when united, amounted to 30 persons. We then, by general consent, put ourselves under the management and control of Col. Boon, who was to be our pilot and conductor through the wilderness, to the promised land; perhaps no adventurers since the days of Don Quixote, or before, ever felt so cheerful and elated in prospect; every heart abounded with joy and excitement in anticipating the new things we would see, and the romantic scenes through which we must pass; and, exclusive of the novelty of the journey, the advantages and accumulations ensuing on the settlement of a new country was a dazzling object with many of our company. Under the influence of these impressions we went our way rejoicing with transporting views of our success, taking our leave of the civilized world for a season.

About the 10th of March we put off from the Long Island, marked out our track with our hatchets, crossed Clinch and Powell's river, over Cumberland mountain, and crossed Cumberland river — came to a watercourse called by Col. ——— Rockcastle river; killed a fine bear on our way, camped all night and had an excellent supper.

On leaving that river, we had to encounter and cut our way through a country of about twenty miles, entirely covered with dead brush, which we found a difficult and laborious task. At the end of which we arrived at the commencement of a cane country, traveled about thirty miles through thick cane and reed, and as the cane ceased, we began to discover the pleasing and rapturous appearance of the plains of Kentucky. A new sky and strange earth seemed to be presented to our view. So rich a soil we had never seen before; covered with clover in full bloom, the woods were abounding with wild game — turkeys so numerous that it might be said they appeared but one flock, universally scattered in the woods. It appeared that nature, in the profusion of her bounty, had spread a feast for all that lives, both for the animal and rational world. A sight so delightful to our view and grateful to our feelings, almost inclined us, in imitation of Columbus, in transport to kiss the soil of Kentucky, as he hailed and saluted the sand on his first setting his foot on the shores of America. The appearance of the country coming up to the full measure of our expectations, and seemed to exceed the fruitful source of our imaginary prospects.

We felt ourselves as passengers through a wilderness just arrived at the fields of Elysium, or at the garden where was no forbidden fruit. Nothing can furnish the contemplative mind with more sublime reflections, than nature unbroken by art; we can there trace the wisdom of the Great Architect in the construction of his work in nature's simplicity, which, when he had finished, he pronounced all good. But, alas! the vision of a moment made dream of a dream, and the shadow of a shade! Man may appoint, but One greater than men can disappoint. A sad reverse overtook us two days after, on our way to Kentucky river. On the 25th of March, 1775, we were fired on by the Indians, in our camp asleep, about an hour before day. Capt. Twetty was shot in both knees, and died the third day after. A black man, his body servant, killed dead; myself badly wounded; our company dispersed. So fatal and tragical an event cast a deep gloom of melancholy over all our prospects, and high calculations of long life and happy days in our newly-discovered country were prostrated; hope vanished from the most of us, and left us suspended in the tumult of uncertainty and conjecture. Col. Boon, and a few others, appeared to possess firmness and fortitude. In our calamitous situation, a circumstance occurred one morning after our misfortunes, that proved the courage and stability of our few remaining men (for some had gone back). One of our men, who had run off at the fire of the Indians on our camp, was discovered peeping from behind a tree, by a black woman belonging to Colonel Callaway, while gathering some wood. She ran in and gave the alarm of Indians. Colonel Boon instantly caught his rifle, ordered the men to form, take trees, and give battle, and not to run till they saw him fall. They formed agreeably to his directions, and I believe they would have fought with equal bravery to any Spartan band ever brought to the field of action, when the man behind the tree announced his name and came in. My situation was critical and dangerous, being then a youth, three hundred miles from white inhabitants. My friend and guardian, Captain Twetty, taken dead from my side, my wounds pronounced by some to be mortal, produced very serious reflections. Yet withal I retained firmness to support me under the presure of distress, and did not suffer me to languish in depression of mind.

But where shall I begin, or where can I end, in thanks and grateful acknowledgment to that benign and merciful Protector who spared and preserved me in the blaze of danger and in the midst of death! I trust I shall remember that singular and protecting event, with filial sensations of gratitude, while I retain my recollections. We remained in the same place twelve days; I could not be removed sooner without the danger of instant death. At length I was carried in a litter between two horses, twelve miles, to Kentucky river, where we made a station, and called it Boonsborough, situated in a plain on the south side of the river, wherein was a lick with two sulphur springs strongly impregnated. On entering the plain we were permitted to view a very interesting and romantic sight. A number of buffaloes, of all sizes, supposed to be between two and three hundred, made off from the lick in every direction; some running, some walking, others loping slowly and carelessly, with young calves playing, skipping and bounding through the plain. Such a sight some of us never saw before, nor perhaps may never again. But to proceed, Colonel Richard Henderson, Colonel Luttrell, from North Carolina; Captain William Cock, since the Honorable Judge Cock, of Tennessee, and Colonel Thomas Slaughter, of Virginia, arrived in the month of April with a company of about thirty men. Our military forces, when united, numbered about sixty or sixty-five men, expert riflemen. We lived plentifully on wild meat, buffalo, bear, deer, and turkey, without bread or salt, generally in good health, until the month of July, when I left the country.

Colonel Richard Henderson, being the chief proprietor in the purchase of the bloody ground (indeed so to us), acted as Governor, called an assembly, by election of members, out of our small numbers; organized a government, convened the assembly in May, 1775, consisting of eighteen members, exclusive of the speaker, passed several laws for the regulation of our little community, well adapted to the policy of an infant government.

This assembly was held under two shade trees, in the plains of Boonsborough. This was the first feature of civilization ever attempted in what is now called the Western Country.

This small beginning, that little germ of policy, by a few adventurers from North Carolina, has given birth to the now flourishing State of Kentucky. From that period the population increased with such rapidity, that in less than twenty years it became a State.

Appendix

In justice to Colonel Henderson, it may be said, that his message or address to the assembly alluded to was considered equal to any of like kind ever delivered to any deliberate body in that day and time.

In the sequel and conclusion of my narrative I must not neglect to give honor to whom honor is due. Colonel Boone conducted the company under his care through the wilderness, with great propriety, intrepidity and courage; and was I to enter an exception to any part of his conduct, it would be on the ground that he appeared void of fear and of consequence — too little caution for the enterprise. But let me, with feeling recollection and lasting gratitude, ever remember the unremitting kindness, sympathy, and attention paid to me by Col. Boone in my distress. He was my father, my physician, and friend; he attended me as his child, cured my wounds by the use of medicines from the woods, nursed me with paternal affection until I recovered, without the expectation of reward. Gratitude is the only tribute I can pay to his memory. He is now beyond the praise or the blame of mortals, in that world unknown from whose bourne no traveler returns. I also was kindly treated by all my companions, particularly John Kennedy. From Captain Cock I received kind and friendly attentions.

We continued in our station; our men were out viewing and exploring the country choosing such tracts of land as suited them, plenty for all, and thought all was our own.

Colonel James Herod, my old acquaintance in North Carolina, come up to see me tarried a few days. Being a little recovered, I went home with him to his station, since called Herodsbough, where he had a few men. I tarried there two weeks, and returned to Boonsborough. These two stations contained the whole population of that country, which did not exceed in number one hundred men.

The company in our station continued to traverse the country through woods and wilds, choosing their lots of future inheritance, until the month of July, when I returned home to my father's residence in North Carolina, and have not seen Kentucky since, which I have often regretted.

I have been often solicited to make a publication of this adventure, but still declined. Until late, there appears something like it in the newspapers, which is not correct.

I, therefore thought it incumbent on me, as one of the company, and in possession of all the facts, to make this statement, and give it publicity, which I know to be truth by hard experience; and perhaps I may be the last solitary individual of that number left to give a correct relation of that adventure.

H

BOONE'S LETTER OF APRIL 1, 1775.

ADDRESSED TO "COLONEL RICHARD HENDERSON — THESE WITH CARE."

(From the Original, copied by Judge James Hall in 1835.)

APRIL THE FIRST, 1775.

Dear Colonel:

After my compliments to you I shall acquaint you of our misfortune. On March the 25 a party of Indians fired on my Company about half an hour before day and killed Mr. Twetty and his negro and wounded Mr. Walker very deeply, but I hope he will recover. On March the 28 as we were hunting for provisions we found Samuel Tate's son, who gave us an account that the Indians fired on their camp on the 27 day. My brother and I went down and found two men killed and sculped, Thomas McDowell and Jeremiah McPeters.

Appendix

I have sent a man down to all the lower companies in order to gather them all to the mouth of Otter Creek. My advise to you, sir, is to come or send as soon as possible. Your company is desired greatly, for the people are very uneasy, but are willing to stay and venture their lives with you, and now is the time to flusterate their intentions and keep the country, whilst we are in it. If we give way to them now, it will ever be the case. This day we start from the battle ground, for the mouth of Otter Creek, where we shall immediately erect a fort, which will be done before you can come or send—then we can send ten men to meet you, if you send for them. I am sir your most obedient

DANIEL BOONE.[1]

N. B.—We stood on the ground and guarded our baggage till day, and lost nothing. We have about fifteen miles to Cantuck at Otter Creek.

I

JUDGE RICHARD HENDERSON'S JOURNAL OF A TRIP TO "CANTUCKEY" AND OF EVENTS AT BOONESBOROUGH IN 1775.

(From the Original in the Library of the Wis. S. Historical Society.[2])

Monday March 20th 1775 Having finished my treaty with the Indians at Wataugah set out for Louisa.

Tuesday 21st. Went to Mr. John Seviers.

---

[1] Boone's signature, opposite page 89, is a *fac-simile* from the original of this letter.

[2] The original of the journal here given in part, comprising eighty pages of a memorandum book used by Judge Henderson, was loaned by Pleasant Henderson to Mann Butler when that writer was preparing his History of Kentucky. Mr. Butler seems to have deposited the little book

Thursday 23d Still at Mr. Seviers because our horses were lost though not uneasy as Messrs. Hart and Luttrell made a poor hand of traveling.

Friday 24th. Set off in pursuit of Hart and Luttrell, overtook them both, and lodged at Capt. Bledsoes.

Saturday 25th Came to Mrs. Callaways.

Monday 27th Employed in storing away goods.

Wednesday 29th Continued our journey.

Thursday 30th Arrived at Capt Martins in Powells Valley.

Friday 31st—Employed in making house to secure the wagons as we could not possibly clear the road any further My wagon & Saml. Henderson came up,—also Mr. Luttrell in the evening.

Saturday April 1st. — Employed in making ready for packing. Mr Hart came up.

Tuesday 4th—Waiting for the wagon—the same evening the wagon arrived though so late we could not proceed.

Wednesday 5th Started off with our pack horses ab't 3-o'Clock. Traveled about 5 miles to a large spring—the same evening Mr Luttrell went out hunting and has not yet returned. Nathl Henderson & Jas Durring went in pursuit of him—The same evening Saml Hendersons & John Farrars horses took a scare with their packs and ran away with same.

Next morning Saml. Henderson & Farrar went in pursuit of their horses.

Thursday 6th Traveled about six miles to the last settlement in Powells Valley, where we were obliged to stop and kill a beef

with the Kentucky Historical Society about the year 1839, after which it came into the hands of the late Lyman C. Draper of the Wis. His. Society. It is one of the very few souvenirs extant of the Transylvania Company and of the founding of Boonesborough. The copy we present was made directly from the original, and, while not entire, is the most complete ever published in historical form, including, as it does, every thing of real value and relevancy in the original that pertains to our subject.

Appendix

wait for Saml Henderson &c. Saml Henderson & John Farrar returned to us with their horses packs and everything safe — we having waited at our camp 10 miles below Martins for them.

Friday 7th About break of day begun to snow. About 11 o'clock received a letter from Mr Luttrells camp that five persons were killed on the road to the Cantuckee, by Indians. Capt Hart, upon the receipt of this news retreated back with his company and determin'd to settle in the Valley to make corn for the Cantuckey people.

The same day received a letter from Daniel Boone that his company was fired upon by Indians who killed two of his men though he kept the ground and saved the baggage &c.

Saturday 8th. Started about 10 o'clock. Crossed Cumberland Gap. about 4 miles away met about 40 persons returning from the Cantuckey on account of the late murders by the Indians. Could prevail on one only to return. Several Virginians who were with us returned home.

Sunday 9th Arrived at Cumberland River where we met Robt Wills & his son returning.

Monday 10th Dispatched Capt Cocke to the Cantuckey to inform Capt Boone that we were on the road. Continued at camp that day on account of the badness of the weather.

Tuesday 11th Started from Cumberl'd. made a very good days travel of near 20 miles, kill'd beef &c.

Wednesday 12th Traveled about 5 miles — prevented going any further by the rains and high water at Richland Creek.

Thursday 13th Last night arrived near our camp Stewart and ten other men who camped within half mile of us on their return from Lousia. Camped that night at Sorrel River — they had well nigh turned three or four of our Virginians back.

Saturday 15th Travel'd about 18 miles and camped on the

North side of Rock Castle River—this river a fork of Cumberland. Lost an ax this morning at camp.

Sunday 16th About 12 oclock met James McAfee with 18 other persons returning from Cantuckey. Travel'd about 22 miles and camped on the head of Dicks River where Luna from McAfees camp came to us resolved to go to the Louisa.

Monday 17th. Started. About 3 o'clock prevented by rain. Travel'd 7 Miles. Tuesday 18th Travel'd about 16 miles. Met Michael Stoner with pack horses to assist us. Camp't that night in the eye of the rich land. Stoner brought us excellent beef in plenty.

Wednesday 19th Travel'd about 16 miles and camped on Otter Creek—a good mill place.

Thursday 20th Arrived at Fort Boone on the mouth of Otter Creek, Cantukey River where we were saluted by a running fire of about 25 Guns, all that was then at Fort—The men appeared in high spirits and much rejoiced on our arrival.

Friday 21st On Viewing the Fort, and finding the plan not sufficient to admit of building for the reception of our company and a scarcity of ground suitable for clearing at such an advanced season, was at some loss how to proceed, Mr Boone's company having laid off most of the adjacent good lands into lots of two acres each and taking as it fell to each individual by lot was in actual possession and occupying them. After some perplexity resolved to erect a fort on the opposite side of a large lick near the river bank which would place us at the distance of about 300 yards from the other fort the only commodious place near or where we could be of any service to Boone's men or *vice versa*. On communicating my thoughts to Mr Luttrell on this subject with my reasons for preferring this place to a large spring over a hill about three quarters of a mile from Fort Boone, he readily gave his assent and seemed pleased with the choice. Mr. Hart said in a very cold indifferent manner "he thought it might do well enough." Accordingly 'twas resolved, that a fort should be built at said place and we moved our tents to the ground—i. e. Mr Luttrell and myself and our particular company lodged there Saturday night 22d.

Sunday 23d Passed the day without public worship as no place provided for that purpose. Monday proceeded with the assistance of Capt. Boone & Col. Callaway in laying off lots, finished 19 besides one reserved round a fine spring. Tuesday finished the lots in all 54 i e new ones.

Saturday 22d finished running off all the lots we could conveniently get, to-wit 54 & gave notice of our intention of having them drawn for in the evening but as Mr Robt McAfee, his brother Saml & some more were not well satisfied whether they would draw or not, wanting to go down the river about 50 miles near Capt Harrods settlement where they had begun improvements and left them on the late alarm. Informed by myself in hearing of all attending, that such settlements should not entitle them to lands from us. Appeared much concerned and at a loss what to do. On which the lottery was deferred til next morning at sun rise; thereby giving them time to come to a resolution.

Sunday 23 Drew lots.

Tuesday 25. Had a second lottery at the end of which every body seemed well satisfied. I had been able by one way or other to obtain 4 lots for the fort garden &c.

Wednesday 26 Other people coming, employed in showing lots for their use. Sowed small seed, planted cucumbers &c.

Thursday 27 Employed in clearing Fort lot &c. Mr Luttrell, Nat Henderson & Saml Henderson all that assisted me. Mr Hart having made choice of a piece of ground for his own & people's cultivation adjacent to the town lands said, Mr Luttrell reported, that he would have nothing to say to the Fort, things were managed in such a manner, tho' cannot guess the reason of his discontent.

Friday 28th Mr Luttrell chose a piece of ground about ¾ of a mile from the fort and set three of his people to work. Two remained with me to assist in clearing about where the fort is to stand.

Saturday 29—Built or rather begun a little house for magazine but did not finish it.

Wednesday May 3d Finished the magazine. Capt John Floyd arrived here conducted by one Jo. Drake from a camp on Dicks River where he had left about 30 men in his company from Virginia, and said he was sent by them to know on what terms they might settle our lands—That if terms were reasonable they would pitch on some place on which to make corn, or otherwise go on the north side of the River. Was much at a loss on account of his message as he was Surveyor of Fincastle under Col Preston who had exerted himself against us. We thought it most advisable to secure them to our interest if possable. Accordingly though the season was too far advanced to make much corn, yet promised them land.

We restrained these men to settle some where in a compact body for mutual defense, and to be obedient to such laws as should from time to time be made for the Government of all the adventurers on our purchase and gave them leave to make choice of any lands not before marked by any of our men, or a certain Capt & his men who were settled some where about 50 miles west of us on the head of Salt River of whom we could form no conjecture, but thought it best to prevent any interuption to him or his men 'til we should know, what he intended with respect to us and our titles. The day before this one Capt Collomes and Mr Berry with five other men arrived here from Virginia, and gladly treated with us for lands and other indulgences which we granted.

Thursday 4th Capt Floyd returned home, seemed highly pleased with gaining his point and expressed great satisfaction on being informed of the plan we proposed for legislation which is no more than the peoples sending delegates to act for them in Gen. Convention &c.

Friday 5th—Nothing material—let Mr Wm Cocke have five yards & a half oznaburgs off my old tent for which I charge him 5s 6d Va. money.

Sunday 7th Went into the woods with my brother's Nat, Saml. and Capt Boone after a horse left out on Saturday night. Stayed till night & on our return found Capt Harrod & Col Thomas Slaughter from Harrods Town on Dicks River.

Monday 8th Rainey. Was much embarrassed with a dispute between the above mentioned. Capt Harrod with about 40 men settled on Salt River last year, was driven off and joined the army with 30 of his men and being determined to live in this country had come down this spring from Monongahala accompanied by about 50 men, most of them young persons without families. They came on Harrods invitation. These men had got possession some time before we got here. The reception our plan of legislation met with from these gentlemen as well as Capt Floyd gave us great pleasure and we therefore immediately set about the business and appointed a meeting for Tuesday the 23d Instant at Boonesborough and according made out writings for the different towns to sign and wrote to Capt Floyd appointing an election. Harrodsburgh & the Boiling Spring settlement received their summons verbally by the gentlemen aforesaid.

Tuesday 9th Col Slaughter & Capt Harrod took their departure in great good humor. Our plantation business went on as usual, some people planting others preparing &c— We found it very difficult at first to stop great waste in killing meat. Some would kill three, four, five or ½ a dozen buffaloes and not take half a horse load from them all. For want of a little obligatory law our game as soon as we got here, if not before, was driven off very much. Fifteen or 20 miles was as short a distance as good hunters thought of getting meat, nay sometimes they were obliged to go thirty though by chance once or twice a week buffaloe was killed within 5 or six miles. It was some pleasure to find wonton men were afraid of discovery & I am convinced this fear saved the lives of many buffaloes, elks and deer—as to bear, no body wasted any that was fit to eat nor did we care about them.—

Wednesday 10th Nothing remarkable.

Thursday 11th—Common occurrences.

Friday 12th—Old story.

Saturday 13, No scouring of floors, sweeping of yards or scalding bedsteads here.

Sunday 14—No Divine service, our church not being finished—that is to say, about 50 yards from the place where I am writing and right before me to the south (the River about 50 yards behind my camp and a fine spring a little to the west) stands one of the finest elms, that perhaps nature ever produced in any region.—This tree is placed in a beautiful plain surrounded by a turf of fine white clover forming a green to its very stock to which there is scarcely anything to be likened. The trunk is about 4 feet through to the first branches which are about 9 feet high from the ground from thence above it so regularly extends its large branches on every side at such equal distances as to form the most beautiful tree that imagination can suggest. The diameter of its branches from the extream ends is 100 feet—and

Appendix

every fair day it describes a semicircle on the heavenly green around it, of upward of 400 feet and any time between the hours of 10 & 2 100 persons may commodiously seat them selves under its branches.

This divine tree or rather one of the many proofs of the existance from all eternity of its Divine Author, is to be our church, state-house,—council chamber &c and having many things on our hands have not had time to erect a pulpit, seats &c but hope by Sunday, Sennight, to perform divine service for the first time—in a public manner and that to a set of scoundrels who scarcely believe in God or fear a devil if we were to judge from most of their looks, words and actions.

Monday 15th. Express arrived, ten men, including Maj. Bowman, Capt. Bowman and one Capt. Moore.

Tuesday 16th continue, eating meat without bread, and Should be very contented were it not for the absence of four men who went down the River by land on Fryday.

Wednesday 17th Hunters not returned. No meat but fat bear. Almost starved. Drank a little coffee & trust to luck for dinner. — Am just going to our little plant patches in hopes the greens will bear cropping, if so a sumptuous dinner indeed. Mr Calloways men got a little spoild buffaloe and elk, which we made out with pretty well depending on amendment tomorrow.

Thursday 18th. 'Tis now 12 o'clock and no news of the hunters or the absentees. 3 o'clock. Hunters came in but no news of the lost men.

Friday 19th. Sent off Mr. Stoner with Capt. Calloway and some of his men in search of persons above mentioned.

Saturday 20th The election for Boonesborough was held this afternoon with great regularity when Squire Boone, Daniel Boone, William Cocke, Samuel Henderson, William Moore, and Richard Callaway were elected.

Sunday 21st. Capt. Callomees men returned — had been lost. Gave great pleasure.

Monday 22d One Capt. Thos. Guess arrived from above Pittsburg with six or seven men.

Tuesday 23d Delegates met from every town. Pleased with their stations and in great good humor.

Wednesday 24th The Convention met. Sent a message acquainting me that they had chosen Col. Thos Slaughter Chairman, and Mr Matt Jouett Clerk of which I approved. Open'd the business by a short speech &c.

Thursday 25th — Three of the members of the committee waited on the proprietors with a very sensible address — which asked leave to read; read it and delivered in return an answer &c — business went on &c. This day four bills were fabricated & read — 1 for establishing tribunals of justice & recovery of debts — 2d for establishing a militia, — 3d for preventing the distruction of game &c fourth a law, concerning fees. The delegates very good men and much disposed to serve their country.

Saturday 27th — Finished convent'n in good order — Every body pleas'd.

Sunday 28th Divine service for the first time by the Rev. John Lyth, minister of the Gospel, of England. Most of the Delegates returnd home.

Monday 29 — No letters from our friends. — Letter with an account of the battle at Boston.

Friday 2d June. Hunters returned, very good meal.

Sunday 4th Divine service by Mr. Lyth.

Monday 5 Made out commissions for Harrodsburg, Boiling Spring and St. Asaph, both military and civil.

Tuesday 6 Abundance of people going away—Selling their lots &c.

Tuesday 13th Col. Boone set off for his family and the young men went with him for salt.

Saturday 17 Muster of men at the fort by Capt. Moore. Thirty two appeared under arms.

Sunday 18 Corn planted 26 or 27 of April was tasseled or shot. Had a mess of snap beans. Peas ripe. No meat. Two men from Va. Found bacon on which with the beans we had an excellent dinner.

Wednesday 21 Returned home late at night from hunting with a load of buffalo.

Friday 23d Bro. Samuel and two others set off down the river in a canoe to hunt elk, our horses being too much fatigued with constant riding.

28th Scarcity of meat.

30th Meat plenty and many joyful countenances.

Saturday July 1—1775 Dry weather. People going away. Mr. Luttrell and myself set off for Harrodsburg. Were four days bogning in the woods seeking the way. Went too near the river and much plagued with the hills, cane and bad ways.

Wednesday July 5 Arrived at Capt. Harrods and found all well.

Friday 7th set off back in company with Mr Slaughter and about 12 others who were going in to bring out their families or stock. Harrodsburg seemed quite abandoned; only five men left on the spot to guard the crop &c. We suffered in this journey a little for want of provisions.—The weather very dry and the springs being scarce, water was rarely to be gotten.—Buffaloe had abandond their range & were gone into other parts.—When we got to this place we found all well, but a scarcity of meat. Sundry people gone since we left home & more going.

Wednesday 12th—Horses being almost worn out my Brothers Nathaniel and Samuel with some others went up the river in a canoe to get meat if possable. Our salt quite out except about a quart which I brought from Harrodsburg. The men sent for salt not yet returnd, nor any news from the East—Times a little melancholy, provisions very scarce, no salt, to enable us to save meat at any distance from home, no accou't or arrival from within; Weather very dry — and we not able to raise above fourteen or fifteen fighting men at any one time unless they were all summond, which could not easily be done without long notice they being much dispersed, Hunting &c

Thursday 13th July. Things as usual. Meat a little difficult to get.

Thursday 20th Capt. Linn & his company set off down the river to Lee's settlement with whom I sent two men for a little salt, our men being not yet return'd.

Sunday 23d Nothing uncommon more than a fellow calld Grampus belonging to Mr Luttrel ran away on Thursday which was thought nothing of at first — supposing he would return, but on Saturday it was discovered that he had stolen Mr Luttrels mare (his only riding beast) and was totally gone.

Monday 24th Mr Luttrel took a resolution of following his man, and immediately set off. I have intentions of going home as soon as a sufficient number of people come to defend the fort.

Tuesday 25th — Weather dry & are still in great want.—By Capt Linn we are informd that 5 or six men were gone down the Ohio to the Falls by order of Capt Bullet. Mr Bullets orders & his mens resolutions were to pay no regard to our title but settle the land nolens volens. They also inform me that Major Conelly is resolved on the same conduct.

*   *   *   *   *   *   *   *

The Occurrences of tomorrow & so on you'l find in another stitched book cover'd with brown paper & begins with Wednesday 26th July 1775.[1]

---

[1] This note concludes all that is known to be extant of this journal. The "stitched book" referred to, which would probably complete the journal, has never been discovered.

Appendix

J

PROCLAMATION OF LORD DUNMORE (MARCH 21, 1775) AGAINST "RICHARD HENDERSON AND HIS ABETTORS."

(From the Virginia Gazette in the Library of Congress.)

By his Excellency the Right Hon. John, Earl of Dunmore, his Majesty's Lieutenant and Governor General of the Colony and dominion of Virginia, and Vice Admiral of the same:

A PROCLAMATION.

Virginia, to wit.

Whereas his Majesty did, at the request of the Assembly of this colony, permit the Western boundary thereof to be extended, as the same has been run and ascertained by Col. Donelson, and other surveyors deputed for the purpose; and whereas his Majesty, both for the greater convenience of, & the prevention of litigation and disputes, among such persons as shall be inclined to settle upon any of his vacant lands, ordered that all that tract of land, included within the aforesaid boundary, and all other vacant lands within this colony, be surveyed in districts, and laid out in lots of from one hundred to one thousand acres, and as far as the said surveys shall be completed, by the surveyors duly authorized, and the surveys thereof returned, that the lands so surveyed and allotted be put up to public sale, at such time and place as shall be appointed by public notice; and that the highest bidder for such lots and parcels of land, at such sales be the purchaser thereof, and be entitled to a grant in fee simple of the land so purchased as aforesaid, by letters patent under the great seal of the Colony, subject to no conditions or reservations whatever, other than the payment of the annual quitrent of one half penny sterling per acre, and also of all mines of gold, silver, & precious stones; and whereas advice has been received that one Richard Henderson, and other disorderly persons, his associates, under pretense of a purchase made from the Indians, contrary to the aforesaid orders and regulations of his Majesty, do set up a claim to the lands of the Crown within the limits of this Colony; I have thought fit, therefore, to issue this my proclamation, strictly charging all justices of peace, sheriffs, and other officers, civil and military, to use their utmost endeavours to prevent the unwarrantable and illegal designs of the said Henderson and his abettors: and if the said Henderson, or others concerned with him, shall take possession of, or occupy any lands within the limits of his Majesty's government of Va. merely under any purchase, or pretended purchase, made from Indians, without any other title, that he or they be required, in his Majesty's name forthwith to depart, and relinquish the possession so unjustly obtained; and in case of refusal, and of violent detaining such possession, that he or they be immediately fined & imprisoned in the manner the laws in such cases direct.

Given under my hand, and the seal of the Colony, this 21st day of March, in the 15th year of his Majesty's reign. (1775)

God save the King.

DUNMORE.

K

JUDGE HENDERSON TO HIS PARTNERS IN NORTH CAROLINA.

EXTRACTS FROM LETTER WHILE EN ROUTE TO KENTUCKY.

(From Hall's Romance of Western History.)

Gentlemen : POWELL'S VALLEY, April 8, 1775.

Few enterprises of great consequence continue at all times to wear a favorable aspect ; ours has met with the common fate, from the incautious proceedings of a few headstrong and unthinking people. On the twenty-fifth of March last, the Indians fired upon a small party of men, in camp, near the Louisa, killed two and put four others to the route ; and on the 27th, did likewise on Daniel Boone's camp, and killed a white man and a negro on the spot, but the survivors maintained their ground and saved their baggage. But for a more particular account I refer you to Mr. Boone's original letter on that occasion, which came to hand last night. You scarcely need information that these accidents have a bad effect with respect to us. * * * You observe from Mr. Boone's letter the absolute necessity of our not losing one moment, therefore don't be surprised at not receiving a particular account of our journey with the several little misfortunes and cross accidents, which have caused us to be delayed so that we are still one hundred and thirty or one hundred and forty miles from our journey's end. We are all in high spirits, and on thorns to fly to Boone's assistance, and join him in defense of so fine and valuable a country. My only motives for stopping, are, first, that you should receive a just representation of the affair, and secondly, to request your immediate assistance ; for want of workmen our wagons are laid aside at Captain Martin's in this valley ; the chief of our salt and all our saltpetre and brimstone are left behind.

L

LETTER OF JUDGE HENDERSON (JUNE 12, 1775) TO PROPRIETORS REMAINING IN NORTH CAROLINA.

(From the Original, Loaned by James Alves to James Hall.)

Gentlemen, BOONSBOROUGH, June 12, 1775.

It would be needless in me to enter into a detail of every little occurrence and cross accident which has befallen us since we left Wattauga; they can afford no instruction, and are too trifling for your amusement. No doubt but you have felt great anxiety since the receipt of my letter from Powell's Valley. At that time, things wore a gloomy aspect; indeed it was a serious matter, and became a little more so, after the date of the letter than before. That afternoon I wrote the letter in Powell's Valley, in our march this way, we met about 40 people returning, and in about four days the number was little short of 100. Arguments and persuasions were needless; they seemed resolved on returning, and traveled with a precipitation that truly bespoke their fears. Eight or ten were all that we could prevail on to proceed with us, or to follow after; and thus, what we before had, counting every boy and lad, amounted to about 40, with which number we pursued our journey, with the utmost diligence, for my own part never under more real anxiety. Every person almost that we met, seemed to be at pains to aggravate the danger of proceeding; and had we given them all a fair hearing, I believe they would, in return for the favor, have gotten all our men. Many seemed to be of opinion (who had been with Boone) that the men assembled at the mouth of Otter creek would get impatient and leave him before we could possibly get there, if no other accident befell them; and with me, it was beyond a doubt, that our right, in effect, depended on Boone's maintaining his ground — at least until we could get to him. Here, gentlemen, your imagination must take the burden off my hands, and paint what I am unable to describe. You need not be afraid of giving scope to your fancy; it is impossible to make the picture worse than the original. Every group of travelers we saw, or strange bells which were heard in front, was a fresh alarm; afraid to look or inquire, lest Captain Boone or his company was amongst them, or some disastrous account of their defeat. The slow progress we made with our packs, rendered it absolutely necessary for some person to go on and give assurance of our coming, especially as they had no certainty of our being on the road at all; or had even heard whether the Indians had sold to us or not. It was owing to Boone's confidence in us, and the people's in him, that a stand was ever attempted in order to wait for our coming. The case was exceedingly distressing : we had not a fellow that we could send on a forlorn hope in our whole camp : all our young men had sufficient employ with the packhorses ; and, the truth is, very few would have gone, if they had been totally idle. Distress generally has something in store when it is least expected; it was actually the case with us. Mr. William Cocke, (with whom some of you are acquainted,) observing our anxiety on that account, generously offered to undertake the journey himself, and deliver a letter to Captain Boone, with all the expedition in his power. This offer, extraordinary as it was, we could by no means refuse — it was not a time for much delicacy ; a little compliment and a few very sincere thanks, instantly given, preceded a solemn engagement to set off next morning ; and if he escaped with his life, to perform the trust. The day proved dark and rainy ; and I own, Mr. Cocke's undertaking appeared a little more dangerous than the evening before — in spite of affectation, it was plain he thought so — whether it was from the gloominess of the weather, or the time of setting off being actually come, or what, I cannot tell; but perhaps a little of both. Indeed, I rather suspect there is some little secondary mischievous passion personating courage, hankering about the heart of man, that very often plays him a double game, by causing him to view dangers at a little distance through the wrong end of the glass; and as soon as cool deliberation, by the help of caution, has shifted the telescope, and brought the object home to a nearer view, and perhaps the dangerous features a little magnified, this monkey passion most shamefully deserts and leaves the affair to be managed as it can. Be that as it may, in these cases we are not always without a friend. *Pride* will, if possible, take up the cudgels; and let the world say what it will of her, she answers the end of genuine innate courage, (if there be such a thing,) and for aught I know, it is the thing itself. But to return to our subject: no time was lost; we struck whilst the iron was hot, fixed Mr. Cocke off with a good Queen Ann's musket, plenty of ammunition, a tomahawk, a large cuttoe knife, a Dutch blanket, and no small quantity of jerked beef. Thus equipped, and mounted on a tolerably good horse, on the   day of April, Mr. Cocke started from Cumberland river, about 130 miles from this place, and carried with him, besides his own enormous load of fearful apprehensions, a considerable burden of my own uneasiness. The probability of giving Mr. Boone and his men word of our being near them, administered great pleasure, and we made the best use of our time, following on.

The general panic that had seized the men we were continually meeting, was contagious; it ran like wild fire; and, notwithstanding every effort against its progress, it was presently discovered in our own camp; some hesitated and stole back, privately;

others saw the necessity of returning to convince their friends that they were still alive, in too strong a light to be resisted; whilst many, in truth, who have nothing to thank but the fear of shame, for the credit of intrepidity, came on, though their hearts, for some hours, made part of the deserting company. In this situation of affairs, some few, of genuine courage and undaunted resolution, served to inspire the rest; by help of whose example, assisted by a little pride and some ostentation, we made a shift to march on with all the appearance of gallantry, and, cavalier like, treated every insinuation of danger with the utmost contempt. It soon became hibitual; and those who started in the morning, with pale faces and apparent trepidation, could lie down and sleep at night in great quiet, not even possessed of fear enough to get the better of indolence. There is a mistaken notion amongst the vulgar, with respect to courage, which cannot be eradicated but by dint of experiment; all watching, when it comes to be put in practice, has to them the appearance of cowardice; and that it is beneath a soldier to be afraid of any thing, especially when a little fatigued. They would all agree in the morning, that it would be highly prudent and necessary to keep sentinels around our camp at night; but a hearty meal or supper (when we could get it) and good fires, never failed putting off the danger for at least 24 hours; at which time it was universally agreed, on all hands, that a watch at night would be indispensably necessary. Human nature is eternally the same; a death-bed repentance and a surprised camp are so nearly assimilated, that you may safely swear they arise from the same cause. Without further speculation, we have been so fortunate, hitherto, as to escape both. I wish from my soul, that they may not be in league to come together. Never was fairer opportunity, as to the one, and you may form a tolerable judgment as to the other; the western waters having, as yet, produced no visible alteration with respect to morals or Christian charity amongst us. It will no doubt surprise you, but it is nevertheless true, that we are in no posture of defence or security at this time; and, for my own part, do not much expect it will ever be effected, unless the Indians should do us the favor of annoying us, and regularly scalping a man every week until it is performed; if the intervals should be longer, the same spirit of indolence and self-security, which hath hitherto prevailed, would not only continue, but increase. To give you a small specimen of the disposition of the people, it may be sufficient to assure you, that when we arrived at this place, we found Captain Boone's men as inattentive on the score of fear, (to all appearances), as if they had been in Hillsborough. A small fort only wanting two or three days' work to make it tolerably safe, was totally neglected on Mr. Cockes arrival; and unto this day remains unfinished, notwithstanding the repeated applications of Captain Boone, and every representation of danger from ourselves. The death of poor Tivitty and the rest, who at the time you were informed, became sacrifices to indiscretion, had no more effect than to produce one night's watching after they got to Otter creek; not more than ten days after the massacre. Our plantations extend near two miles in length, on the river and up a creek. Here people work in their different lots; some without their guns, and others without care or caution. It is in vain for us to say any thing more about the matter; it cannot be done by words. We have a militia law, on which I have some dependence; if that has no good effect, we must remain for some time much at the mercy of the Indians. Should any successful attempt be made on us, Captain Hart, I suppose, will be able to render sufficient reasons to the surviving company, for withdrawing from our camp, and refusing to join in building a fort for our mutual defence. This representation of our unguarded and defenceless situation is not all that seems to make against us. Our men, under various pretences, are every day leaving us. It is needless to say any thing against it; many of them are so much determined that they sell their rights for saving land on our present terms, to others who remain in their stead, for little or nothing; nay, some of them are resolved to go, and some are already gone, and given up all pretensions for this season, and depend on getting land on the next fall's terms. Our company has dwindled from about eighty in number to about fifty odd, and I believe in a few days will be considerably less. Amongst these I have not heard one person dissatisfied with the country or terms; but go, as they say, merely because their business will not admit of longer delay. The fact is, that many of them are single, worthless fellows, and want to get on the other side of the mountains, for the sake of saying they have been out and returned safe, together with the probability of getting a mouthful of bread in exchange for their news.

Having given you a slight view of one side of the question, it may not be amiss to turn the subject over and see what may be said on the other hand. Notwithstanding all our negligence, self-security, scarcity of men, and whatever else may be added against us, I cannot think but we shall carry the matter through, and be crowned with success. My reasons for this opinion, calls for in you, a kind of knowledge of the geography of our country. Those who have no just idea of this matter may be aided by Captain Hart. We are seated at the mouth of Otter creek, on the Kentucky, about 150 miles from the Ohio. To the west, about 50 miles from us, are two settlements, within six or seven miles one of the other. There were, some time ago, about 100 at the two places; though now, perhaps, not more than 60 or 70, as many of them are gone up the Ohio for their families, &c.; and some returned by the way we came, to Virginia and elsewhere. These men, in the course of hunting provisions, lands, &c., are some of them constantly out, and scour the woods from the banks of the river near forty or fifty miles southward. On the opposite side of the river, and north from us, about 40 miles, is a settlement on the crown lands, of about 19 persons; and lower down, towards the Ohio, on the same side, there are some other settlers, how many, or at what place, I can't exactly learn. There is also a party of about 10 or 12, with a surveyor, who is employed in searching through that country, and laying off officers' lands; they have been more than three weeks within ten miles of us, and will be several weeks longer ranging up and down that country. Now, taking it for granted, that the Cherokees are our friends, which I most firmly believe, our situation exempts us from the first attempt or attack of any other Indians. Colonel Harrod, who governs the two first mentioned settlements, (and is a very good man for our purpose), Colonel Floyd, (the surveyor), and myself, are under solemn engagements to communicate, with the utmost despatch, every piece of intelligence respecting danger or sign of Indians, to each other. In case of invasion of Indians, both the other parties are instantly to march and relieve the distressed, if possible. Add to this, that our country is so fertile, the growth of grass and herbage so tender and luxuriant that it is almost impossible for man or dog to travel, without leaving such sign that you might, for many days, gallop a horse on the trail. To be serious, it is impossible for any number of people to pass through the woods without being tracked, and of course discovered, if Indians, for our hunters all go on horseback, and

Appendix

could not be deceived if they were to come on the trace of footmen. From these circumstances, I think myself in a great measure secure against a formidable attack; and a few skulkers could only kill one or two, which would not much affect the interest of the company.

Thus, gentlemen, you have heard both sides of the question, and can pretty well judge of the degree of danger we are in. Let your opinions be as they may on this point, by no means betray the least symptom of doubt to your most intimate friends. If help is ever wanting, it will be long before succour can come from you, and therefore every expense of that kind superflous and unnecessary. If we can maintain our ground until after harvest in Virginia, I will undertake for ever after to defend the country against every nation of red people in the world, without calling on the company for even a gun-flint.

Here I must beg the favor of your turning back with me to Powell's Valley. Our anxiety at that time is now of very little concern to you; but the impressions still remain on my mind, and indeed I would not wish to get clear of them in a little time. It learnt me to make an estimate of the probable value of our country; to see the imminent danger of losing it forever, and presented me with a full view of the ridiculous figure we should cut in the world, in case of failure. With respect to the real consequence of such a disappointment, I could not so well judge for the company in general, as for myself, but thought it too serious an affair with respect to us all, to be tamely given up without the fire of a single gun, or something like an attempt to take possession and defend our rights, so long, at least, as we should find our posts tenable.

Though the danger Mr. Cocke exposed himself to in rendering this piece of service to the company, dwelt on me for some time, yet having despatched a messenger to Captain Boone was a matter of such consolation, that my burthen from that time was much lightened. We soon found, by his letters on the road, that he had a companion, and went on very well (a small stoppage by waters excepted). On Thursday, the 20th April, found him with Captain Boone and his men at the place appointed, where he had related the history of his adventures, and come in for his share of applause; here it was that the whole load, as it were, dropped off my shoulders at once, and I questioned if a happier creature was to be found under the sun. Why do I confine it to myself; it was general; the people in the fort, as well as ourselves, down to an old weather-beaten negro, seemed equally to enjoy it. Indeed it was natural for us, after being one whole month, without intermission, traveling in a barren desert country, most of the way our horses packed beyond their strength; no part of the road tolerable, most of it either hilly, stony, slippery, miry, or bushy; our people jaded out and dispirited with fatigue, and what was worse, often pinched for victuals. To get clear of all this at once, was as much as we could well bear; and though we had nothing here to refresh ourselves with, but cold water and lean buffalo beef, without bread, it certainly was the most joyous banquet I ever saw. Joy and festivity was in every countenance, and that vile strumpet, envy, I believe, had not found her way into the country.

By this time, gentlemen, I make no doubt but you would be glad that I would change my subject, and enter on something more interesting. You want a description of our country, soil, air, water, range, quantity of good land, disposition of the people here, what probability of keeping possession and availing ourselves of the purchase, how much money can be immediately raised towards defraying the first purchase, and, if any, overplus that will remain on hand for the use of the copartners, &c. &c. &c. These, sirs, are matters of the utmost importance, and many of them deserve your most serious attention. With respect to the country, Mr. Hart, who brings this, will give you ample satisfaction. All that I shall say about it is, that it far exceeds the idea which I had formed of it; and indeed it is not surprising, for it is not in the power of any person living to do justice to the fertility of the soil, beauty of the country, or excellence of its range; let it suffice, that we have got a country of good land, with numberless advantages and inducements to a speedy population; that this country is large enough, and surely will be settled immediately on some principles or other: the grand affair, on our part, is to manage matters so as to have our rights acknowledged, and continue lords of the soil. Every thing has succeeded to my wish with respect to title. The torrent from Virginia appears to be over, and gentlemen of considerable fortune, from thence, are some of them come, and others coming, with design to purchase under us, as they cannot come within the indulgences to adventurers of this season; and applications are daily making for the next year's price. Many of them are returned home, and would have been much dissatisfied, if I had not promised them, on my word and honor, that the terms should be immediately published in all the Williamsburg papers.

M

LETTER TO PATRICK HENRY FROM HENDERSON & CO., APRIL 26, 1775.

(Copied by James Hall from the Original.)

HILLSBOROUGH, April 26, 1775.

Sir,—The late meeting of the delegates, from the several counties, cities, and boroughs, in his majesty's antient Colony and Dominion of Virginia, at Richmond, was an event which raised the expectations and attracted the attention of the whole British America, as well on account of the acknowledged wisdom and public integrity of the delegates, as the important and interesting purposes of that numerous and respectable Convention. The copartners in the purchase of lands, on Louisa, from the Indians, neither intending by their distant and hazardous enterprize, to revolt from their allegiance to their sovereign, nor yet to desert the grand and common cause of their American brethren and fellow subjects, in their manly and glorious struggle for the full enjoyment of the natural rights of mankind, and the inestimable liberties and priviledges of our happy constitution, were anxious to know the result of the wise and mature deliberations of the Convention, and particular in their enquiries concerning the several matters which became the subject of consideration in that august assembly. It was not long before we learnt the particulars from some of the members, and that the minute circumstances of our contract with the Cherokee Indians had occasionally been moved and debated. The true point of view in which, we are told, you, with several other gentlemen, conceived the nature of the contract, and the eloquence and good sense with which you defended, and the liberal principles on which you supported our claim to the benefit of our engagement with the Indians, in addition to the universal applause of the whole continent, for your noble and patriotick exertions, give you an especial claim to our particular acknowledgements, of which we take this earliest opportunity of begging your acceptance. It would, Sir, have afforded us the most singular satisfaction to have had it in our power to give you a more substantial evidence of our gratitude. Yet we conceive the generous disinterestedness of your principles and publick conduct to be such, that even our thanks may be more than you expected or wished for. We hope, however, that our wishes to make known our gratitude to you, will be considered as a sufficient apology for our having given you the trouble of this letter.

Convinced that our purchase is neither against the laws of our country, nor the principles of natural justice and equity, and conscious to ourselves of the uprightness of our intentions, we totally disregard the reproaches thrown out against us by ill-informed or envious and interested persons; and now encouraged by the approbation of the respectable Provincial Congress of Virginia, we shall hereafter pursue with eagerness what we at first adopted with caution.

We beg that you will pardon the length of this letter, and that you will do us the honor to believe, that we are, with the highest sense of gratitude for the part you have taken in favor of our hazardous enterprise, and with the greatest respect and esteem for your eminent and distinguished character and reputation, among the vigilant guardians and illustrious patrons of American liberty,

Sir your most obliged and very mo. devoted h'ble serv'ts,

RICHARD HENDERSON.	NATH'L HART.
THOMAS HART.	DAVID HART.
JOHN WILLIAMS.	LEND. H. BULLOCK.
JAMES HOGG.	JOHN LUTTRELL.
	WM. JOHNSTON.

To Patrick Henry, Esq., Hanover County, Va.

N. B.—A copy of the above letter sent to Thos. Jefferson, Esqr., Virginia.

Boonesborough

N

JOURNAL OF THE PROCEEDINGS OF THE HOUSE OF DELEGATES OR REPRESENTATIVES OF THE COLONY OF TRANSYLVANIA,

BEGUN ON TUESDAY THE 23D OF MAY, IN THE YEAR OF OUR LORD CHRIST 1775, AND IN THE FIFTEENTH YEAR OF THE REIGN OF HIS MAJESTY, KING OF GREAT BRITAIN.

(Copy of the Original. Furnished by James Alves[1] to Mann Butler in 1835.)

The proprietors of said colony having called and required an election of Delegates or Representatives to be made for the purpose of legislation, or making and ordaining laws and regulations for the future conduct of the inhabitants thereof, that is to say, for the town of Boonesborough six members, for Harrodsburg three, for the Boiling Spring settlement four, for the town of St. Asaph four, and appointed their meeting for the purpose aforesaid, on the aforesaid 23d of May, *Anno Domini* 1775 :—

It being certified to us here this day, by the secretary, that the following persons were returned as duly elected for the several towns and settlements, to-wit:

For Boonesborough,	*For Harrodsburg,*
Squire Boone,	Thomas Slaughter,
Daniel Boone,	John Lythe,
William Cocke,	Valentine Harmon,
Samuel Henderson,	James Douglass;
William Moore, and	
Richard Callaway;	

[1] James Alves was a descendant of James Hogg and the legal representative of Hogg and other members of the Transylvania Company in the matter of lots in the town of Henderson, Kentucky. Certain papers of said Company and of Judge Henderson were in Mr. Alves'.possession.

For Boiling Spring,	*For St. Asaph,*
James Harrod,	John Todd,
Nathan Hammond,	Alexander Spotswood Dandridge,
Isaac Hite, and	
Azariah Davis;	John Floyd, and
	Samuel Wood.

Present — Squire Boone, Daniel Boone, Samuel Henderson, William Moore, Richard Callaway, Thomas Slaughter, John Lythe, Valentine Harmon, James Douglass, James Harrod, Nathan Hammond, Isaac Hite, Azariah Davis, John Todd, Alexander Spotswood Dandridge, John Floyd, and Samuel Wood, who took their seats at convention.

The House unanimously chose Colonel Thomas Slaughter Chairman, and Matthew Jouett Clerk, and after divine service was performed by the Rev. John Lythe, the House waited on the proprietors and acquainted them that they had chosen Mr. Thomas Slaughter Chairman, and Matthew Jouett Clerk, of which they approved; and Colonel Richard Henderson, in behalf of himself and the rest of the proprietors, opened the convention with a speech, a copy of which, to prevent mistakes, the Chairman procured.

Ordered, that said speech be read—read the same which follows:

Mr. Chairman, and Gentlemen of the Convention :

You are called and assembled at this time for a noble and an honorable purpose — a purpose, however ridiculous or idle it may appear at first view, to superficial minds, yet is of the most solid consequence; and if prudence, firmness, and wisdom are suffered to influence your councils and direct your conduct, the peace and harmony of thousands may be expected to result from your deliberations; in short, you are about a work of the utmost importance to the well-being of this country in general, in which the interest and security of each and every individual is inseparably connected; for that state is truly sickly, politically speaking, whose laws or edicts are not careful equally of the different members, and most distant branches, which constitute the one united whole.

Nay, it is not only a solecism in politics, but an insult to common sense, to attempt the happiness of any community, or composing laws for their benefit, without securing to each individual his full proportion of advantage arising out of the general mass; thereby making his interest (that most powerful incentive to the actions of mankind) the consequence of obedience: this at once not only gives force and energy to legislation, but as justice is, and must be eternally the same, so your laws, founded in wisdom, will gather strength by time, and find an advocate in every wise and well-disposed person.

You, perhaps, are fixing the palladium, or placing the first corner-stone of an edifice, the height and magnificence of whose superstructure is now in the womb of futurity, and can only become great and glorious in proportion to the excellence of its foundation. These considerations, gentlemen, will, no doubt, animate and inspire you with sentiments worthy the grandeur of the subject.

Our peculiar circumstances in this remote country, surrounded on all sides with difficulties, and equally subject to one common danger, which threatens our common overthrow, must, I think, in their effects, secure to us an union of interests, and, consequently, that harmony in opinion, so essential to the forming good, wise, and wholesome laws. If any doubt remain amongst you with respect to the force or efficacy of whatever laws you now, or hereafter make, be pleased to consider that all power is orginally in the people; therefore, make it their interest, by impartial and beneficial laws, and you may be sure of their inclination to see them enforced. For it is not to be supposed that a people, anxious and desirous of having laws made,—who approve of the method of choosing delegates, or representatives, to meet in general convention for that purpose, can want the necessary and concomitant virtue to carry them into execution.

Nay, gentlemen, for argument's sake, let us set virtue for a moment out of the question, and see how the matter will then stand. You must admit that it is, and ever will be, the interest of a large majority that the laws should be esteemed and held sacred; if so, surely this large majority can never want inclination or power to give sanction and efficacy to those very laws, which advance their interest and secure their property. And now, Mr. Chairman, and gentlemen of the convention, as it is indispensably necessary that laws should be composed for the regulation of our conduct, as we have a right to make such laws without giving offense to Great Britain, or any of the American colonies, without disturbing the repose of any society or community under heaven; if it is probable, nay, certain, that the laws may derive force and efficacy from our mutual consent, and that consent resulting from our own virtue, interest, and convenience, nothing remains but to set about the business immediately, and let the event determine the wisdom of the undertaking.

Among the many objects that must present themselves for your consideration, the first in order, must, from its importance, be that of establishing courts of justice, or tribunals for the punishment of such as may offend against the laws you are about to make. As this law will be the chief corner-stone in the ground-work or basis of our constitution, let us in a particular manner recommend the most dispassionate attention, while you take for your guide as much of the spirit and genius of the laws of England, as can be interwoven with those of this country. We are all Englishmen, or, what amounts to the same, ourselves and our fathers have, for many generations, experienced the invaluable blessings of that most excellent constitution, and surely we can not want motives to copy from so noble an original.

Many things, no doubt, crowd upon your minds, and seem equally to demand your attention; but next to that of restraining vice and immorality, surely nothing can be of more importance than establishing some plain and easy method for the recovery of debts, and determining matters of dispute with respect to property, contracts, torts, injuries, etc. These things are so essential, that if not strictly attended to, our name will become odious abroad, and our peace of short and precarious duration; it would give honest and disinterested persons cause to suspect that there was some colorable reason, at least, for the unworthy and scandalous assertions, together with the groundless insinuations contained in an infamous and scurrilous libel lately printed and published, concerning the settlement of this country, the author of which avails himself of his station, and under the specious pretense of proclamation, pompously dressed up and decorated in the garb of authority, has uttered invectives of the most malignant kind, and endeavors to wound the good name of persons, whose moral character would derive little advantage by being placed in competition with his, charging them, among other things equally untrue, with a design "of forming an asylum for debtors and other persons of desperate circumstances;" placing the proprietors of the soil at the head of a lawless train of abandoned villains, against whom the regal authority ought to be exerted, and every possible measure taken to put an immediate stop to so dangerous an enterprise.

I have not the least doubt, gentlemen, but that your conduct in this convention will manifest the honest and laudable intentions of the present adventurers, whilst a conscious blush confounds the willful calumniators and officious detractors of our infant, and as yet, little community.

Next to the establishment of courts or tribunals, as well for the punishment of public offenders as the recovering of just debts, that of establishing and regulating a militia, seems of the greatest importance; it is apparent, that without some wise institution, respecting our mutual defense, the different towns or settlements are every day exposed to the most imminent danger, and liable to be destroyed at the mere will of the savage Indians. Nothing, I am persuaded, but their entire ignorance of our weakness and want of order, has hitherto preserved us from the destructive and rapacious bands of cruelty, and given us an opportunity at this time of forming secure defensive plans to be supported and carried into execution by the authority and sanction of a well-digested law.

There are sundry other things, highly worthy your consideration, and demand redress; such as the wanton destruction of our game, the only support of life amongst many of us, and for want of which the country would be abandoned ere to-morrow, and scarcely a probability remain of its ever becoming the habitation of any Christian people. This, together with the practice of many foreigners, who make a business of hunting in our country, killing, driving off, and lessening the number of wild cattle and other game, whilst the value of the skins and furs is appropriated to the benefit of persons not concerned or interested in our settlement: these are evils, I say, that I am convinced can not escape your notice and attention.

Mr. Chairman and gentlemen of the convention, you may assure yourselves that this new-born country is an object of the most particular attention of the proprietors here on the spot, as well as those on the other side of the mountains; and that they will most cheerfully concur in every measure which can in the most distant and remote degree promote its happiness or contribute to its grandeur. RICHARD HENDERSON.

May 23, 1775.

Ordered, that Colonel Callaway, Mr. Lythe, Mr. Todd, Mr. Dandridge, and Mr. Samuel Henderson, be a committee to draw up an answer to the proprietors' speech.

May 25th. Mr. Todd produced to the house an answer (drawn up by the committee) to the proprietors' speech, and being approved of by the committee, ordered, that Mr. Todd, Mr. Cocke, and Mr. Harrod, wait on the proprietors with an answer to their address which is as follows:

Colonel Richard Henderson and Company — Gentlemen —

We received your speech with minds truly thankful for the care and attention you express towards the good people of this infant country, whom we represent. Well aware of the confusion which would ensue the want of rules for our conduct in life, and deeply impressed with a sense of the importance of the trust our constituents have reposed in us, though laboring under a thousand disadvantages, which attend prescribing remedies for disorders, which *already* call for our assistance, as well as those that are lodged in the womb of futurity. Yet the task, arduous as it is, we will attempt with vigor, not doubting but unanimity will insure us success.

That we have an absolute right, as a political body, without giving umbrage to Great Britain, or any of the colonies, to frame rules for the government of our little society, can not be doubted by any sensible, unbiassed mind — and being without the jurisdiction of, and not answerable to any of his Majesty's courts, the constituting tribunals of justice shall be a matter of our first contemplation; and as this will be a matter of the greatest importance, we will still keep in the genius and spirit of the English laws, which happy pattern it shall be our chief care to copy after.

Next to the restraint of immorality, our attention shall be directed towards the relief of the injured as well as the creditor, nor will we put it in the power of calumny and scurrility to say, that our country is an asylum for debtors or any disorderly persons.

Nor shall we neglect, by regulating a militia, as well as the infancy of our country will permit, to guard against the hostilities and incursions of our savage enemies, and at the same time, to be cautious to preserve the game of our country, so essentially necessary for the subsistence of the first adventurers.

Conscious, gentlemen, of your veracity, we can not express the satisfaction we experience, that the proprietors of this promising colony are so ready to concur with us in any measure which may tend to promote its happiness and contribute to its grandeur.

THOMAS SLAUGHTER, *Chairman*.

To which Colonel Henderson returned the following answer:

Mr. Chairman and Gentlemen of the Convention —

From the just sense of the nature and importance of the trust reposed in you by your constituents, and your laudible and truly patriotic resolution of exerting your abilities in the service of your country, we derive the most sanguine hopes.

Arduous as the task is, every difficulty must give way to perseverance, whilst your zeal for the public good is tempered with that moderation and unanimity of opinion, so apparent in your conduct.

We, gentlemen, look with infinite satisfaction on this happy presage of the future felicity of our infant country, and hope to merit a continuation of that confidence you are pleased to express in our veracity and good intentions.

While our transactions have credit for the integrity of our desires, we can not fail uniting with the delegates of the good people of this country, fully persuaded that the proprietors are zealously inclined to contribute every thing in their power which may tend to render it easy, prosperous, and flourishing.

RICHARD HENDERSON,

May 25th, 1775.   For himself and the company.

On motion made, ordered, that Mr. Todd have leave to bring in a bill for the establishment of Courts of Judicature, and regulating the practice therein; ordered, that Mr. Todd, Mr. Dandridge, Mr. Calloway, and Mr. Henderson, do bring in a bill for that purpose.

On motion of Mr. Douglass, leave is given to bring in a bill for regulating a militia; ordered, that Mr. Floyd, Mr. Harrod, Mr. Cocke, Mr. Douglass, and Mr. Hite, be a committee for that purpose.

On motion of Mr. Daniel Boone, leave is given to bring in a bill for preserving game, &c.; ordered, that Mr. Boone, Mr. Davis, Mr. Harmon, Mr. Hammond, and Mr. Moore, be a committee for that purpose.

The bill for establishing courts of judicature, and regulating the practice therein, brought in by the committee, and read by Mr. Todd — passed the first time — ordered to be referred for a second reading.

The bill for establishing and regulating a militia, brought in by the committee, read by Mr. Floyd — ordered to be read by the clerk — passed the first time — ordered to be referred for a second reading.

The bill for preserving game, brought in by the committee, ordered to be read by the clerk — read, and passed the first time — ordered to be referred for a second reading.

Ordered, that the convention be adjourned until to-morrow, six o'clock.

26th May. Met according to adjournment.

Mr. Robert M'Afee appointed sergeant at arms.

Ordered, that the sergeant at arms bring John Guess before this convention, to answer for an insult offered Colonel Richard Calloway.

The bill for regulating a militia, read the second time, and ordered to be engrossed.

The bill for establishing courts of judicature, and regulating the practice therein, read a second time — ordered to be recommitted, and that Mr. Dandridge, Mr. Todd, Mr. Henderson, and Mr. Calloway, be a committee to take it into consideration.

On motion of Mr. Todd, leave is given to bring in an attachment bill — ordered, that Mr. Todd, Mr. Dandridge, and Mr. Douglass, be a committee for that purpose.

The bill for establishing writs of attachment, read by the clerk, and passed the first time — ordered to be referred for a second reading.

On motion of Mr. Dandridge, leave is given to bring in a bill to ascertain clerks' and sheriffs' fees.

The said bill was read, and passed the first time — ordered to be referred for the second reading.

On motion made by Mr. Todd, ordered, that Mr. Todd, Mr. Lythe, Mr. Douglass, and Mr. Hite, be a committee to draw up a compact between the proprietors and the people of this colony.

On motion of Mr. Lythe, leave is given to bring in a bill to prevent profane swearing and Sabbath breaking — The same read by the clerk, ordered, that it be recommitted, and that Mr. Lythe, Mr. Todd, and Mr. Harrod, be a committee to make amendments.

Mr. Guess was brought before the convention, and reprimanded by the chairman.

Ordered, that Mr. Todd and Mr. Harrod wait on the proprietors, to know what name for this colony would be agreeable. Mr. Todd and Mr. Harrod reported, that it was their pleasure that it should be called *Transylvania*.

The bill for ascertaining clerks' and sheriffs' fees, read a second time, passed — and ordered to be engrossed.

The attachment bill read a second time, and ordered to be engrossed.

A bill for preserving game, read the second time, and passed — ordered to be recommitted, and that Mr. Todd, Mr. Boone, and Mr. Harrod, be a committee to take it into consideration.

The militia bill read a third time, and passed.

On motion of Mr. Todd, leave is given to bring in a bill for the punishment of criminals — ordered, that Mr. Todd, Mr. Dandridge, and Mr. Lythe, be a committee for that purpose.

The bill for establishing courts of judicature, and regulating the practice therein, read a second time, and ordered to be engrossed.

On motion of Mr. Boone, leave is given to bring in a bill for improving the breed of horses. Ordered that Mr. Boone, Mr. Davis, and Mr. Hammond, bring in a bill for that purpose.

The bill for ascertaining clerks' and sheriffs' fees, read a third time, and passed.

The bill for establishing writs of attachment, read a third time and passed.

On motion, ordered that Mr. Todd have leave to absent himself from this house.

The bill for the punishment of criminals, brought in by the committee, read by the clerk, passed the first time, and ordered to be read a second time.

The bill for establishing courts of judicature, and regulating the practice therein, read the third time with amendments, and passed.

The bill for improving the breed of horses, brought in by Capt. Boone, read the first time, passed, and ordered to be for consideration, etc.

Ordered, that the convention adjourn until to-morrow, six o'clock.

Met according to adjournment.

The bill to prevent profane swearing and Sabbath-breaking, read the second time, with amendments; ordered to be engrossed.

The bill for the punishment of criminals, brought in and read; passed the second time, and ordered to be engrossed.

The bill for the improvement of the breed of horses was read a second time, and ordered to be engrossed.

Ordered, that Mr. Harrod, Mr. Boone, and Mr. Cocke, wait on the proprietors, and beg they will not indulge any person whatever in granting them lands on the present terms unless they comply with the former proposals of settling the country, etc.

On motion of Squire Boone, leave is given to bring in a bill to preserve the range; ordered, that he have leave to bring in a bill for that purpose.

The following message was received from the proprietors, to wit:

To give every possible satisfaction to the good people, your constituents, we desire to exhibit our title deed from the aborigines and first owners of the soil in Transylvania, and hope you will cause an entry to be made of the exhibition in your journals, including the corners and abutments of the lands or country contained therein, so that the boundaries of our colony may be known and kept on record.

RICHARD HENDERSON.

Transylvania, 27th May, 1775.

Ordered, that Mr. Todd, Mr. Douglass, and Mr. Hite, inform the proprietors that their request will be complied with; in conseqence of which Colonel Henderson personally attended the convention with Mr. John Farrow, attorney in fact for the head warriors or chiefs of the Cherokee Indians, who, in presence of the convention, made livery and seisin of all the lands, in a deed or feofment then produced, bearing date the 7th day of March last, 1775. [We omit the boundaries which are here set forth on the record, having already given them to our readers in another place.]

A bill for preserving the range, brought in by the committee and read, passed the first time; ordered to be laid by for second consideration.

The bill to prevent profane swearing and Sabbath-breaking, read the third time, and passed.

Ordered, that Mr. Calloway and Mr. Cocke wait on the proprietors with the laws that have passed, for their perusal and approbation.

The committee, appointed to draw up the compact between the proprietors and the people, brought in and read it, as follows, viz:

Whereas, it is highly necessary, for the peace of the proprietors and the security of the people of this colony, that the powers of the one and the liberties of the other be ascertained; We, Richard Henderson, Nathaniel Hart, and J. Luttrel, on behalf of ourselves, as well as the other proprietors of the colony of

Transylvania, of the one part and the representatives of the people of said colony, in convention assembled, of the other part — do most solemnly enter into the following contract or agreement, to wit:

1. That the election of delegates in this colony be annual.

2. That the convention may adjourn, and meet again on their own adjournment; Provided, that in cases of great emergency, the proprietors may call together the delegates before the time adjourned to; and, if a majority do not attend, they may dissolve them and call a new one.

3. That, to prevent dissension and delay of business, one proprietor shall act for the whole, or some one delegated by them for that purpose, who shall always reside in the colony.

4. That there be perfect religious freedom and general toleration; Provided, that the propagators of any doctrine or tenets, evidently tending to the subversion of our laws, shall, for such conduct, be amenable to, and punished by, the civil courts.

5. That the judges of the superior or supreme courts be appointed by the proprietors, but be supported by the people, and to them be answerable for their malconduct.

6. That the quit-rents never exceed two shillings sterling per hundred acres.

7. That the proprietors appoint a sheriff, who shall be one of three persons recommended by the court.

8. That the judges of the superior courts have, without fee or reward, the appointment of the clerks of this colony.

9. That the judges of the inferior courts be recommended by the people, and approved by the proprietors, and by them commissioned.

10. That all other civil and military officers be within the appointment of the proprietors.

11. That the office of surveyor-general belong to no person interested or a partner in this purchase.

12. That the legislative authority, after the strength and maturity of the colony will permit, consist of three branches, to wit: the delegates or representatives chosen by the people; a council, not exceeding twelve men, possessed of landed estate, who reside in the colony, and the proprietors.

13. That nothing with respect to the number of delegates from any town or settlement shall hereafter be drawn into precedent, but that the number of representatives shall be ascertained by law, when the state of the colony will admit of amendment.

14. That the land office be always open.

15. That commissions, without profit, be granted without fee.

16. That the fees and salaries of all officers appointed by the proprietors, be settled and regulated by the laws of the country.

17. That the convention have the sole power of raising and appropriating all public moneys, and electing their treasurer.

18. That, for a short time, till the state of the colony will permit to fix some place of holding the convention which shall be permanent, the place of meeting shall be agreed upon between the proprietors and the convention.

To the faithful and religious and perpetual observance of all and every of the above articles, the said proprietors, on behalf of themselves as well as those absent, and the chairman of the convention on behalf of them and their constituents, have hereunto interchangeably set their hands and affixed their seals, the twenty-seventh day of May, one thousand seven hundred and seventy-five.

    RICHARD HENDERSON. [*Seal.*]
    NATHANIEL HART. [*Seal.*]
    J. LUTTRELL. [*Seal.*]
    T. SLAUGHTER, Chair'n. [*Seal.*]

Appendix

A bill for improving the breed of horses, read the third time and passed.

The bill for the punishment of criminals, read the third time and passed.

The bill to preserve the range, read the second time, and ordered to be engrossed.

Ordered, that Mr. Lythe wait on Colonel Henderson and the rest of the proprietors, with the bill for establishing courts of justice and regulating the practice therein.

The bill to preserve the range, read the third time and passed.

Ordered, that Colonel Calloway wait on the proprietors with the bill for preserving the range.

Ordered, that a fair copy of the several bills, passed into laws, be transmitted to every settlement in this colony that is represented.

Ordered, that the delegates of Boonesboro be a committee to see that all the bills that are passed be transcribed, in a fair hand, into a book for that purpose.

Ordered, that the proprietors be waited on by the chairman, acquainting them that all the bills are ready for signing.

The following bills this day passed and signed by the proprietors, on behalf of themselves and their partners, and the chairman of the convention, on behalf of himself and the other delegates:

1. An act for establishing courts of jurisdiction and regulating the practice therein.
2. An act for regulating a militia.
3. An act for the punishment of criminals.
4. An act to prevent profane swearing, and Sabbath breaking.
5. An act for writs of attachment.
6. An act for ascertaining clerks' and sheriffs' fees.

7. An act to preserve the range.

8. An act for improving the breed of horses.

9. An act for preserving game.

All of the above mentioned acts were signed by the chairman and proprietors, except the act for ascertaining clerks' and sheriffs' fees, which was omitted by the clerks not giving it in with the rest.

Ordered, that at the next meeting of delegates, if any member be absent and doth not attend, that the people choose one to serve in the room of such absent member.

Ordered, that the convention be adjourned until the first Thursday in September next, then to meet at Boonesboro.

MATTHEW JEWITT, Clerk.

O

MEETING OF THE TRANSYLVANIA PROPRIETORS IN NORTH CAROLINA, SEPTEMBER 25, 1775.

MINUTES OF PROCEEDINGS, APPOINTMENTS, REGULATIONS, DONATIONS OF LAND, ELECTION OF DELEGATE TO CONTINENTAL CONGRESS, MEMORIAL TO THE CONGRESS, AND PETITION FOR ADMISSION AS FOURTEENTH COLONY.

(American Archives, Volume IV.)

At a meeting of the Proprietors of Transylvania held at Oxford, in the County of Granville, on Monday the 25th day of September, Anno Domoni, 1775.

Pres: Colonel Richard Henderson, Col. Thos. Hart, Col. John Williams, Capt. John Luttrell, William Johnston, James Hogg and Leonard H. Bullock.

Col. Henderson being unanimously chosen president, they took into their consideration the present state of the said Colony and made the following resolve, viz:

Resolved, that Col. John Williams be appointed Agent for the Transylvania Company to transact their business in the said Colony, and he is accordingly invested with full power by letter of Attorney.

Ordered, That Mr. Williams shall proceed to Boonesborough in the said Colony as soon as possible, and continue there until the twelfth day of April next; and to be allowed for his services, one hundred and fifty pounds, Proclamation money of North Carolina, out of the profits arising from the sale of lands, after discharging the Company's present engagements.

N. B.—In case the Settlement should be broken up by attack of Indians, or other enemies so as to render it impossible for Mr. Williams to continue there and execute the trust reposed in him, it is agreed by the Company, that he shall still be paid the above salary at the expiration of three years.

Resolved: That Mr. Williams be empowered to appoint one or more Surveyors, and the other officers of the Land Office, for the said Colony, as he may find it necessary.

Clerks, Surveyors and Chain-Carriers, to be sworn before they act.

Resolved, In case of the death or removal of Mr. Williams, that Col. Richard Henderson, Capt. Nathaniel Hart, and Capt. John Luttrell, or any one of them, be and are hereby, declared Agents for the said Company with the same powers as are given to Mr. Williams until a new appointment shall be made by the Proprietors.

Resolved, That the Agent shall not grant any Lands adjoining Salt springs, gold, silver, copper, lead, or sulphur mines, knowing them to be such.

Resolved, That a reservation to the Proprietors, of one-half of all gold, silver, copper, lead, and sulphur mines, shall be made by the Agent, at granting deeds.

Resolved, That the Agent shall take a counterpart of all deeds granted by him, and shall transmit them to the proprietors, residing in the Province of North Carolina, to be audited, with his other proceedings, by the Company.

Resolved, that all surveys shall be made by the four Cardinal points, except where rivers or mountains so intervene as to render it too inconvenient; and that in all cases where one survey comes within the distance of eighty poles from another, their lines shall join without exception; and that every survey on navigable rivers shall extend two poles out for one pole along the river; and that each survey not on navigable rivers shall not be above one-third longer than its width.

Resolved, That a present of two thousand acres of land be made to Col. Daniel Boone, with the thanks of the Proprietors, for the signal services he has rendered to the Company.

Resolved, That the thanks of this Company be presented to Col. Richard Calloway, for his spirited and manly behavior in behalf of the said Colony; and that a present of six hundred and forty acres of land be made to his younger son.

Resolved, that James Hogg, Esq., be appointed Delegate to represent the said Colony in the Continental Congress, now sitting at Philadelphia; and that the following Memorial be presented to that august body.

To the Honorable the Continental Congress Now Sitting at Philadelphia.

The Memorial for Richard Henderson, Thomas Hart, John Williams, Nathaniel Hart, John Luttrell, William Johnson, James

Appendix

Hogg, David Hart and Leonard Henly Bullock, Proprietors of Transylvania, sheweth:

That on the seventeenth day of March last, for a large and valuable consideration, Your Memorialists obtained from the Cherokee Indians, assembled at Watauga, a grant of a considerable territory, now called Transylvania, lying on the South side of the river Ohio.

They will not trouble the Honorable Congress with a detail of the risks and dangers to which they have been exposed, arising from the nature of the enterprise itself, as well as from the wicked attempts of certain Governments and their emissaries; they beg leave, only, to acquaint them that, through difficulties and dangers, at a great expense, and with the blood of several of their followers, they have laid the foundation of a Colony, which, however mean in its origin, will, if one may guess from present appearances, be one day considerable in America.

The Memorialists, having made this purchase from the Aborigines and immemorial possessors, the sole and uncontested owners of the country in fair and open treaty, and without the violation of any British or American law whatever, are determined to give it up only with their lives. And though their country be far removed from the reach of ministerial usurpation, yet they cannot look with indifference on the late arbitrary proceedings of the British Parliament. If the United Colonies are reduced, or will tamely submit to be slaves, Transylvania will have reason to fear.

The Memorialists by no means forget their allegiance to their Sovereign, whose constitutional rights and pre-eminences they will support at the risk of their lives. They flatter themselves that the addition of a new Colony in so fair and equitable way, and without any expense to the Crown, will be acceptable to His Most

Gracious Majesty, and that Transylvania will soon be worthy of his Royal regard and protection.

At the same time, having their hearts warmed with the same noble spirit that animates the United Colonies, and moved with indignation at the late Ministerial and Parliamentary usurpation, it is the earnest wish of the Proprietors of Transylvania to be considered by the Parliaments as brethren, engaged in the same great cause of liberty and of mankind. And, as by reason of several circumstances, needless to be here mentioned, it was impossible for the Proprietors to call a convention of the settlers in such time as to have their concurrence laid before this Congress, they here pledge themselves for them, that they will concur in the measure now adopted by the Proprietors.

From the generous plan of liberty adopted by the Congress, and that noble love of mankind which appears in all their proceedings, the Memorialists please themselves that the United Colonies will take the infant Colony of Transylvania into their protection; and they, in return, will do everything in their power, and give such assistance in the general cause of America as the Congress shall judge to be suitable to their abilities.

Therefore, the Memorialists hope and earnestly request, that Transylvania may be added to the number of the United Colonies, and that James Hogg, Esq., be received as their delegate, and admitted to a seat in the honorable the Continental Congress.

By order of the Proprietors.

RICHARD HENDERSON, President.

Resolved, That Mr. Hogg be empowered to treat and contract with any person or persons who may incline to purchase Lands from the Company, and that he be allowed his expenses for transacting the above business.

Appendix

Resolved, That the united thanks of this Company be presented to Col. Richard Henderson, Capt. Nathaniel Hart, and Capt. John Luttrell for their eminent services and public spirited conduct in settling the aforesaid Colony.

Resolved, That from this time to the first day of June, one thousand seven hundred and seventy-six, the lands in the said Colony shall be sold on the following terms: No survey of land shall contain more than six hundred and forty acres, (except in particular cases); and the purchaser shall pay for the entry and warrant of survey two dollars; for surveying the same and a plot thereof, four dollars; and for the deed and plot annexed, two dollars. And also shall pay to the said proprietors, their Agent, or Receiver, for the time being, at the time of receiving a deed, two pounds, ten shillings, sterling, for each hundred acres contained in such deed; also an annual quit-rent of two shillings, like money, for every one hundred acres, commencing in the year 1780. And that any person who settles on the said Lands before the first day of June, 1776, shall have the privilege, on the aforesaid conditions, of taking up for himself any quantity not above six hundred and forty acres; and for each taxable person he may take with him, and settle there, three hundred and twenty acres, and no more.

Resolved, That Colonel Richard Henderson, survey and lay off, within the said Colony, in such places and in such quantities as he shall think proper, not less than two hundred thousand acres, hereafter to be equally divided amongst the copartners or their representatives, according to their rateable part, (as fully set forth in the Articles of Agreement entered into by the copartners); and that each copartner be permitted, by himself or his deputy, to make choice of, and survey in one or more places, any quantity of vacant Land in the aforesaid Colony, for his or their particular use; but not above two thousand acres, and that agreeable to the aforesaid rateable proportions, unless on the same terms, and under the same regulations and restrictions as laid down for other purchasers.

Resolved, That not more than five thousand acres shall be sold to any one person who does not immediately settle on the said Land; and that at three pounds, ten shillings sterling per hundred, and not more than one hundred thousand acres in the whole on these terms.

Resolved, That the Agent deliver what money he may have received for the sale of lands to Col. Thomas Hart, when he leaves the said Colony, and that Col. Hart pay what money may be due from the Company to the people at Watauga on his return; and that the remainder be applied to the payment of the Company's other debts.

Also that the Agent shall take the first safe opportunity of remitting what further sums he may receive thereafter to William Johnston, Treasurer, to be by him applied towards paying off the Company's debts.

Resolved, That William Johnston be empowered to bargain and contract with any persons inclining to purchase Lands in the said Colony.

Ordered, That Mr. Johnston do in behalf of the Proprietors, accomodate Mr. Peter Hay, merchant, (at Cross Creek, Cumberland County, North Carolina), with a present of one thousand acres of Land in the said Colony, for his friendly behavior towards the Company; or in lieu thereof, that Mr. Hay be permitted to purchase ten thousand acres, without being obliged to settle the same, at two pounds, ten shillings, sterling, per hundred acres, subject to office fees and quit-rents.

Resolved, That a present of six hundred and forty acres of

Land be made to the Reverend Mr. Henry Patillo, on condition that he will settle in the said Colony.

Resolved, That the Agent duly attend to the above Resolves, unless when the interest of the Company makes the contrary necessary.

By order of the Proprietors:

RICHARD HENDERSON, President.

P

LETTER FROM SILAS DEANE TO JAMES HOGG (NOVEMBER 2, 1775) REGARDING THE GOVERNMENT OF TRANSYLVANIA.

(From Volume IV of American Archives.)

NOVEMBER 2ND, 1775.

Dear Sir: At the time of granting the New England Charters, the Crown of Great Britain had no idea of any real interest or property in the American Lands. The Pope, as Vicar of Christ, pretended very early to have an absolute right in fee simple, to the earth and all that was therein, but more particularly to the Countries and persons of heretics, which he constantly gave away among his favorites. When the Crown of Great Britain threw off its submission to the Pope, or, in other words, by setting itself at the head of the Church, became Pope of Great Britain, this old, whimsically arrogant nation, was, in degree, restrained; and Queen Elizabeth, in the year 1579, most graciously gave to Sir Walter Raleigh all North America, from the lattitude 34° North to 48° north; and extending West to the great Pacific Ocean; to which immense territory she had no more right or title than she had to the empire of China.

On Sir Walter's attainder, this was supposed to revert to the Crown, and in 1606, James I, in consequence of the same principle, granted the South part of the above, to a Company then called the London Company; and in 1620, granted the Northernmost part to a Company called the Plymouth Company, containing within its bounds all the lands from 40° to 45° north lattitude, and West to the South Seas. This Company granted, 1631, to certain persons, that tract described in this charter, which you will see was very liberal, and rendered them (as in reality they were) independent of the Crown for holding their lands; they having, at their own expense, purchased or conquered them from the natives, the original or sole owners.

The Settlement of Connecticut began in 1634 when they came into a Voluntary Compact of Government, and governed under it, until their Charter, in 1662, without any difficulty. They were never fond of making many laws; Nor is it good policy in any State, but the worst of all in a new one. The laws, or similar ones to those which I have turned down to, are necessary in a new Colony, in which the highest wisdom is to increase, as fast as possible, the inhabitants, and at the same time to regulate them well.

The first is to secure the general and inalienable rights of man to the settlers; without this, no inhabitants, worth having, will adventure. This, therefore, requires the Closest and earliest attention.

Next to this, is the mode or rule by which civil actions may be brought, or the surest ways and means by which every individual may obtain his right.

Then a provision for the safety of the Community against high handed offenders, house breakers, etc.

There are two ways of regulating a Community; one by correcting every offender, and the other to prevent the offense itself;

to effect the latter, education must be attended to as a matter of more importance than all the laws which can be framed, as it is better to be able to prevent, than after to correct a disease.

Peace officers will be necessary, and these ought to be chosen by the people, for the people are more engaged to support an officer of their own in the execution of his trust, than they will ever be in supporting one forced upon them.

Some regulation of civil course ought early to be made the most simple and least expensive is best; an honest judge will support his dignity without a large salary, and a dishonest one can have no real dignity at any rate.

The General Assembly must be the supreme fountain of power in such a state, in constituting which, every free man ought to have his voice. The elections should be frequent, at least annually; and to this body every officer ought to be amenable for his conduct. Every impediment in the way of increase of people should be removed, of course marriage must be made easy.

Overgrown estates are generally the consequence of an unequal division of interest, left by a subject at his decease. This is prevented by an equal, or nearly equal right of inheritance. This has taken place in all the New England Colonies, and in Pennsylvania to their great emolument.

All fees of office ought to be stated and known, and they should be stated as low as possible.

Some crimes are so dangerous in their tendency, that capital punishments are necessary; the fewer of these, consistent with the safety of the State, the better.

There ought to be some terms on which a man becomes free of the community. They should be easy and simple; and every one encouraged to qualify himself in character and interest, to comply with them; and these terms should be calculated to bind the person in the strongest manner, and engage him in its interest.

A new Colony, in the first place, should be divided into small townships or districts, each of which ought to be empowered to regulate their own internal affairs; and to have and enjoy every liberty and privilege not inconsistent with the whole.

Tenure of lands is a capital object, and so is the mode of taking out grants for, and laying them out. If individuals are permitted to engross large tracts, and lay them out as they please, the population of the country will be retarded.

Precarious must be the possession of the finest country in the world, if inhabitants have not the means and skill of defending it. A militia regulation must, therefore, in all prudent policy, be one of the first.

Though entire liberty of conscience ought everywhere to be allowed, yet the keeping up among a people a regular and stated course of Divine worship has such beneficial effects that the encouragement thereof deserves the particular attention of the Magistrate.

Forms of oath are ever best, as they are concise, and carry with them a solemn simplicity of appeal to the Divine Being; and to preserve their force, care should be had to avoid too frequent a repetition of them, and on ordinary occasions.

The preservation of the peace being the capital object of government, no man should be permitted on any occasion, to be the avenger of the wrongs he has, or conceives he has, received; but if possible, every one should be brought to submit to the decision of the law of the country in every private as well as public injury.

Providing for the poor is an act of humanity, but to prevent their being numerous and burdensome to society is at once humane and an act of the highest and soundest policy; and to effect it, the education of children, and the manners of the lower orders are constantly to be attended to.

Appendix

As, in a well ordered government, every one's person and property should be equally secure, so each should pay equally, or on the same scale, for the expenses in supporting the same.

In a new and wild country it will be deemed, perhaps, impossible to erect schools; but the consequences are so great and lasting that every difficulty ought to be encountered rather than give up so necessary, so important an institution. A school will secure the morals and manners, and at the same time tend to collect people together in society, and promote and preserve civilization.

The throwing a country into towns, and allowing these towns particular privileges like corporations in England and America, tends to unite the people, and, as in the least family there is, generally, the best economy, so these towns will conduct the internal and domestic crudentials better than larger bodies, and give strength, soundness and solidity to the basis of the State.

Sir, you have in the foregoing, the outlines of the policy of the Connecticut Government, in as concise a view as I could; the great and leading principles of which will, I conceive, apply to any new State; and the sooner they are applied the better it will be for the health and prosperity of the rising community.

An equal and certain security of life, liberty and property, an equal share in the rights of legislation, and an equal distribution of the benefits resulting from society; with an early attention to the principles, morals and manners of the whole, are the great first principles of a good Government, and these well fixed, lesser matters will easily and advantageously adjust, as I may say, themselves. I am far from thinking our system is entirely fit for you, in every point. It has grown up and enlarged itself, as we have grown. Its principle features are worth your attending to; and, if I had leisure, would point out, more particularly which part I think you might adopt immediately, what additions are necessary, and why some parts should be rejected. But I will, if possible, give you after your perusal of this, the general head of what, from my little reading and observation, I think to be the most simple, and consequently, the best plan of government.

I am, Sir, yours,

Thursday morning, November 2nd, 1775. S. DEANE.

Two laws, I see I have run over without noting upon; the one is for punishing vagabonds, by setting them to hard labor. The other, for the punishment of theft, which you may think too light, but I think too severe; or, in other words, I would avoid infamous punishments, such as cropping, branding, whipping, etc., and substitute hard labor in their stead.

Q

JAMES HOGG TO RICHARD HENDERSON, JANUARY, 1776.

REPORT OF THE TRANSYLVANIA "EMBASSY" TO THE CONTINENTAL CONGRESS.

(American Archives, Volume IV.)

JANUARY, 1776.

Dear Sir: On the 2nd of December I returned hither from Philadelphia; and I have now set down to give you an account of my embassy, which you will be pleased to communicate to the other gentlemen, our co-partners, when you have an opportunity. I waited for Messrs. Hooper and Hewes a day and a half at Richmond, but they were detained by rainy weather for several days, so that they did not overtake me till I was

Appendix 225

near Philadelphia, where I was kept two days by heavy rain, though they had it dry where they were. It was the 22nd of October when we arrived at Philadelphia. In a few days they introduced me to several of the Congress gentlemen, among the first of whom were, accidentally, the famous Samuel and John Adams; and as I found their opinion friendly to our new Colony, I showed them our map, explained to them the advantage of our situation, etc., etc. They entered seriously into the matter, and seemed to think favorably of the whole; but the difficulty that occurred to us soon appeared to them. "We have petitioned and addressed the King," said they, "and have entreated him to point out some mode of accomodation. There seems to be an impropriety in embarrassing our reconciliation with anything new; and the taking under our protection a body of people who have acted in defiance of the King's proclamations, will be looked on as a confirmation of that independent spirit with which we are daily reproached." I then showed them our memorial, to convince them that we did not pretend to throw off our allegiance to the King, but intended to acknowledge his sovereignty whenever he should think us worthy of his regard. They were pleased with our memorial, and thought it very proper; but another difficulty occurred. By looking at the map they observed that we were within the Virginia Charter. I then told them of the fixing of their boundaries, what had passed at Richmond in March last, and that I had reason to believe the Virginians would not oppose us; however, they advised me to sound the Virginians, as they would not choose to do anything in it without their consent. All the Delegates were, at that time, so much engaged in the Congresses from morning till night that it was some days before I got introduced to the Virginians; and before then I was informed that some of them had said, whatever was their own opinion of the matter, they would not consent that Transylvania should be admitted as a Colony, and represented in Congress until it originated in their Convention, and should be approved by their constituents. Some days after this, I was told that Messrs. Jefferson, Wythe, and Richard Henry Lee, were desirous of meeting with me, which was accordingly brought about; but, unfortunately, Mr. Lee was, by some business, prevented from being with us, though I had some conversation with him afterwards. I told them that the Transylvania Company, suspecting that they might be misrepresented, had sent me to make known to the gentlemen of the Congress our friendly intentions towards the cause of liberty, etc., etc., but said nothing of our memorial, or my pretentions to a seat in Congress. They said nothing in return to me, but seriously examined our map, and asked many questions. They observed that our purchase was within their charter, and gently hinted, that by virtue of it, they might claim the whole. This led me to take notice, that a few years ago, I had been informed that their assembly had petitioned the Crown for leave to purchase from the Cherokees, and to fix their boundaries with them, which was accordingly done, by a line running from six miles east of the Long Island in Holston, to the mouth of the Great Kanawha, for which they had actually paid twenty five hundred pounds to the Cherokees; by which purchase, both the Crown and their Assembly had acknowledged the property of those islands to be in the Cherokees. Besides, said I, our settlement of Transylvania will be a great check on the Indians, and consequently be of service to the Virginians.

They seemed to waive the argument concerning the right of property; but Mr. Jefferson acknowledged, that in his opinion, our Colony could be no loss to the Virginians, if properly united

Appendix

to them; and said, that if his advice was followed, all the use they should make of their Charter would be, to prevent any arbitrary or oppressive government to be established within the boundaries of it; and that it was his wish to see a free Government established at the back of theirs, properly united with them; and that it should be extended westward to the Mississippi, and on each side of the Ohio, to their Charter line, but he would not consent that we should be acknowledged by the Congress, until it had the approbation of their constituents in Convention, which he thought might be obtained; and that, for that purpose, we should send one of our Company to their next Convention. Against this proposal, several objections occurred to me, but I made none.

This was the substance of our conference, with which I acquainted our good friends, Messrs. Hooper and Hewes, who joined me in opinion that I should not push the matter further; and they hinted to me, that, considering the present very critical situation of affairs, they thought it was better for us to be unconnected with them. These gentlemen acted a most friendly part all along, and gave a favorable account of our proceedings. Indeed I think the Company under great obligations to them, and I hope they will take it under their consideration. I was frequently with parties of the Delegates, who in general think favorably of our enterprise.

All the wise ones of them, with whom I conversed on the subject, are clear in opinion that the property of these lands are vested in us by the Indian grant; but some of them think, that by the common law of England, and by the common usage in America, the Sovereignty is in the King, agreeable to a famous law opinion, of which I was so fortunate as to procure a copy. The suffering traders, and others, at the end of last war, obtained a large tract of land from the Six Nations, and other Indians. They formed themselves into a Company, (called, I believe, the Ohio,) and petitioned the King for a patent, and desired to be erected into a Government. His Majesty laid their petition before Lord Chancellor Camden and Mr. Charles York, then Attorney General, and afterwards Chancellor. Their opinion follows:

"In respect to such places as have been, or shall be acquired by treaty or grant from any of the Indian Princes or Governments, your Majesty's letters patent are not necessary; the property of the soil vested in the grantee by the Indian grants, subject only to your Majesty's rights of Sovereignty over the settlements, as English settlements, and over the inhabitants as English subjects, who carry with them your Majesty's law whereever they form Colonies, and receive your Majesty's protection by virtue of your Royal charters."

After an opinion so favorable for them, it is amazing that this Company never attempted to form a settlement, unless they have procured a charter; with the hopes of which, it seems, they were flattered, from time to time. However, our example has roused them, I am told, and they are now setting up for our rivals. Depending on the opinion, another company of gentlemen, a few years ago, purchased a tract between the Mississippi and Ohio, beginning about a league below Fort Chartres, and running over towards the mouth of the Wabash; but whether or not their boundary line is above or below the mouth of the Wabash, the gentlemen who showed me their deed could not tell, as it is not mentioned, but is said to terminate at the old Shawanese town, supposed to be only thirty-five leagues above the mouth of the Ohio. And the said Company purchased another larger tract, lying on the Illinois River. It was from one of this Company that I procured a copy of the above opinion, which he assured me was the genuine one, and is the very same which you have heard was in possession of Lord Dunmore, as it was their Company that sent it to him, expecting he would join them.

I was several times with Mr. Deane, of Connecticut, the gentleman of whom Mr. Hooper told you, when here. He says he will send some people to see our country; and if their report be favorable, he thinks many Connecticut people will join us.

This gentleman is a scholar, and a man of sense and enterprise, and rich; and I am apt to believe, has some thoughts of heading a party of Connecticut adventurers, providing things can be made agreeable to him. He is reckoned a good man and much esteemed in Congress; but he is an enthusiast in liberty, and will have nothing to do with us unless he is pleased with our form of Government. He is a great admirer of the Connecticut Constitution, which he recommended to our consideration, and was so good as to favor me with a long letter on that subject, a copy of which is enclosed.[1] You would be amazed to see how much in earnest all these speculative gentlemen are about the plan to be adopted by the Transylvanians. They entreat, they pray, that we make it a free Government, and beg that no mercenary or ambitious views in the Proprietors may prevent it. Quit-rents, they say, is a mark of vassalage, and hope they will not be established in Transylvania. They even threaten us with their opposition, if we do not act upon liberal principles when we have it so much in our power to render ourselves immortal. Many of them advised a law against negroes.

Enclosed I send you a copy of a sketch by John Adams,[2] which I had from Richard Henry Lee.

[1] The letter is herewith published in Appendix P.
[2] See footnote, page 43.

R

REPLY OF JOHN WILLIAMS, AGENT OF THE TRANSYLVANIA PROPRIETORS, TO THE HARRODSBURG REMONSTRANCE OF DECEMBER, 1775.

(Calendar Virginia State Papers.)

BOONESBOROUGH, January 1, 1776.

To the Gentlemen Inhabitants in & about Harrodsburg :—

Gentlemen: By the hands of Messrs Col. Abraham Hite Jos Bowman Jno Wharton & Wm McAfee we received an Instrument of writeing, purporting to be an address to us directed, for the relief of Grievances subsisting in the Colony of Transylvania. Respecting the letting our Lands within the said Colony. Nothing could have astonished us more than a Remonstrance of this Kind, at a time when we were Endeavoring to pursue every practicable measure to prevent any dispute or disquietude in the minds of the Inhabitants of this Young and yet feeble Colony and for that End had Established rules for the purpose of granting the Lands within the same upon as favorable Terms as we can well afford from the large price which we purchased them at, the numberless Expenses which have, and still must accrue upon the Occasion and the many disadvantages we have put Ourselves to, without mentioning the many dangers resulting from such hazardous Enterprizes. Conscious to ourselves of the integrity of our Intentions and the uprightness of our Conduct in purchasing more Lands and fully satisfied with the Right we have Acquired from the Aborigines first and Sole Occupants thereof — the Cherokee Indians — From the Chief's of whom, by and with the Consent of the whole Nation in fair & open Treaty for a large & valuable Consideration, we obtained a Deed of Feafment with actual livery and Seasin in due

Appendix

form of law with Quiet and Peacable possession which we still Retain and than which right we know of no better, the premises acceded to. We flattered ourselves that the modes and Terms on which we purpose on letting our Lands within said Colony would have met the approbation of every reasonable honest and well disposed person who wished to become a purchaser under us and an Inhabitant of said Colony. And it is with surprise we find persons now Expecting Lands on the Inferior Terms which we let them Last Spring to such Persons who ventured out with us to take Possession of the Country & Defend us against our Savage Enemies untill we Could build Forts make Corn &c and thereby give encouragement to others to Emigrate hither as many since have done & more about to do. To whom we proposed letting Lands (on what we think reasonable Terms) To every Person who shall remove here to reside before the year 1777 for himself 640 Acres of Land and for each Taxable Person he shall bring with him & Employ in cultivating land or other business within said Colony 320 Acres at 50 S. Sterling pr hundred exclusive of the office fees & an Annual quit rent of 2.S like money pr hundred acres, to commence in the year 1780. For which we make an indefeasible Right in Fee Simple with General Warranty. This being the lowest price we can take, we conceive it can never be considered as exorbitant when in fact all who see the lands and their situation the fertility of the soil, the Luxuriance of the range the purity of the air and healthiness of the Climate with every promising prospect of a rapid population and of course in a very short time a flourishing Country must know the lands, even at this Time to be of Infinite more Value, Exclusive of the money advantages needless here to mention, the above being our Right, which well understood we hope will give satisfaction to all, Yet if any Doubt we wish them to satisfy themselves of a right so generally acknowledged and of which we entertain not the least Scruple before they pretend to become inhabitants of this Country as it is highly expedient that each and every Person inhabiting this new and at present weak Country should unanimously join in one general Cause for the safety and protection of the whole which I am Convinced Every Gentleman every honest man and every good citizen would desire to do, And when-ever any person comes in otherwise disposed they thereby raise disentions and Animosities by which they loose and Weaken the bands of Society and of course must render us an Easy prey to our Savage Enemies whenever they may see cause to take the advantage of our disunited situation to prevent which we not only wish to see every person in this Colony lending his aid but assure you Gentlemen that nothing within our power shall be wanting to Accomplish so Good an End.

JNO WILLIAMS Agt for ye Com'y.

A True Copy.

S

JOHN WILLIAMS' REPORT (JANUARY 3, 1776) OF TRANSYLVANIA AFFAIRS TO THE PROPRIETORS IN NORTH CAROLINA.

(American Archives, Volume IV.)

Gentlemen: BOONESBOROUGH, January 3, 1776.

In my last of the 27th inst., I promised in my next a more circumstancial account than I was capable then of giving, under the confused situation of mind I was then in, occasioned by the unhappy catastrophe of my brother's death, which happened before that. To comply in some measure with that promise, and to discharge a duty encumbered upon me, as well as the promptitude of mind that I feel to discharge that duty, I cheerfully enter on the task and endeavor to render some account of what I have been after since my arrival at this place, now upwards of a month since; and as a primative intention of sending me to Transylvania was to establish a land office, appoint the necessary officers to the said office, surveyors, etc., Upon the best footing in my power, and to make the sale of the lands within the said Colony, upon such terms as might be most advantageous to the Proprietors and satisfactory to the inhabitants thereof; my first step was to fall on some method of appointing a person to the office of surveyor, who shall give general satisfaction to the people; I thought none more likely to do so, than calling a Convention and taking their recommendation for the person who I would appoint. From the dispersed situation of the people, and the extreme badness of the weather, we failed in convening a majority; however, I took the sense of those who appeared, and who unanimously recommended Col. John Floyd, a gentleman generally esteemed, and I am persuaded, truly worthy, and him I have commissioned surveyor of the Colony at present, though, perhaps, it may be advisable at a future day, to divide the Colony into two districts, and to appoint another surveyor to one of the Districts. The Entering Office I have disposed of to Mr. Nathaniel Henderson, and the Secretaries to Mr. Richard Harrison; though, upon consideration, I have thought that the numerous incidental expenses were so great that some way ought to be fallen upon to defray them without breaking in upon the moneys arrising from the sale of the lands, and that the two dollars for entering, etc., and the other two for filling up the deeds, counterparts, annexing seals and plots, etc., was more money than services of those offices absolutely required; I, therefore, have reserved out of each office, one dollar, to answer the purpose of defraying those extraordinary expenses; and the offices are left well worth the acceptance of persons capable of filling them with credit. The number of entries on our book is now upwards of nine hundred, a great part of which was made before I came to this place, when people could make entries without money and without price; the country abounded with land-mongers; since there is two dollars exacted on the entry made, people are not quite so keen, though I make no doubt but all who can comply with the terms will endeavor to save their lands; and as many people who have got entry on the book are now out of the country, and can not possibly pay up the entry money immediately, I have thought proper to advertise that every person who has made entry on the book, and paid no money, that they come in and pay up the entrance money by the first of April, and take out their warrants of survey, or their several entries will, after that time, be considered as vacated, and liable to be entered by any other person whatever.

The surveyors have now begun to survey and some few people have been desirous of getting out their deeds immediately; but they generally complain of a great scarcity of money, and doubt their being able to take their deeds before next June, or even before next fall; though, in a general way, people seem to be well reconciled to the terms, and desirous to take up on them, except some few whom I have been obliged to tamper with, and a small party about Harodsburg, who, it seems, have been entering into a confederacy not to hold lands on any other terms than those of the first year. As this party is composed of people in general, of small consequence, and I have taken some steps to remove some of their principal objections, I make no doubt but

Appendix

to do all that way; and for that purpose, have formed a design of removing myself, with the office to Harodsburg, some time in February next, unless I should find, from a trip I purpose immediately taking there, that I can not do it with safety. The principal man, I am told, at the head of this confederacy, is one Hite; and him I make no doubt but to convince he is in error. Among other things, one of the great complaints was that the Proprietors, and a few gentlemen, had engrossed all the lands at and near the Falls of Ohio, which circumstance I found roused the attention of a number of people of note; I, therefore, found myself under the necessity of putting a stop to all clamors of that kind, by declaring that I would grant no large bodies of land to any person whatever, which lay contiguous to the Falls; which I have done in a solemn manner. This I am far from thinking will be injurious to the Proprietors, but quite the reverse; and a circumstance which will render more general satisfaction, and be of as much utility to the Colony, as any step heretofore taken. You will observe that I am going on to justify the measure before I inform you what it is. But to be brief, it is this; the Falls, it is certain, is a place which, from its situation, must be the most considerable mart in this part of the world; the lands around are generally rich and fertile, and most agreeably situated; which had occasioned many people to fix their affections on that place. Many applications have been made for large grants at and about that place, and refused. Since which, twenty thousand acres, and upwards, have been entered there for the Company; forty thousand or fifty thousand more, in large tracts, by a few other gentlemen; a partially was complained of; a general murmuring ensued. Upon considering the matter, I thought it unjust; I thought it a disadvantage to the partners in general, and that some step ought to be taken to pacify the minds of the people. I, therefore entered into a resolution that I would grant to no one man, living within a certain distance of the Falls, more than one thousand acres of land, and that to be settled and improved in a certain space of time, under the penalty of forfeiture; that every person who had more entered than one thousand acres, might retain his one thousand out of which spot he pleased; that the several officers, who have claims there, may each, on application and complying with our terms, be entitled to a one thousand within his survey. That a town be immediately laid out, and a lot reserved to each proprietor, and then the first settlers to take the lots which they may choose, enter and improve; which improvement must be done in a certain limited time, or the lot forfeited, and again to be sold, etc. These proposals seem to have given general satisfaction, and every one who had entered large quantities within these limits, gives it up with the greatest alacrity; and I am in hopes will meet the general approbation of the company; if so, I shall be happy; if not, I shall be very sorry, though the necessity must justify the measure.

The Falls of the Ohio is a place of all others within the Colony, will admit of a town, which, from its particular situation, will immediately become popular and flourishing; the land contiguous thereto rich and fertile, and where a great number of gentlemen will most certainly settle, and be the support and protection of a town at that place; a place which should meet with every encouragement, to settle and strengthen in as much as it will, most certainly be the terror of our savage enemies, the Kickeboos Indians, who border more nearly on that place than any other part of the Colony; and as I think it absolutely necessary that the afforesaid proposed town at the Falls, be laid off the ensuing spring, if I find it practicable, to raise a party about the first of March, and go down and lay out upon the future tranquility of our situation between this and then, for I assure you the little attack made upon us by the Indians the 23rd of last month, has made many people, who are ashamed to confess themselves afraid, find out that their affairs on your side the mountains will not dispense with their staying here any longer at present; and I am well convinced, once they get there, that every alarm, instead of precipitating, will procrastinate their return. When I mention the little attack made on the 23rd of last month, in this cursory manner, it is because I have heretofore sent you a particular account of that massacre, in a letter of the 27th ult. Though as that letter may fail, and not get to hand, I will now briefly endeavor to relate the circumstances.

On Saturday about noon, being the 23rd, Col. Campbell, with a couple of lads, (Saunders and McQuinney) went across the river. On the opposite bank they parted. Campbell went up the river about two hundred yards and took up a bottom. The two lads, without a gun, went straight up the hill. About ten minutes after they parted a gun and a cry of distress was heard, and the alarm given that the Indians had shot Col. Campbell. We made to his assistance. He came running to the landing with one shoe off, and said he was fired on by a couple of Indians. A party of men was immediately dispatched under the command of Col. Boone, who went out, but could make no other discovery than two Moccasin tracks, whether Indians or not could not be determined. We had at that time over the river, hunting, etc., ten or a dozen, in different parties, part or all of whom we expected to be killed, if what Col. Campbell said was true; but that by many was doubted. Night came on; several of the hunters returned, but had neither seen nor heard of the

Indians nor yet of the two lads. We continued in this state of suspense until Wednesday, when a party of men sent out to make search for them found McQuinney killed and scalped in a corn field, at about three miles distance from town on the north side of the river. Saunders could not be found and has not yet been heard of.

On Thursday a ranging party of fifteen men, under the command of Jesse Benton, was dispatched to scour the woods, twenty or thirty miles round and see if any further discovery could be made. To those men we gave two shillings per day, and five pounds for every scalp they should produce.

After they went out our hunters returned, one at a time, till they all came in safe, Saunders excepted, who no doubt had shared McQuinney's fate.

On Sunday, the 31st day of the month, our rangers returned without doing any thing more than convincing themselves that the Indians had, immediately on doing the murder, ran off far northward, as they discovered their tracts thirty or forty miles towards the Ohio making that way.

On the above massacre being committed we began to doubt there was a body of Indians about, who intended committing outrage on our inhabitants. However, we are perfectly satisfied since, that their number was only six or seven men, who set off from Shawanee town before the treaty at Fort Pitt, with an intent, as they termed it, to take a look at the white people on Kentucky; and King Cornstalk at the treaty, informed the commissioners on this and said, for the conduct of these men, before they returned, he could not be responsible for that he did not know, but that they might do some mischief, and that if any of them should get killed by the whites he should take no notice at all of it.

Appendix

For this, we have undoubted authority, and do not at present think ourselves in any great danger here than if the above massacre had not been committed.

Another circumstance is that our ammunition grows scant. I do not think there is enough to supply this place till the last of March; supposing we should have no occasion of any to repulse an enemy. If we should, God only knows how long it will last.

If any powder can possibly be procured it would certainly be advisable to do it; if not, some person who can manufacture the materials we have on the way for the purpose of making powder, Most part of those are at the block house, or at least within two or three miles of there — the rest in Powell's Valley. Those (if we had any person who knew how properly to manufacture them into gun-powder) it would be necessary to have at this place. We have no such person, and of course they would be of but little service here. Nothwithstanding, I should have sent for them before now; but people here expect the most exorbitant wages for trivial services. Not less than a dollar a day, which will prevent my sending till I find the necessity greater, or men to be hired cheaper.

T

FORM OF HENDERSON & CO.'S SURVEY WARRANT, 1776.

(From an Original held by Robert Pogue, deceased, of Mason County, Kentucky.[1])

TRANSYLVANIA, } ss. RICHARD HENDERSON & Co.,
BOONESBOROUGH, }   Proprietors of the Colony of Transylvania,

{ SEAL }   To JOHN FLOYD, Esquire,
            Surveyor of the said Colony.

You are hereby authorized and required to survey and lay off for Wm. Pogue Six Hundred and forty acres of land lying on the west branches of Clark Creek known by the name of Gilmer's Lick abt. three miles west of Wm. Whitleys place where he lives and marked on a tree with powder,—W. Pogue. And the same having surveyed persuant to the rules of our office laid down and our instructions by the Surveyor to be observed; two fair and correct plots of the same you make or cause to be made with your proceedings thereon, into our office within three months from the date hereof, wherever then held within our said Colony.

Given under our Seal at Boonesborough the fifteenth day of January 1776.

JNO. WILLIAMS, Ag't, &c.

Endorsed—No 676 Wm. Pogues Warn't for 640 acres of land, Gilmer's lick.

[1] Collins, page 516, Vol. II.

Appendix

U

PETITION OF TRANSYLVANIANS TO THE VIRGINIA CONVENTION. (RECEIVED MAY, 1776.)

(From Journal Va. Convention.)

To the Honorable the Convention of Virginia:

The petition of the inhabitants, and some of the intended settlers of that part of North America, now denominated Transylvania, humbly sheweth:

Whereas some of your petitioners became adventurers in that country from the advantageous reports of their friends who first explored it, and others since allured by the specious shew of the easy terms on which the land was to be purchased from those who stile themselves proprietors, have, at a great expense, and many hardships, settled there, under the faith of holding the lands by an indefeasible title, which those gentlemen assured them they were capable of making. But your petitioners have been greatly alarmed at the late conduct of those gentlemen, in advancing the price of the purchase money from twenty shillings to fifty shillings sterling, per hundred acres, and at the same time have increased the fees of entry and surveying to a most exorbitant rate; and, by the short period prefixed for taking up the lands, even on those extravagant terms, they plainly evince their intentions of rising in their demands as the settlers increase, or their insatiable avarice shall dictate. And your petitioners have been more justly alarmed at such unaccountable and arbitrary proceedings, as they have lately learned from a copy of the deed made by the Six Nations with Sir William Johnson, and the commissioners from this Colony, at Fort Stanwix, in the year 1768, that the said lands were included in the cession or grant of all that tract which lies on the south side of the river Ohio, beginning at the mouth of Cherokee or Hogohege river, and extending up the said river to Kettaning. And, as in the preamble of the said deed, the said confederate Indians declare the Cherokee river to be their true boundary with the southard Indians, your petitioners may, with great reason, doubt the validity of the purchase that those proprietors have made of the Cherokees — the only title they set up to the lands for which they demand such extravagant sums from your petitioners, without any other assurance for holding them than their own deed and warrantee; a poor security, as your petitioners humbly apprehend, for the money that, among other new and unreasonable regulations, these proprietors insist should be paid down on the delivery of the deed. And, as we have the greatest reason to presume that his majesty, to whom the lands were deeded by the Six Nations, for a valuable consideration, will vindicate his title, and think himself at liberty to grant them to such persons, and on such terms as he pleases, your petitioners would, in consequence thereof, be turned out of possession, or obliged to purchase their lands and improvements on such terms as the new grantee or proprietor might think fit to impose; so that we can not help regarding the demand of Mr. Henderson and his company as highly unjust and impolitic, in the infant state of the settlement, as well as greatly injurious to your petitioners, who would cheerfully have paid the consideration at first stipulated by the company, whenever their grant had been confirmed by the crown, or otherwise authenticated by the supreme legislature.

And, as we are anxious to concur in every respect with our brethren of the united colonies, for our just rights and privileges, as far as our infant settlement and remote situation will admit of,

Appendix

we humbly expect and implore to be taken under the protection of the honorable Convention of the Colony of Virginia, of which we can not help thinking ourselves still a part, and request your kind interposition in our behalf, that we may not suffer under the rigorous demands and impositions of the gentlemen stiling themselves proprietors, who, the better to effect their oppressive designs, have given them the color of a law, enacted by a score of men, artfully picked from the few adventurers who went to see the country last summer, overawed by the presence of Mr. Henderson.

And that you would take such measures as your honors in your wisdom shall judge most expedient for restoring peace and harmony to our divided settlement; or, if your honors apprehend that our cause comes more properly before the honorable the General Congress, that you would in your goodness recommend the same to your worthy delegates, to espouse it as the cause of the Colony. And your petitioners, &c.

James Harrod,	John Beesor,	Wm. Myars,
Abm. Hite, Jun.	Conrod Woolter,	Peter Paul,
Patrick Dorane,	John Moore,	Henry Simons,
Ralph Nailor,	John Corbie,	Wm. Gaffata,
Robt. Atkinson,	Abm. Vanmetre,	James Hugh,
Robt. Nailor,	Saml. Moore,	Thos. Bathugh,
John Maxfield,	Isaac Pritcherd,	John Connway,
Saml. Pottinger,	Joseph Gwyne,	Wm. Crow,
Barnerd Walter,	Geo. Uland,	Wm. Feals,
Hugh M'Million,	Michl. Thomas,	Benja. Davis,
John Kilpatrick,	Adam Smith,	Beniah Dun,
Robt. Dook,	Saml. Thomas,	Adam Neelson,
Edward Brownfield,	Henry Thomas,	Wm. Shepard,

Wm. House,	John Mills,	James Calley,
Jno. Dun,	Elijah Mills,	Joseph Parkison,
Jno. Sim, Sen.	Jehu Harland,	Jediah Ashraft,
John House,	Leonard Cooper,	John Hardin,
Sime. House,	Wm. Rice,	Archd. Reves,
Chas. Creeraft,	Arthur Ingram,	Moses Thomas,
James Willie,	Thos. Wilson,	J. Zebulon Collins,
John Camron,	William Wood,	Thos. Parkinson,
Thos. Kenady,	Joseph Lyons,	Wm. Muckleroy,
Jesse Pigman,	Andrew House,	Meridith Helm, Jun.,
Simon Moore,	Wm. Hartly,	Andw. House,
John Moore,	Thomas Dean,	David Brooks,
Thos. Moore,	Richard Owan,	John Helm,
Herman Consoley,	Barnet Neal,	Benja. Parkison,
Silas Harland,	John Severn,	Wm. Parkison,
Wm. Harrod,	James Hugh,	Wm. Crow.
Levi Harrod,		

V

PETITION OF "THE COMMITTEE OF WEST FINCASTLE" TO THE CONVENTION OF VIRGINIA (HARRODSBURG, JUNE 20, 1776).

(From Journal of Va. Convention.)

To the Honourable the Convention of Virginia:

The Humble petition of the Committee of West Fincastle of the Colony of Virginia, Being on the North and South Sides of the River Kentucke (or Louisa). Present, John Gabriel Jones, Esqr., chairman, John Bowman, John Cowen, William Bennet,

Appendix

Joseph Bowman, John Crittenden, Isack Hite, George Rodgers Clark, Andrew McConnel, Hugh McGary, James Harrod, Silas Harland, William McConnel and John Maxwell, gentlemen. The Inhabitants of this remote part of Virginia who are equally desirous of contributing to the utmost of their power to the Support of the present laudable cause of American Freedom and willing to prove to the World, that tho they live so remote from the Seat of Government, that they Feel in the most Sensible manner for the Suffering Brethern, and that they most Ardently desire to be looked upon as part of the Colony notwithstanding the Base proceedings of a Detestible, Wicked and Corrupt Ministry to prevent any more County's to be laid off without the inhabitants would be so Pusilanimous as to give up the Right of appointing proper Persons to Represent 'em in Assembly or Convention, and as we further conceive that as the Proclamation of His Majesty for not settling on the Western Waters of this Colony is not founded upon Law, it can have no Force. And if we submit to that Proclamation as well as to have other Counties laid off without sending any representatives to ye Convention, it's in our Opinion manifesting an Acquiesence to the Will of an Abandoned Ministry and leaving an Opening to their Wicked and Diabolical designs as then this Immense and Fertile Country would afford an Assylum to those whose Principles are inimical to American Freedom, And if Counties are not laid off as Fincastle County now Reaches and already Settled near Three Hundred and Eighty Miles from East to West it would be impossible that two Delegates can be Sufficient to Represent such a Respectable body of People, or that Such a number of Inhabitants should be Bound to Obey without being heard, and as those very People would most cheerfully Co operate in every measure tending to the Publick Peace and American Liberty if their Delegates now chosen by the Free voice of the Inhabitants on the Western Waters of Fincastle (on Kentucke) and which Election was held for Eight days at Harrods Town after the Preparatory Notice of Five Weeks given to the Inhabitants, and on the Pole being Closed, Captain John Gabriel Jones and Captain George Rodgers Clark having the Majority were returned, and not doubting the acceptance of 'em as our Representatives by the Honourable ye Convention, to serve in that Capacity, as we conceive the Precedent Established in West Augusta will Justify our Proceedings; And we cannot but observe how impolitical it would be to Suffer such a Respectable Body of Prime Rifle Men to remain in a state of Neutrality, when at this time a Certain Set of men from North Carolina stiling 'emselves Proprietors and claiming an Absolute Right to these very Lands taking upon 'emselves the Legislative Authority, Appointing Offices both Civil and Military, having also opened a Land Office Surveyors General & Deputys appointed & act, conveyances made, and Land sold at an Exhorbitant Price, with many other unConstitutional practices tending to disturb the Inhabitants, those who are well disposed to the whole some Government of Virginia, and creating factions and Divisions amongst them. * as we have not hitherto been Represented in Convention as well knowing ye Frailty of Human Nature that Interest will often Predominate, and that the Tyrannick Ministry would not stop at any means to reduce the loyal americans to their detestable ends that if these pretended Proprietors have leave to continue to act in their arbitrary manner out the controul of this Colony the end must be evident to every well wisher to American Liberty. At this time of Danger we cannot take too much Precaution against

Appendix

the Inroads of ye Savages and to prevent the Effusion of Innocent Blood. We the Committee (after receiving a messuage from the Chiefs of the Delaware's who are now settled near the Mouth of the Waubash) informing us that a League would be held at Opost, by the English and ye Kiccapoos Indians and that they would attend to know the purport of the same, if their Brothers of the Long Knife would send a man they could rely on, they would on their Return inform 'em of the same & they were Apprehensive the Kiccapoos would strike their Brothers ye Long Knife therefore we thought it most prudent and shall send immediately a Certain James Harrod and Garrett Pendergrass, to converse with 'em on ye same. And as it's the Request of the Inhabitants that we should point out a Number of Men Capable and most acquainted with the Laws of this Colony to act as Magistrates, a List of the same we have inclosed, and For other Matters Relative to this Country we Conceive that Captain Jones and Captain Clark our Delegates will be able to inform the Honourable the Convention, not doubting but they will listen to our Petition and take us under their Jurisdiction—And your Petitioners as in Duty Bound &c.

Signed by order of the Committee.

JNO. GA JONES, *Chairman*,
ABRAHAM HITE, JUNR, *Clerk*.

HARRODSBURG, June 20, 1776.

W

PROCLAMATION OF TRANSYLVANIA COMPANY AGAINST SETTLEMENT OF DISPUTED LANDS (JUNE 26, 1776).

(From Cal. Va. State Papers, Vol. 1.)

TRANSYLVANIA OR WEST KENTUCKY.

Whereas disputes have arisen respecting the Title of the proprietors of Transylvania to the Soil of that Country and as some short time will elapse before they may be fully and satisfactorily determined (being anxious to avoid all cause of complaint) the said proprietors earnestly desire, that no person may in the mean time take possession of any entered or surveyed lands in said Country, with expectation of procuring a title in consequence thereof, as such lands ought, of right, to be granted to the respective persons in whose names those entries were made: and should the absolute title be adjudged in favour of the Subscribers on the present dispute, (as they have no doubt will be the case) they hereby declare their intention of granting such lands, on application to the proper claimants, according to the rules of their office. And the proprietors have hitherto reserved the lands below Green river, and as high up Cumberland on both sides as Manskors' Lick, for themselves, until they could lay uff a small quantity therein for their separate use, they hope that no person will make improvement within the said bounds before such surveys shall be made, as such improvement may possibly interfere with choice of some of the copartners, and consequently, not be granted. And as it is unsafe at this time to settle the Country in small detached parties, and the alarming reports with respect to the hostile intention of the Cherokee Indians, on the frontiers, will no doubt prevent emigration for some time, to that Country, care will be taken to cause those lands to be laid off as soon as conveniently may be: so that when, from the more pacific disposition of those people, a removal to that Country may be thought safe, every person on Application to the books of the land office at Boonsborough, may be informed of the entered and reserved lands as aforesaid, and direct their choice accordingly.

JOHN LUTTRELL,   THOMAS HART,
JAMES HOGG,   NATHANIEL HART,
DAVID HART,   JOHN WILLIAMS,
LEONARD H. BULLOCK, WILLIAM JOHNSTON.
RICHARD HENDERSON,

X

CAPTURE OF THE GIRLS AT BOONESBOROUGH.

(Extract from a Letter of John Floyd to William Preston of Virginia.)

My Dear Sir: BOONESBOROUGH, July 21, 1776.

The situation of our country is much altered since I wrote you last. The Indians seem determined to break up our settlements; and I really doubt, unless it is possible to give us some assistance, that the greater part of the people may fall a prey to them. They have, I am satisfied, killed several whom, at this time I know not how to mention. Many are missing who some time ago went out about their business of whom we can hear nothing. Fresh sign of Indians is seen almost every day. I think I mentioned to you before some damage they had done at Lee'stown. On the seventh of this month they killed one Cooper on Licking Creek and on the fourteenth a man whose name I know not at your Salt Spring on the same creek.

On the same day they took out of a canoe within sight of this place Miss Betsy Callaway, her sister Frances, and a daughter of Daniel Boone, the two last about thirteen or fourteen years old and the other grown. The affair happened late in the afternoon. They left the canoe on the opposite side of the river from us, which prevented our getting over for some time to pursue them. We could not that night follow more than five miles. Next morning by daylight we were on their track; but they had entirely prevented our following them by walking some distance apart through the thickest cane they could find. We observed their course and on which side we had left their sign, and travelled upwards of thirty miles. We then supposed they would be less cautious in travelling, and making a turn in order to cross their track we had gone but a few miles when we found their tracks in a buffalo path—pursued and overtook them in going about ten miles, just as they were kindling a fire to cook. Our study had been how to get the prisoners without giving the Indians time to murder them after they discovered us. We saw each other nearly at the same time. Four of us fired and all rushed on them by which they were prevented from carrying anything away except one shot gun without any ammunition. Mr. Boone and myself had each a pretty fair shot as they began to move off. I am well convinced I shot one through the body. The one he shot dropped his gun—mine had none. The place was covered with thick cane, and being so much elated on recovering the three poor little heart-broken girls, we were prevented from making any further search. We sent the Indians off almost naked—some without their moccasins and none of them with so much as a knife or tomahawk. After the girls came to themselves sufficiently to speak they told us there were only five Indians—four Shawanese and one Cherokee. They could speak good English and said they would then go to the Shawanese towns. The war club we got was like those I have seen of that nation. Several words of their language, which the girls retained, were known to be Shawanese. * * *

JOHN FLOYD.

Y

THE BOWMAN LETTER (TO COLONEL GEORGE ROGERS CLARK) ON THE LAST SIEGE OF BOONESBOROUGH.

(From original, held by the late John B. Bowman.)

Dear Sir— HARRODSBURGH, October 14, 1778.

This day I received yours by Wm. Miers and with difficulty I shall furnish him with a horse to ride to the settlement on.

The Indians have pushed us hard this summer. I shall only begin on the 7th of September when three hundred and thirty Indians with eight Frenchmen came to Boonesborough, raised a flag and called for Capt. Boone who had lately come from them and offered terms of peace to the Boonesborough people. Hearing that the Indians gladly treated with you at the Illinois gave them reason to think that the Indians were sincere; two days being taken up in this manner till they became quite familiar with one another; but finding the Boonesborough people would not turn out and having Col. Callaway, Maj. Smith, Capt. Boone,

Capt. Buchanan and their subalterns eight in number, in the Lick where they had their table, (you know the distance, about eighty yards) the Indians getting up, Blackfish made a long speech, then gave the word go, instantly a signal gun fired, the Indians fastened on the eight men to take them off, the white people began to dispute the matter though unarmed, and broke loose from the Indians, though there were two or three Indians to one white man. In running the above distance upwards of two hundred guns fired from each side and yet every man escaped but Squire Boone who was badly wounded though not mortally; he got safe to the fort. On this a hot engagement ensued for nine days and nights, constant fire without any intermission, no more damage was done however but one killed and two wounded. The Indians then dispersed to the different forts where they still remain in great numbers and waylaying our hunters. General McIntosh who commands the army intended against Detroit I understand received instructions to strike the Indians and not meddle with Detroit. For other northern news I refer you to the Gazettes I herewith send you.

The Indians have done more damage in the interior settlements this summer than was ever done in one season before. Absolute necessity obliges me to send Capt. Harrod for salt that we may be able to lay up a sufficient quantity of provision for the next summer. I hope you will send us one hundred bushels for that purpose, send an account of the same and I will send you the money by Capt. Montgomery in the Spring. Your compliance in this matter will enable us to keep our ground if not we shall be obliged to break up for want of provision for necessity will break through stone walls. I was obliged to promise six shillings per day to every man that returns with Capt. Harrod that I sent. I beg this as a favor to let every

Appendix

man of them have the value of forty dollars in goods as may best suit them and I will pay it with the above.

I am, dear sir, your humble servant JNO. BOWMAN.

N. B. Pray forward the newspapers to my brother after your looking over them.

P. S. We have been reinforced from Washington County with eighty men but their time was near out before they came this length so they return immediately again.

COL. G. R. CLARK.

Z

THE TRANSYLVANIA PURCHASE DECLARED VOID BY VIRGINIA IN 1778.

(From Journal Virginia House of Delegates.)

In the House of Delegates, Wednesday, the 4th of November, 1778.

Resolved, That all purchases of lands, made or to be made, of the Indians, within the chartered bounds of this commonwealth, as described by the constitution or form of government, by any private persons not authorized by public authority, are void.

Resolved, That the purchase heretofore made by Richard Henderson and Company, of that tract of land called Transylvania, within this commonwealth, of the Cherokee Indians, is void; but as the said Richard Henderson and Company have been at very great expense in making the said purchase, and in settling the said lands, by which this commonwealth is likely to receive great advantage, by increasing its inhabitants, and establishing a barrier against the Indians, it is just and reasonable to allow the said Richard Henderson and Company a compensation for their trouble and expense.

Tuesday, November 17th, 1778: Agreed to by the Senate.

I

AN ACT TO VEST CERTAIN LANDS ON THE OHIO AND GREEN RIVERS, IN FEE-SIMPLE, IN RICHARD HENDERSON AND COMPANY AND THEIR HEIRS.

Passed at the Session of the General Assembly of Virginia Begun at Williamsburg October 5, 1778, and in the Third Year of the Commonwealth.

(From Henning's Statutes at Large, Vol. IX, p. 571.)

Whereas it has appeared to this Assembly that Richard Henderson and Company have been at very great expense in making a purchase of the Cherokee Indians and although the same has been declared void yet as this Commonwealth is likely to receive great advantage therefrom by increasing its inhabitants and establishing a barrier against the Indians it is therefore just and reasonable the said Richard Henderson and Company be made a compensation for their trouble and expense.

Be it enacted by the General Assembly that all that tract of land situate, lying and being on the waters of the Ohio and Green rivers bounded as follows, to wit: Beginning at the mouth of Green River, thence running up the same twelve and a half miles when reduced to a straight line, thence running at right angles with the said reduced lines twelve and a half miles on each side of the said river, thence running lines from the termination of the line extended on each side the said Green River at right angles with the same till the said lines intersect the Ohio, which said river Ohio shall be the western boundary of the said tract, be, and the same is hereby granted to the said Richard Henderson and Company and their heirs as tenants in common subject to the payment of the same taxes as other lands within this Commonwealth are

Appendix

but under such limitations of time as to settling the said lands as shall be hereafter directed by the General Assembly but this grant shall and is hereby declared to be in full compensation to the said Richard Henderson and Company and their heirs for their charge and trouble and for all advantage accruing therefrom to this Commonwealth and they are hereby excluded from any farther claim to lands on account of any settlement or improvements heretofore made by them or any of them on the lands so as aforesaid purchased from the Cherokee Indians.

II

CAPTAIN JOHN HOLDER'S COMPANY AT AND NEAR BOONESBOROUGH IN JUNE, 1779.

(From the John B. Bowman papers.)

Holder, John, *Cap't.*
Ark, Uriel.
Bailey, Thos.
Ballard, Bland.
Baughman, John.
Bedinger, G. M.
Berry, James.
Bryan, James.
Bunten, James.
Butler, John.
Callaway, John.
Collins, Elijah.
Collins, Josiah.
Collins, William.
Constant, John.
Cook, David.
Coombs, William.
Cradlebaugh, Wm.
Dunpard, John.
Estill, James.
Fear, Edmund.
Gass, David.
Hancock, Stephen.
Hancock, Wm.
Hawiston, John.
Hays, William.
Hodges, Jesse.
Horn, Jeremiah.
Kirkham, Robert.
Kirkham, Samuel.
Lee, John.
Lockhart, Charles.
McCullum, John.
McGee, Wm.
Morgan, Ralph.
Morris, Wm.
Perry, James.
Pleck, John.
Porter, Samuel.
Proctor, Nicholas.
Proctor, Reuben.
Rollins, Pemberton.
Ross, Hugh.
Searcy, Bartlett.
Searcy, Reuben.
South, John, Sr.
South, John, Jr.
South, John, y'ng'r.
South, Thomas.
Stagner, Barney.
Stearns, Jacob.
Stephenson, John.
Vallandigham, Benoni.
Weber, John.
Wilcoxson, Daniel.
Wilson, Moses.

III

AN ACT FOR ESTABLISHING THE TOWN OF BOONSBOROUGH IN THE COUNTY OF KENTUCKEY.

PASSED AT THE SESSION OF THE GENERAL ASSEMBLY OF VIRGINIA HELD AT WILLIAMSBURG, COMMENCING OCT. 4, 1779, AND IN THE FOURTH YEAR OF THE COMMONWEALTH.

(From Henning's Statutes at Large, Vol. X, p. 134.)

Whereas it hath been represented to this present General Assembly that the inhabitants of the township called Boonsborough lying on Kentuckey river in the County of Kentuckey have laid off twenty acres of land into lots and streets and have petitioned this Assembly that the said lots and streets together with fifty acres of land adjoining thereto may be laid off into lots and streets and established a town for the reception of traders and that Six Hundred and forty acres of land allowed by law to every township for a common may also be laid off adjoining thereto. Be it therefore enacted, That the said fifty acres of land adjoining the said forty lots already laid off shall be and the same is hereby vested in Richard Callaway, Charles Mimms Thruston, Levin Powell, Edmund Taylor, James Estre, Edward Bradley, John Kennedy, David Gist, Pemberton Rollins, and Daniel Boone, gentlemen, trustees to be by them or any six of them laid out into lots of half an acre each with convenient streets which together with the lots and streets so laid off in the said township shall be and the same is hereby established a town by the name of Boonsborough.

And be it further enacted, That so soon as the said fifty acres of land shall be so laid out into lots and streets the said trustees shall cause a plan thereof together with a plan of the said township as the same is already laid off to be returned to the court of the said County of Kentuckey there to be recorded, &c. &c. * * *

Appendix

IV

MEMORIAL TO CONGRESS OF THE TRANSYLVANIA COMPANY, JANUARY 6, 1795.

(American Archives.)

To the Honorable the Congress of the United States:

The Memorial of Thomas Hart, of the State of Kentucky, John Williams, Leonard Henley Bullock, and James Hogg, of the State of North Carolina, sheweth,

That in the fall of the year 1774, your Memorialists, in company with Richard Henderson, William Johnston, Nathaniel Hart, John Luttrell, and David Hart, all now deceased, entered into bargain with the Overhill Cherokee Indians, for a purchase of some of their lands; and agreeably to preliminaries then agreed to, they, in March 1775, met at Watauga with the chiefs of the said Indians, attended by upwards of twelve hundred of their people; and then and there, in fair and open treaty, after several day's conference, and full discussion of every matter relating to the purchase, in presence of, and assisted by interpreters chosen by the said chiefs, and in consideration of a very large assortment of clothes and other goods, then delivered by the said Company to the said chiefs, and by them divided among their people, they the said Company obtained from the said Indians two several deeds, signed by Okonistoto their king or chief warrior, Atakullakulla and Savonooko or Coronoh, the next in the nation to Okonistoto in rank and consideration, for themselves, and on behalf, and with the warm approbation of the whole nation. These two grants comprehended, besides a great tract of land on the back of Virginia, a vast territory within the chartered limits of North Carolina, lying on the rivers of Holston, Clinch, Powell, and Cumberland, and their several branches, to the amount of many millions of acres.

This purchase from the aborigines and immemorial possessors of the said lands, being concluded more than a year before the Declaration of Independence, before the very existence of the Americans as States, or their claim to such lands, and not contrary to any then existing law of Great Britain or her Colonies, your memorialists and their copartners with confidence concluded that they had obtained a just, clear and indefeasible title to the said lands; and being then by the said Indians put into the actual possession of the said country, they immediately hired between two and three hundred men, and proceeded across their territory, to the river Kentucky, which with all its branches was comprehended in their purchase; and there about the 20th of April in the said year of 1775, began a settlement to which they gave the name of Boonsborough. The raising of necessary accommodations for their infant Colony, and building forts for their defence against the Shawanese and other hostile Indians, on the northwest of the Ohio, added much to the prime cost of their lands, and was attended with imminent risk and danger, and even with the massacre of some of the proprietors and several of their friends and followers.

After thus possessing and defending their property at a vast expense, trouble and danger, for several years against the savages, the Company were much astonished to find that first the Assembly of Virginia, and some years afterwards, the Assembly of North Carolina, began to call in question the rights of the said Company. It would be to no purpose at this time, to trouble Congress with any thing relating to the negotiation of the said Company with the Assembly of Virginia, as the compensation in lands, made to them by that state, remains untouched and unclaimed by any person or persons whatever against the Company, as far as has come to their knowledge. But the different fate of the lands granted them by the Assembly of North Carolina, makes some detail necessary.

This Assembly, in their May session of 1782, enacted that a great part of the lands lying on the river Cumberland and branches thereof, all within the said Company's purchase, should be laid off and reserved for the officers and soldiers of the North Carolina line, and soon thereafter, opened a land office for the sale of their whole purchase. However, after repeated remonstrances, presented to them by the Company, the Assembly, by way of compensation for their trouble and expense, agreed that the Company should retain 200,000 acres on the waters of Powell and Clinch rivers, part of the Company's purchase, with the grant or guarantee of the state for the same. The Company felt themselves grossly aggrieved by being thus arbitrarily dealt with; but they saw no alternative: they had not power to do themselves justice; and there was then no tribunal to which they could appeal. One of the conditions of this grant or guarantee was, that it should be surveyed within a certain limited time. The Company, therefore, found it necessary to have the survey made within the time prescribed; and though the Indians were then hostilely disposed, they ventured to depute one of their partners with a surveyor, chain carriers and guards; but after incurring an expense of £300 and upwards, the survey and plot were found defective, owing to the hurry in which the business was done. This misfortune obliged the Company to apply to the Assembly for further time to have a new survey. Time was accordingly given, and agreeably thereto, at the expense of £200 more and upwards, the survey was completed, and soon thereafter conferred by the Assembly.

But while these things were doing, the General Assembly, in the year 1789, had ceded their western lands to the United States, and the United States in 1790, accepted this cession, on certain conditions, one of which was, that all entries made by, and grants made to, any persons within the limits ceded, should have the same force and effect as if the cession had not been made. Within this cession the whole of the Company's grant from the General Assembly was comprehended; and though, in the opinion of the Company, it was a compensation very inadequate to their trouble and risk and expense, yet being now in possession of a State right as well as Indian right, they flattered themselves their title to it was beyond a cavil. They concluded it to be of considerable value; and as the Holston settlements were rapidly advancing around it, they were pursuaded they could venture to form settlements on it, or at least dispose of it to advantage. They therefore had a bill of partition filed in the district court of Washington; and being now in view of a speedy partition and of receiving some small compensation for their great expenditures and trouble, they could not help being greatly astonished and extremely mortified, when they learnt that almost the whole of their grant from the Assembly was ceded to the Cherokee Indians by the United States at the treaty of Holston, made on the   day of   179

Such a seizure and disposal of the property of citizens without any previous stipulation with the proprietors, nay without the least notice given them or any crime alleged against them, appeared to your Memorialists not only improper but unjust; but for the honor of the States, your Memorialists hope, that at the time this cession was made to the Indians, the government was not aware that such private property was comprehended in it. At any rate, if for political reasons, and for the interest of the States, it was found expedient to make such a sacrifice of the rights of a private company, it is to be hoped that Congress will be disposed to make ample compensation.

Twenty years have nearly elapsed since the Company made their purchase from the Indians. The expenses of this purchase from first to last have been great, and have been the means of reducing some of the Company to great difficulties; for, owing to the facts and circumstances above set forth, they have not to this day, been able to receive the smallest recompense.

The injustice and oppression complained of are flagrant, and the facts and circumstances above set forth are notorious, at least they are well known to the Senators and Representatives in Congress from the state of North Carolina, and the deeds and other vouchers are ready to be produced. And that all difficulty and dispute may hereafter be done away, your memorialists are willing, upon receiving proper compensation, to relinquish all claim to the lands purchased by them from the Indians within the chartered limits of North Carolina, an extensive territory now held by the United States in which the Indian claim was extinguished by fair purchase, at the expense of your Memorialists. Your Memorialists therefore, without further detail, beg leave to submit their case to the wisdom and justice of the Congress of the United States, and from them hope for speedy and ample redress.

Your Memorialists have only further to request, that whatever compensation Congress may be pleased to give them, may be directed to be dealt out to your Memorialists and Company, and their representatives or assigns, respectively, in proportion to the share to which each is entitled by the copartnership.

Signed for and in behalf of the Company, by

JNO. WILLIAMS, Chairman.

6th January, 1795.

INDEX.

	PAGE
Abingdon	37
Adams, Charles Francis	44
Adams, John	43, 229
Adventurers	58, 166
Aikin, Samuel	130
Alleghanies	30
Alves, James	151, 196
Ambuscades	16, 88
American Pioneer	69
Anderson, Nicholas	108
Anthony, James	108
Appendix	139
Ark, Uriel	255
Arrows Blazing	96
Artillery, Dread of	82, 119
Ash Hopper	41
Athens, Kentucky	121, 131
Attacullaculla	8, 151, 161
Attempt to Burn Fort	59, 96, 101
Bacon, J. P.	156
Bailey, Thomas	255
Ballard, Bland	116, 255
Baubin, Charles	65, 86
Baughman, John (Boffman)	121, 255
Bear Meat	163, 166, 176
Bedinger, G. M	255
Bennet, William	244
Benton, Jesse	45, 238
Berry, James	255
Bible Class	49
Big Hill, Kentucky	10
Big Sandy	5
Big Turtle (Boone)	65

Index

Bird, Henry..108, 119
Black Bird..72, 86
" Black Dan "...32, 36
Black Fish..........56, 65, 66, 68, 72, 80, 81, 84, 87, 88, 103, 108, 109
Blackfish Ford...76
Black's Fort...37
Black Hoof..74
Bledsoe, Captain..170
Block Houses.......................................35, 79, 88, 107
" Block House, The "..36, 37
Blue Grass..18
Blue Licks, Battle of..129
Blue Licks, Lower...64
Blue Licks, Upper.......................................51, 75, 82
Blue Ridge, The..2, 4
Boffman's Creek..121
Boiling Spring..28
Boone, Daniel, and Cherokees..................................2, 3
Boone, Daniel, and the Henderson Scheme............2, 3, 4, 5, 7, 9
Boone, Daniel, and Wilderness Road............6, 9, 10, 16, 17, 165
Boone, Daniel, Appointed Lieutenant Colonel.....................122
Boone, Daniel, at Battle of Blue Licks.........................129
Boone, Daniel, at Watauga...................................2, 7, 9
Boone, Daniel, Autograph..................................89, 111
Boone, Daniel, Before 1775....................................145
Boone, Daniel, Brings His Family to Boonesborough......37, 40, 178
Boone, Daniel, Captured at Blue Licks.......................65, 68
Boone, Daniel, Characteristics of..............................167
Boone, Daniel, Coolness....................................12, 21
Boone, Daniel, Early Life,......................................9
Boone, Daniel, Escapes Capture at Boone's Station..............131
Boone, Daniel, Escapes from the Indians........................69
Boone, Daniel, Exonerated.....................................105
Boone, Daniel, Family at Snoddy's..............................38
Boone, Daniel, First Attempt to Colonize Kentucky...........2, 146
Boone, Daniel, Helps to Rescue the Girls.......................50
Boone, Daniel, in Command at Boonesborough..................56, 98
Boone, Daniel, in " The Great Siege "..........................87

Index

Boone, Daniel, Leaves Kentucky...131
Boone, Daniel, Letter of April 1, 1775...168
Boone, Daniel, Letter to Governor of Virginia...129
Boone, Daniel, Name...111
Boone, Daniel, Order to the Lower Companies...12
Boone, Daniel, Portrait of...10
Boone, Daniel, Returns with Family from North Carolina...120
Boone, Daniel, Relics of...66
Boone, Daniel, Robbed...120
Boone, Daniel, Settles Boone's Station...120
Boone, Edward, Killed...120
Boone, Israel...121
Boone, James, Killed...146
Boone, Jemima,...40, 41, 49, 67, 77
Boone, Jemima, Captured...49
Boone, Mrs. ...40, 41, 67
Boone, Mrs., Returns to North Carolina...67
Boone, Squire...9, 52, 67, 77, 87, 90, 107
Boone's Creek...121
Boone's Gap...11
Boone's Narrative...34, 49, 57, 72
Boone's Path Post-office...14
Boone's Station...121, 128, 129
Boone's Trace...59, 192
Boonesborough a Deserted Village...137
Boonesborough an Open Town...132
Boonesborough, Burials at...60, 117
Boonesborough Ferry...110, 134
Boonesborough, Floods at...132, 133
Boonesborough Fort, Aid Asked...71
Boonesborough Fort, Appearance of it in 1778...89
Boonesborough Fort Battery...93
Boonesborough Fort Besieged...57, 75
Boonesborough Fort, Boys in...77, 129
Boonesborough Fort, Books at...63
Boonesborough Fort, Cabin Equipments...62
Boonesborough Fort Commenced...25
Boonesborough Fort Completed...34, 52, 69

Index

Boonesborough Fort, Conveniences of 62
Boonesborough Fort, Food 63
Boonesborough Fort, Friendly Savages at 82, 83
Boonesborough Fort, Garrison of 57, 58, 77
Boonesborough Fort Incomplete................................... 26
Boonesborough Fort Mine 92, 99
Boonesborough Fort, No Remnant of Exists...................... 134
Boonesborough Fort, No Well in............................... 36, 69
Boonesborough Fort, Patriots Rejoice 53, 61, 132
Boonesborough Fort, Plan of............................. 26, 35, 79
Boonesborough Fort, Siege Abandoned........................... 100
Boonesborough Fort, Site of 24, 40, 135, 172
Boonesborough Fort, Sufferings at........... 60, 61, 67, 78, 122, 125
Boonesborough Fort, Surrender Demanded 81
Boonesborough Fort, the Truce 81
Boonesborough Fort, Women of 77, 129
Boonesborough Incorporated.................................. 110, 256
Boonesborough in 1792.. 133
Boonesborough, Land Disposed of by Lot 172
Boonesborough, Location Described 137
Boonesborough, Memorials Proposed............................. 138
Boonesborough Named....................................... 28, 165
Boonesborough, Plat of.. 110
Boonesborough Settled 20
Boonesborough, Site in 1900 .... 25, 135, 136
Boonesborough, Trustees of.................................... 111
Boonesborough, Town Becomes Extinct........................... 134
Boston, Battle at 178
Bowman, Captain... 177
Bowman, John 60, 76, 85, 108, 118, 244
Bowman, John, Letter to Clark............................. 76, 251
Bowman, John, Warning Letter to.............................. 118
Bowman, Joseph 230, 245
Bowman, Major.. 177
Braddock's Defeat 74
Bradford, John 5, 72
Bradley, Edward 111
Brant, Joseph.. 124

Index

Bread, Lack of	32, 177, 192
Bridges, James	161
British Commissary	88
British Flag	88
Brooks, Castleton	156
Brooms, Hickory	40
Brooks, Thomas	57, 66
Brush, Dead	17, 163
Bryan, James	255
Bryan's or Bryant's Station	107, 113, 127, 128
Buchanan, William	87, 127
Buffaloes	17, 19, 22, 166, 176
Buffalo Meat	22, 192
Buffalo Tongues	80
Buffalo Trace	10, 16
Bulger, Edward	118
Bullet, Captain	180
Bullock, Leonard H.	4
Bunker Hill	33
Bunten, James	255
Burton, C. M.	103
Bush, William	51
Butler, John	255
Butler, Mann	108, 169
Butler, Simon	56, 67, 72, 103
Cabin Creek	75
Cabins in the Hollow	20, 33, 40
Cahokia	86
Calk, William	15
Callaway, Elizabeth	49, 52
Callaway, Fanny	49
Callaway, Flanders	51, 76, 87
Callaway, John	255
Callaway, Richard	9, 36, 38, 41, 49, 50, 67, 77, 81, 87, 98, 105, 111, 165
Callaway, Richard, Death of	116
Caldwell, William	127
Canadian Archives	73, 133
Campbell, Arthur	71, 160

Index

Campbell, Colonel 237
Cane 16, 163
Canebrakes 17
Cane Creek, North Carolina 39
Cannon, the Wooden.. 95
Canoe Ridge.. 116
Capture of the Three Girls 49, 249
Caroline County, Virginia 9
Carr, John 72
Carter County, Tennessee 1, 7
Carter, T. W.. 38
Carter's Books 159
Carter's Valley 159
Cartwright, John 108
Cartwright, Robert... 108
Castlewood, Virginia 38
Catahecassa 74
Chaplain, Abraham 118
Chenault, William.. 16, 87, 127
Chenoca 143, 152
Cherokee River... 242
Cherokees 2, 3, 5, 6, 8, 29, 50, 161, 190, 242
Cherokees, Deed to Henderson and Company 29, 151, 149
Cherokee Towns... 2
Chillicothe 68, 71
Chota... 2
Christmas at Boonesborough 46, 125
Clark County 119, 137
Clark Creek... 240
Clark, George Rogers... 47, 48, 57, 67, 71, 76, 86, 107, 118, 121, 130, 245
Clark, Hills of... 50
Clear Creek... 107
Climax of the Treaty 89
Clinch Mountain... 159
Clinch River... 38, 163
Clover, White.. 18, 28, 31, 176
Coburn, Samuel 161
Cocke, William.......................... 13, 15, 16, 20, 21, 37, 185

Index

Collins, Elijah...255
Collins, Josiah 255
Collins, William 255
Collomes, Captain 175
Combahee Ferry, South Carolina 129
Commissioner, the Prostrate.................................... 90
Commissioners, Attempt to Seize 89
Commissioners, Peace 87
Conelly, Major 180
Conference in the Hollow 87
Connecticut, Transylvania Land Fever in........................ 42
Constant, John...255
Continental Congress and Transylvania.......................... 42
Cook, David 255
Coombs, William 255
Cooper...250
Corn, Indian...............23, 71, 74, 107, 111, 113, 115, 126, 130, 179
Corn-makers' Company......................................23, 107
Cornstalk, Chief..46, 238
Cornwallis' Surrender 125
Coronoh 151
Counter Mine, The 94
Court Martial, the Boone 105
Cowen, John..244
Cowpens, Battle of 123
Cradlebaugh, William 255
Crittenden, John...245
Croghan, George 143
Cross Plains 121
Crow, William 243
Cumberland Gap...10, 14
Cumberland Mountain...163
Cumberland River 15, 114, 163, 157
Curious Warfare 97
Currency, Continental 115
Cuttawa 144
Cuttoe-Knife 16, 186
Dandridge, Alex. S...197

Dark and Bloody Ground 144
Darlington 144
Deane, Silas, Letter of 42, 219, 229
De Chaine, Isadore... 73, 85
Declaration of Independence at Boonesborough...................... 53
Deed, Cherokee, to Henderson and Company 151, 230
Deer 2, 19, 166, 176
Deposition of Charles Robertson 157
De Quindre, Dagneaux................... 72, 80, 85, 87, 88, 102, 104
De Quindre, Death of 103
De Quindre, Autograph of 103
Detroit 61, 68, 72, 74, 78, 86, 88, 91, 103
Devil's Race Path... 146
Dick's River.. 172, 174
Dissension at Boonesborough 98
Dixon, Tilman 156
Donelly's Fort 68
Donelson, Colonel 158, 181
Doniphan, A. W... 109
Doniphan, Joseph 109
Dorchester, Lord 43, 133
Douglas, James 196
Douiller, Peter 72, 101, 104
Dragging Canoe 8, 144, 159
Drake, Joe 174
Draper, Lyman C.......................... 4, 9, 72, 76, 105, 170
Drewyer. See Douiller.
Drinking Tube, Revolutionary 135
Drouth of 1782... 126
Dug-out, The... 110, 115
Dunmore, Lord.......................... 13, 29, 32, 44, 181, 229
Dunning, James... 170
Dunpard, John... 255
Du Quesne (see De Chaine).................................... 72, 73
Duree, Mrs... 125
Durrett, R. T.. 10, 66
Durrett, R. T., Preface by... iii
Election at Harrodsburg... 47

Index

Election of Transylvania Delegates	28
Elizabethtown, Tennessee	1, 7
Elk	19, 176
Ellis' Station	128
Ellis, William	107, 119, 128
Elm, the Divine	19, 28, 88, 135, 176
Elm, the Divine, Cut Down	135
Escheat, the Jury of	120
Estill, James	255
Estill's Defeat	126
Estre, James	111
Exeter Township	9
Falls of Ohio	67, 235, 236
Fanning, David	39
Farrar, John	29, 155, 208
Fayette County, Kentucky, Created	122
Fayetteville, North Carolina	2
Fear, Edmund	255
Feast in the Hollow	88
Ferryboat Built	116, 134
Ferry First Established in Kentucky	110, 116, 125, 134, 137
Filson, John	6, 18, 19, 34, 131, 144
Findlay	144
First White Woman on Kentucky River	40
Flag, British	88
Flag of Truce	78, 80, 81
Flag of United States	26
Flax	96
Fleet of Perogues	115
Flint Locks	83, 132, 136
Flints	112, 191
Floyd, John	34, 44, 51, 53, 130, 233
Floyd, John, on Capture of the Girls	249
Floyd's Defeat	124
Ford, Town of	137
Forest Food	61
Fort and Cabins Confused	34
Fort, Attempts to Burn the	59, 96

Index

Fort Boone 20, 33, 172
Fort Chartres 228
Fort Pitt Conference 46
Fort Stanwix 241
Four Sycamores, The 49
Fowey, The 32
Foxtown, Kentucky 127
Frankfort Commonwealth 11
French Alliance 71, 86
French and Indian War Bounty 112
French Canadians 71, 72, 85, 103, 118, 127
French Lick 114, 115
Game 23, 32, 38, 41, 60, 67, 164, 176
Garden, the Fort 32
Garrison of Boonesborough 23, 77, 87
Gass, David 255
George, Whitson 108
Germain, George 78
Gess, David 51
Gess, John 51
Gilmer's Lick 240
Girty, Simon 127
Gist, Christopher 18, 144
Gist, David 111
Goodman, Daniel, Killed 57
Grampus, Slave 180
Grant, John 107, 118
Grant's Station 118
Granville County, North Carolina 4, 42, 115, 212
Granville, John, Earl of 149
Granville, Town of 134
Great Grant, the 8, 151, 257
Great Siege, Last Night of 100
Great Siege of Boonesborough 76
Greenbrier River 69
Green River 55, 106, 114
Guess, Thomas 178
Gun Flints 112

Index

Gunpowder	23, 112, 113, 149, 239
Gunpowder made at Boonesborough	61
Hackberry Ridge	27, 76
Haldimand, Frederick	65, 72
Haldimand MSS	74, 76
Hall, Edward	108
Halley, H. S	135
Hall, James	26, 168, 183
Hall, William	108
Hamilton's Kindness to Boone	68
Hamilton, William	61, 69, 71, 72, 73, 78, 80, 85, 86
Hammond, Nathan	197
Hancock, Stephen	87, 255
Hancock, William	87, 255
Hard Winter, The	122
Harland, Silas	245
Harmon, Valentine	196
Harper, John	108
Harper, Peter	108
Harrison, Richard	44, 233
Harrod, James	167, 175, 190, 243, 245
Harrodsburg	12, 28, 40, 47, 49, 107, 178, 235
Harrodsburg Election in 1776	246
Harrodsburg Remonstrance	45, 47
Harrod's Station	40, 167, 175
Hart, David	4, 51
Hart, John	161
Hart, Nathaniel	4, 7, 13, 36, 51, 108, 171, 173, 188
Hart, Nathaniel, Death of	127
Hart, N., Junior	11
Hart, Thomas	4, 38, 120
Harvey's History	74
Hat-Waving Signal	89
Hawiston, John	255
Hay, Peter	218
Hays, William	255
Haywood's History	114
Hazel Patch	40

Index

Henderson Company Denounced 182
Henderson Company, Great Work of............................. 55
Henderson Company, Land Grant to..55, 114, 115, 151, 194, 230, 242, 254
Henderson Company, Letter to Patrick Henry...................... 194
Henderson Company, Meeting 42
Henderson Company, Members of............................151, 166
Henderson Company, Memorial to Congress........................ 257
Henderson Company, Second Colony of 114
Henderson Company, The................................... 3, 4, 5, 7, 54
Henderson Company, Virginia Against....................... 48, 54, 106
Henderson, Kentucky 55, 115, 196
Henderson, Nathaniel... 44, 233
Henderson, Pleasant 169
Henderson, Richard, at Boonesborough 22, 26, 33, 36
Henderson, Richard, at Williamsburg............................ 47, 54
Henderson, Richard, Autograph................................... 35
Henderson, Richard, Death of.................................... 115
Henderson, Richard, Early Life of............................. 3, 4, 5
Henderson, Richard, Grave of.................................... 115
Henderson, Richard, Journal................................ 169, 180
Henderson, Richard, Leaves for North Carolina................... 39
Henderson, Richard, Letter of, April 8, 1775 183
Henderson, Richard, Letter of, June 12, 1775.................... 184
Henderson, Richard, Master Spirit 55
Henderson, Richard, Plan Fails 54
Henderson, Richard, Residence in North Carolina 115
Henderson, Richard, Speech to House of Delegates................ 197
Henderson, Richard, Trip to Kentucky............................ 12
Henderson, Richard, Trip through Kentucky in 1780 114
Henderson, Samuel.. 3, 51, 52
Henderson's Land Scheme 3, 4, 5, 7
Hendricks 118
Henning's Statutes... 110
Henry, Patrick... 27, 72
Herod, James (Harrod).. 167
Hewes 224
Hicks, William... 161
Hinkston's Station 52

Index

Hite, Abram	230, 243
Hite, Isaac	57, 235, 245
Hodges, Jesse	255
Hogg, James	4, 42, 43, 55, 196
Hogg's Report of His Embassy	43, 224
Hogohege River	242
Holder, John	51, 108, 116
Holder, John, Company, Roll of	108, 127
Holder's Defeat	128
Holston Company, The	80, 104
Holston River, The	6, 163
Holston Salt Wells	38
Holston Settlements	67, 71, 123
Holston Valley	2
Hooper	224
Hope Deferred at Boonesborough	82, 99, 104
Horn, Jeremiah	255
Houghton, Thomas	156
House of Delegates, Answer to Speech of Proprietors	202
House of Delegates, Journal of	196
House of Delegates, Members of	196
House of Delegates, Transylvania	28, 30
Hoy's Station	127, 128
Hunting Grounds	149, 158
Huts	20, 22
Hyder, N. E.	7
Illinois	85
Imlay	18
Immigrants	36, 40, 44, 46, 107, 110, 111, 121, 124, 126
Independence for Kentucky	48
Indian Alliance	46
Indian Chiefs of the Delawares	247
Indian Forces	57, 58, 65, 72
Indian Hand-shake, The	89
Indian Hostilities Threatened	49, 118
Indian Language	69, 90
Indian Losses	51, 57, 58, 59, 101
Indian Love for Boone	77, 85

Index

Indian Outrages. 11, 21, 37, 45, 49, 51, 56, 104, 117, 119, 125, 130, 237, 249
Indian Paint 75
Indians Attack the Road Builders 11
Indian Scalped 37
Indians, Friendly 47, 82, 83
Indians Hide their Dead 58, 59
Indians, History of 74
Indians, Hurons 124
Indians, Illegal Purchases From 48
Indians in Winter of 1777 56
Indians Kickapoos 236, 247
Indians, Miamis 124, 130
Indians, Neutral 45
Indians, Overhills 2, 3
Indians Side with British 51
Interpreters with Indians and British 87
Invasion Threatened, Letter to Bowman 118
Jackson, Joseph 66, 117
Jefferson County, Kentucky, Formed 122
Jefferson, Thomas 27, 43, 195, 226
Jerked Meat 16, 186
Jobe, E. D. 7
Johnson's Indian Tribes 144
Johnson, Thomas 161
Johnson, William 108
Johnstone, William 4, 218
Jones, John Gabriel 47, 244
Jouett, Matthew 178, 197
Judge's Friend 158
Kanawha 72
Kaskaskia 67
Kelley, John 101
Kenneday, John 111
Kenton, Simon 67
Kenton, Simon, at Boonesborough 56
Kenton, Simon, Captured 104
Kenton, Simon, Kills Three Indians 57
Kenton, Simon, Saves Life of Boone 57

Index

Kentucky	1, 3, 5, 8
Kentucky Climate in Pioneer Times	18
Kentucky County Created	54, 56
Kentucky District Formed	131
Kentucky, Extinct Towns of	134
Kentucky, Fertility of	164, 190
Kentucky Forts at Mercy of Artillery	119
Kentucky Historical Society	170
Kentucky River	5, 6, 8, 9, 10, 16, 17, 20, 40, 92, 115, 122, 124, 128
Kentucky River Floods	133, 134
Kentucky, The Name	76, 104, 124, 132, 143, 157, 169, 171, 246
Kentucky, The Name, Account of	143
Kewee, South Carolina	162
Killed at Boonesborough	57, 59, 94, 101, 127
King's Mountain	7, 123
Kirkham, Robert	255
Kirkham, Samuel	255
LaMothe, De Jaine	86
Land Court at Boonesborough	112
Land Entries	234
Land Fever High	112
Land Grants	114, 149, 235, 241
Land, Kentucky Price of	44, 47, 241, 246
Land Law Enacted	112
Land Office at Boonesborough	44, 46, 233
Land of British Subjects Confiscated	120
Last Battle of the Revolution	129
Leavy, William	108
Lee, John	255
Lee, Richard Henry	43, 226, 229
Leestown	249
Leowvisay (Louisa)	161
Letter to Patrick Henry from Henderson Company	27
Lewisburg	69
Lexington, Battle of	31, 178
Lexington, Kentucky	31, 107, 108, 120, 127
Lick	18, 19, 90, 166, 172
Licking Creek	250

Index

Lick Spring, The 19, 59, 83, 87, 90, 135
Linn 180
Lincoln County, Kentucky, Created 122
Little Carpenter 162
Livery of Seisin 29, 207, 230
Live Stock 13, 59, 83, 100, 179, 206
Lockhart, Charles 255
Logan, Benjamin 105
Long Island, Tennessee 6, 9, 37, 163, 226
Long Knife 47, 49, 247
Long Run 124
Lorimer 65
Lossing, Benson J 66
Lost Men, The 177
Loughry's Defeat 129
Louisa, the Name 5, 169, 152, 172
Lulbegrud Creek 74
Lumkin, George 156
Luna 172
Luttrell, John 4, 7, 13, 37, 39, 55, 115
Lythe, John 30, 31, 178, 196
Maddern, George 108
Madison County, Kentucky 11, 87, 137
Magazine, The Boonesborough 174
Maginty, Alex 143
Mansker's Lick 248
Marshall, Humphrey, History 5, 120
Martin, John 51
Martin, Joseph 14, 155
Martin, Josiah 5, 29, 31, 43, 150
Martin's Cabin 14, 38
Martin's Station 107, 119, 170, 183
Maxwell, John 245
Maysville, Kentucky 75
McAfee, James 172
McAfee, Robert 22, 173
McAfee, Samuel 22, 173
McAfee's Station 109, 124

Index

McAfee, William	230
McClelland's Fort Abandoned	56
McConnell, Andrew	245
McConnell, William	245
McCullum, John	255
McDowell, Thomas	11, 169
McGary, Hugh	40, 245
McGee, William	255
McIntosh, General	252
McKee, Alexander	124
McMillan, John	51
McPheeters, Joseph	11, 169
McQuinney	45, 49, 237
Meadow Land, The	144, 145
Meat, Wild	59, 64, 74
Memorials for Boonesborough	138
Memorial to Congress of Transylvania Company	55, 215, 257
Miers, William	251
Mile Trees	10, 17
Militia	47, 56, 60, 64, 77, 84, 86, 99, 118
Mine, The, at Boonesborough	93, 97
Miseries of the Siege	96, 98
Moluntha, Chief	74, 80, 81
Monk, Negro Powder-maker	113
Monongahala	175
Montgomery, Alexander	72, 103
Montgomery, Captain	252
Montgomery, John	60
Moore, Captain	177
Moore, William	177
Morehead's Address	120
Morgan, Ralph	255
Morris, William	255
Mound-Builders	145
Munseka, Chief	65
Negroes Captured by Indians	74, 117
Negro Slaves, Price of	74
Negro Slaves with Settlers	10, 13, 22, 87, 116, 164, 165, 192

Index

Negro with Indians 74, 102
Neil Ford 146
Nelson, Archibald 5
Newspapers 253
News, Slow Progress of, in the Revolution 131
North Carolina 1, 114, 115, 166
North Carolina and Henderson Company Lands 258
North Carolinians Explore Kentucky 1
North Carolina Riflemen 60
Noggins 41
Nourse, James 18
Oconistoto 3, 8, 151
Ohio Company 228
Ohio Indians 33, 78
Ohio River 58, 65, 69, 71, 75, 81, 110, 127
Old Fields, The 1, 7
Oldham, Jesse 108
Opost, League at 247
Orange County, North Carolina 4
Osnaburgs 25, 175
Otter Creek 9, 12, 16, 20, 169, 172, 188
Overflows at Boonesborough 24
Overhill Indians 3
Oxford, North Carolina 42, 212
Pack-Horses 10, 13, 15, 40, 67, 75, 79, 110, 112
Paint Lick Expedition 105
Panics of Settlers 15, 21, 52, 119, 184, 186
Parratt, James 150
Path Deed, The 8, 257
Patillo, Henry 219
Patriots at Boonesborough 35, 53, 100
Patton, James 118
Peace Celebration at Boonesborough 132
Peace Commissioners at Boonesborough 87
Peake, Jesse 108
Peaks of Otter 9
Peck, J. M. 40, 76
Peeke, James 161

Index

Peltry	14, 20, 201
Pendegrass, Garrett	247
Pennsylvania Settlers	125
Perry, James	255
Petition of Committee of West Fincastle	245
Petition of Transylvanians	47, 241
Piggins	41
Pioneers, Carelessness of	188
Piqua Expedition	121
Pleck, John	255
Pogue, William	41, 45, 240
Point Pleasant	5, 21
Pompey, the Negro	74, 94
Porter, Samuel	38, 255
Portwood, Page	16, 192
Powder Magazine	23, 25
Powell, Levin	111
Powell's Mountain	146, 152
Powell's River	147, 163
Powell's Valley	6, 11, 31, 37, 39, 115, 170, 184
Powwows	2, 8
Powwow, The, at Boonesborough	88
Prayer for Royal Family	31
Price, Thomas	156
Proceedings of Transylvania Proprietors	42
Proclamation Money	213
Proclamation of Governor Martin	5, 147
Proclamation of Lord Dunmore	181
Proclamation of Transylvania Company	48, 248
Proctor, Nicholas	255
Proctor, Reuben	255
Proprietary Government	44, 49
Proprietary Government, Opposition to	41, 43, 47, 54
Puckashinwa	72
Queer Conducts of British and Indians	83
Quit Rents	43, 209, 229
Raft, The Drifting	126
Rains and the Great Siege	94, 96, 98, 101

Index

Ramsay's Annals	4, 7
Rawlings, Pemberton, Killed	117
"Rebels of Kentuck"	71, 100
Reese, D. N	7
Regulators, The	4, 145
Reid, Nathan	51
Religious Freedom in Transylvania	209
Reply of John Williams to Harrodsburg Remonstrance	230
Revolution, Spirit of, at Boonesborough	41, 62, 100
Richland Creek	52, 171
Richmond, Kentucky	11
Richmond, Made Capital of Virginia	113
Richmond, Virginia	113
Riflemen	13, 23, 50, 52, 57, 60, 77, 88, 93, 97, 246
Roberts, Benjamin	118
Robertson, Charles, Deposition	54
Robertson's Station	1, 6, 161
Rockcastle River	104, 138, 163
Rollins or Rawlings	111, 116, 117, 255
Roll of Holder's Company	255
Ross, Hugh	255
Ruddle's Station	107, 109
Ruse of Boonesborough People	87
Sallings, John	143
Salt	14, 15, 19, 34, 39, 40, 41, 183
Salt Famine	32, 38, 54, 61, 63, 179
Salt Lick	17, 19, 143
Salt-makers Captured	65, 78, 86, 117
Salt River	40, 175
Salt Spring, the Secret	68
Salt, Value of	64
Saltville, Virginia	38, 64
Sanders	45, 237
Savanooko	8, 151
Scalping	37, 116, 128
Scalps, Reward for	45, 68
School at Boonesborough	109
Searcy, Bartlett	255

Index

Searcy, Reuben 255
Sennight 177
Sermon, the First in Kentucky 30, 177
Sevier, John 169
Shane, John D 72, 130
Shawanese 5, 33, 46, 50, 51, 56, 65, 66, 68, 71, 72, 74, 77,
                                              90, 108, 109, 117, 131
Shawanese at Boone's Station 131
Shelby, Isaac 54
Shelbyville, Kentucky 107
Siege, The Great, of Boonesborough 72, 251
Siege, The Great, of Boonesborough Abandoned 100
Silas Deane's Letter 219
Six Nations, The 143, 228, 241
Skaggs' Trace 121
Slaughter, Thomas 175, 196
Smith, Dan 160
Smith's Ferry 115
Smith, William Bailey 13, 51, 55, 58, 67, 81, 87, 98, 115, 156
Smythe, John F. D 32
Snead, W. B. G 115
Snoddy, John 38
Snoddy's Fort 2, 38, 147
Sons of Liberty 53, 118, 132
Sorrell River 171
South, John, Junior 255
South, John, Senior 255
South, the Younger 255
South, Thomas 255
Spinning Wheel 40
Springs 18, 68, 157, 170, 172
Stafford County, Virginia 108, 109
Stagner, Barney 41, 255
St. Asaph 28
Stearns, Jacob 255
Stephenson, John 255
Stewart 171
Stoner, Michael 25, 57, 172

Index

Store at Boonesborough, The	25, 37
Story of Bryan's Station	127
Stratagems and Tricks	57, 85, 87, 90, 93, 105, 128
Strode's Station	107, 119
Sulphur	15
Sulphur Spring	19, 39, 135, 166
Sulphur Well	135
Sunbonnets	40
Superstitions of Settlers	130
Surrender of Burgoyne Celebrated	62
Sycamore Hollow	20, 24, 87, 104, 134
Sycamore Shoals	1, 6, 7, 9, 20
Sycamores, The Four	49
Sycamore, The Old	136
Sycamore Trees	19, 49, 88, 90, 135, 136
Surveyors	14, 44, 54, 174, 210, 233, 234
Surveys	214, 217
Survey Warrant of Henderson and Company	240
Tanguay, Historian	103
Tate, Samuel	11
Tate's Creek	11
Taylor, Alfred	7
Taylor, Edmund	111
Tellassee	2
Tellico	2
Tenase	157
Tennessee	157
Tennessee River	151
Tents	173, 175
Thoughts on Government	43
Thruston, Charles	111, 256
Thwaits	66
Tivity. See Twetty.	
Tobacco in Kentucky	133
Todd, John	57
Torches, Blazing, Used	95, 101
Tories	32
Trabue, Daniel	87, 105

Index

Trails and Traces	10, 16, 17, 75, 121, 190
Transylvania Colony	27, 29
Transylvania Compact	30
Transylvania Company	3, 4, 7, 9, 12, 16, 27
Transylvania Company, Members of	29, 151
Transylvania Government Abolished	54
Transylvania House of Delegates	29, 41
Transylvania House of Delegates, Journal of	196
Transylvania Land Prices Raised	44
Transylvania Purchase Declared Void	106, 253
Transylvania, The Name	28, 47, 55, 206
Transylvania, Town of	134
Traveling Church	119
Treaty of Paris	127, 131
Treaty of Point Pleasant	5
Treaty of Watauga	8, 157, 161
Treaty at Boonesborough	85, 88
Turey, Valentine	156
Turkeys	164, 166
Twetty, William	10, 11, 161, 164, 168
United State Register	8, 108
Vallandigham, Benoni	255
Vance County, North Carolina	53, 115
Vegetables	32, 61, 83, 179
Vincennes	70, 71, 107
Virginia and Indian Lands	48
Virginia Archives	8, 31, 122, 157
Virginia, Campbell's History	69
Virginia Convention	31, 43, 47
Virginia Convention, Journal of	47, 48
Virginia Gazette	53
Virginia Land Grant to Henderson Company	55, 254
Virginia Ownership of Kentucky	48
Wages	239, 252
Walden's Ridge	3
Walker, Felix	11, 19, 161, 164, 168
Walker, Felix, Narrative	6, 11, 161
Walker, Thomas	5, 143

Index

Wallen's Gap ... 38, 40, 146
Warriors' Path ... 3, 10, 50
Washington County, Virginia ... 71, 252
Watauga ... 1, 2, 3, 6, 7, 123, 161
Watauga Association ... 7
Watauga River ... 1, 7
Watch Tower, the ... 93
Water, Lack of, at Boonesborough ... 36, 59, 63, 70, 82, 97
Watkins, Captain ... 64
Weber, John ... 255
Wedding, First at Boonesborough ... 52
West Fincastle ... 47
Western Review ... 70
Western Waters of Fincastle ... 245
Wharton, John ... 230
Wheeler's History, North Carolina ... 4, 54
White, Benjamin ... 108
White Oak Station ... 36, 128
Wilcoxson, Daniel ... 255
Wilderness Road ... 6, 9, 10, 16, 17, 110, 192
Williamsboro ... 53, 115, 116
Williamsburg ... 54, 113, 193
Williams, Edward ... 108
Williams, John ... 4, 37, 44, 53, 213, 230
Williams, John, Report on Transylvania Affairs ... 232
Wills, Robert ... 171
Wilson, Moses ... 255
Wisconsin Historical Society ... 169, 170
Women at Boonesborough ... 40, 59
Wooden Cannon, The ... 95
Wood, M. B. ... 38
Worthington, E ... 118
Wyandots ... 118, 126
Wythe, George ... 43, 226
Yadkin, The ... 38, 145
Yellow Mountain ... 7

The First American Frontier

*This is a volume in
the Ayer Company collection*

Agnew, Daniel.
A History of the Region of Pennsylvania North of the Allegheny River. 1887.

Alden, George H.
New Government West of the Alleghenies Before 1780. 1897.

Barrett, Jay Amos.
Evolution of the Ordinance of 1787. 1891.

Billon, Frederick.
Annals of St. Louis in its Early Days Under the French and Spanish Dominations. 1886.

Billon, Frederick.
Annals of St. Louis in its Territorial Days, 1804-1821. 1888.

Littel, William.
Political Transactions in and Concerning Kentucky. 1926.

Bowles, William Augustus.
Authentic Memoirs of William Augustus Bowles. 1916.

Bradley, A. G.
The Fight with France for North America. 1900.

Brannan, John, ed.
Official Letters of the Military and Naval Officers of the War, 1812-1815. 1823.

Brown, John P.
Old Frontiers. 1938.

Brown, Samuel R.
The Western Gazetteer. 1817.

Cist, Charles.
Cincinnati Miscellany of Antiquities of the West and Pioneer History. (2 volumes in one). 1845-6.

Claiborne, Nathaniel Herbert.
Notes on the War in the South with Biographical Sketches of the Lives of Montgomery, Jackson, Sevier, and Others. 1819.

Clark, Daniel.
Proofs of the Corruption of Gen. James Wilkinson. 1809.

Clark, George Rogers.
Colonel George Rogers Clark's Sketch of His Campaign in the Illinois in 1778-9. 1869.

Collins, Lewis.
Historical Sketches of Kentucky. 1847.

Cruikshank, Ernest, ed,
Documents Relating to Invasion of Canada and the Surrender of Detroit. 1912.

Cruikshank, Ernest, ed,
The Documentary History of the Campaign on the Niagara Frontier, 1812-1814. (4 volumes). 1896-1909.

Cutler, Jervis.
A Topographical Description of the State of Ohio, Indian Territory, and Louisiana. 1812.

Cutler, Julia P.
The Life and Times of Ephraim Cutler. 1890.

Darlington, Mary C.
History of Col. Henry Bouquet and the Western Frontiers of Pennsylvania. 1920.

Darlington, Mary C.
Fort Pitt and Letters From the Frontier. 1892.

De Schweinitz, Edmund.
The Life and Times of David Zeisberger. 1870.

Dillon, John B.
History of Indiana. 1859.

Eaton, John Henry.
Life of Andrew Jackson. 1824.

English, William Hayden.
Conquest of the Country Northwest of the Ohio. (2 volumes in one). 1896.

Flint, Timothy.
Indian Wars of the West. 1833.

Forbes, John.
Writings of General John Forbes Relating to His Service in North America. 1938.

Forman, Samuel S.
Narrative of a Journey Down the Ohio and Mississippi in 1789-90. 1888.

Haywood, John.
Civil and Political History of the State of Tennessee to 1796. 1823.

Heckewelder, John.
History, Manners and Customs of the Indian Nations. 1876.

Heckewelder, John.
Narrative of the Mission of the United Brethren. 1820.

Hildreth, Samuel P.
Pioneer History. 1848.

Houck, Louis.
The Boundaries of the Louisiana Purchase: A Historical Study. 1901.

Houck, Louis.
History of Missouri. (3 volumes in one). 1908.

Houck, Louis.
The Spanish Regime in Missouri. (2 volumes in one). 1909.

Jacob, John J.
A Biographical Sketch of the Life of the Late Capt. Michael Cresap. 1826.

Jones, David.
A Journal of Two Visits Made to Some Nations of Indians on the West Side of the River Ohio, in the Years 1772 and 1773. 1774.

Kenton, Edna.
Simon Kenton. 1930.

Loudon, Archibald.
Selection of Some of the Most Interesting Narratives of Outrages. (2 volumes in one). 1808-1811.

Monette, J. W.
History, Discovery and Settlement of the Mississippi Valley. (2 volumes in one). 1846.

Morse, Jedediah.
American Gazetteer. 1797.

Pickett, Albert James.
History of Alabama. (2 volumes in one). 1851.

Pope, John.
A Tour Through the Southern and Western Territories. 1792.

Putnam, Albigence Waldo.
History of Middle Tennessee. 1859.

Ramsey, James G. M.
Annals of Tennessee. 1853.

Ranck, George W.
Boonesborough. 1901.

Robertson, James Rood, ed.
Petitions of the Early Inhabitants of Kentucky to the Gen. Assembly of Virginia. 1914.

Royce, Charles.
Indian Land Cessions. 1899.

Rupp, I. Daniel.
History of Northampton, Lehigh, Monroe, Carbon and Schuykill Counties. 1845.

Safford, William H.
The Blennerhasset Papers. 1864.

St. Clair, Arthur.
A Narrative of the Manner in which the Campaign Against the Indians, in the Year 1791 was Conducted. 1812.

Sargent, Winthrop, ed.
A History of an Expedition Against Fort DuQuesne in 1755. 1855.

Severance, Frank H.
An Old Frontier of France. (2 volumes in one). 1917.

Sipe, C. Hale.
Fort Ligonier and Its Times. 1932.

Stevens, Henry N.
Lewis Evans: His Map of the Middle British Colonies in America. 1920.

Timberlake, Henry.
The Memoirs of Lieut. Henry Timberlake. 1927.

Tome, Philip.
Pioneer Life: Or Thirty Years a Hunter. 1854.

Trent, William.
Journal of Captain William Trent From Logstown to Pickawillany. 1871.

Walton, Joseph S.
Conrad Weiser and the Indian Policy of Colonial Pennsylvania. 1900.

Withers, Alexander Scott.
Chronicles of Border Warfare. 1895.